NORTHERN CALIFORNIA
TRAVEL+SMART™ TRIP PLANNER

NORTHERN CALIFORNIA

TRAVEL◆SMART™ TRIP PLANNER

Paul Otteson

John Muir Publications
Santa Fe, New Mexico

Acknowledgments
Special thanks to my many friends around the state who supported my work with ideas and opinions. Thanks especially to Mary, my inspiration.

John Muir Publications, P.O. Box 613, Santa Fe, New Mexico 87504

Printed in the United States of America.
First edition. First printing January 1997

ISSN 1091-5370
ISBN 1-56261-299-9

Editors: Rob Crisell, Dianna Delling, Tama Montgomery
Design: Janine Lehmann, Linda Braun
Graphics Coordination: Tom Gaukel
Cover Photo: Paul Otteson
Back Cover Photos: top—Robert Holmes
                      bottom—Robert Holmes
Map Style Development: American Custom Maps—Albuquerque, NM USA
Map Illustration: Julie Felton
Typesetting: John Ericksen
Production: Marie J. T. Vigil, Nikki Rooker
Printing: Publishers Press

Distributed to the book trade by
Publishers Group West
Emeryville, California

HOW TO USE THIS BOOK

This *Northern California Travel✦Smart Trip Planner* is organized in 16 destination chapters, each covering the best sights and activities, restaurants, and lodging available in that specific destination. Thanks to thorough research and experience, the author is able to bring you only the best options, saving you time and money in your travels. The chapters begin with San Francisco and follow in geographic sequence so you can follow an easy route from one to the next. If you were to visit each destination, you'd enjoy a complete tour of the best of Northern California.

Each chapter contains:
- User-friendly maps of the area, showing all recommended sights, restaurants, and accommodations.
- "A Perfect Day" description—how the author would spend his time if he had just one day in that destination.
- Sightseeing highlights, each rated by degree of importance: ✿✿✿ Don't miss; ✿✿ Try hard to see; ✿ See if you have time; and No stars—Worth knowing about.
- Selected restaurant, lodging, and camping recommendations to suit a variety of budgets.
- Helpful hints, fitness and recreation ideas, insights, and random tidbits of information to enhance your trip.

The Importance of Planning. Developing an itinerary is the best way to get the most satisfaction from your travels, and this guidebook makes it easy. First, read through the book and choose the places you'd most like to visit. Then, study the color map on the inside cover flap and the mileage chart (page 12) to determine which you can realistically see in the time you have available and at the travel pace you prefer. Using the Planning Map (pages 10–11), map out your route. Finally, use the lodging recommendations to determine your accommodations.

Some Suggested Itineraries. To get you started, six itineraries of varying lengths and based on specific interests follow. Mix and match according to your interests and time constraints, or follow a given itinerary from start to finish. The possibilities are endless. *Happy travels!*

SUGGESTED ITINERARIES

With the *Northern California Travel♦Smart Trip Planner* you can plan a trip of any length—a one-day excursion, a getaway weekend, or a three-week vacation—around any special interest. To get you started, the following pages contain six suggested itineraries geared toward a variety of interests. For more information, refer to the chapters listed—chapter names are bolded and chapter numbers appear inside black bullets. You can follow a suggested itinerary in its entirety, or shorten, lengthen, or combine parts of each, depending on your starting and ending points.

Discuss alternative routes and schedules with your travel companions—it's a great way to have fun, even before you leave home. And remember: don't hesitate to change your itinerary once you're on the road. Careful study and planning ahead of time will help you make informed decisions as you go, but spontaneity is the extra ingredient that will make your trip memorable.

Robert Holmes

Best of Northern California Tour

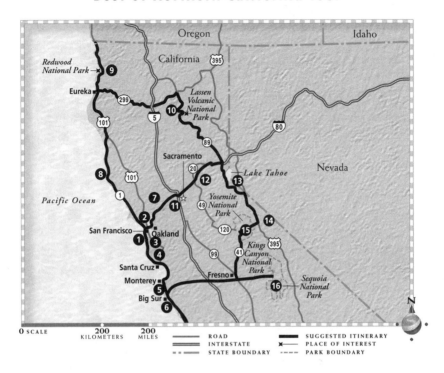

If you've got a couple of weeks to spend touring Northern California, this route will show you the best the area has to offer—from beaches to forests and big cities to small towns.

1. San Francisco
2. Marin County
3. Berkeley and Oakland
4. South Bay and the Peninsula
5. Monterey Peninsula
6. Big Sur
7. Wine Country
8. North Coast
9. Redwood Parks
10. Volcanoes
11. Sacramento
12. Gold Country
13. Lake Tahoe
14. Mono Lake and Owens Valley
15. Yosemite
16. Sequoia and Kings Canyon

Time needed for this trip: 2 to 3 weeks

Nature Lover's Tour

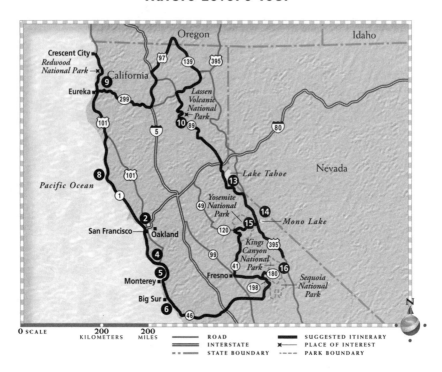

Northern California's diverse natural wonders are scattered about the region. For an unforgettable road trip, drive a full loop on CA 1, U.S. 101, CA 299, CA 89, and U.S. 395, with national park stops along the way. If you want to target your efforts, your scenic priorities should include Big Sur, Yosemite and Mono Lake, Lake Tahoe, Lassen and Shasta, and a redwood park.

6 **Big Sur**
5 **Monterey Peninsula** (Seventeen-Mile drive, Monterey Aquarium)
4 **South Bay** (Ano Nuevo)
2 **Marin** (Marin Headlands, Point Reyes)
8 **North Coast** (state parks and beaches)
9 **Redwood Parks**
10 **Volcanoes** (Lassen Volcanic National Park)
13 **Lake Tahoe** (D. L. Bliss State Park, Emerald Bay)
14 **Mono Lake** and **Owens Valley** (ancient bristlecone forest)
15 **Yosemite National Park**
16 **Sequoia** and **Kings Canyon National Park**

Time needed for this trip: 2 weeks

Arts and Culture Tour

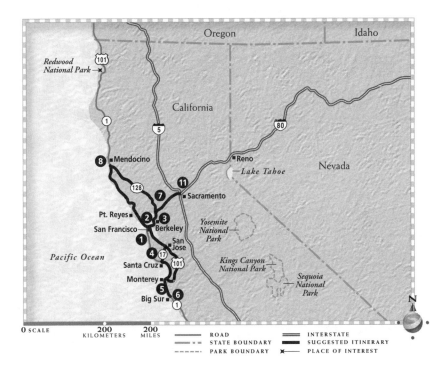

San Francisco is the centerpiece of any trip with a focus on the fruits of civilization. Use the city as a home base for day trips to the museums, universities, historic sites, and cultural enclaves of the Bay Area. Two- to 3-day tours to the north or south offer scenic splendor, fine restaurants, delightful inns, wonderful galleries, and charming towns.

❶ San Francisco
❷ Marin County (Tiburon, Sausalito)
❸ East Bay (University of California at Berkeley)
❹ South Bay (Stanford University, San Jose)
❺ Monterey Peninsula (Seventeen-Mile Drive, Carmel)
❻ Big Sur (galleries)
❼ Wine Country
❽ North Coast (Mendocino)
⓫ Sacramento

Time needed for this trip: 1 week (or a lifetime)

Family Fun Tour

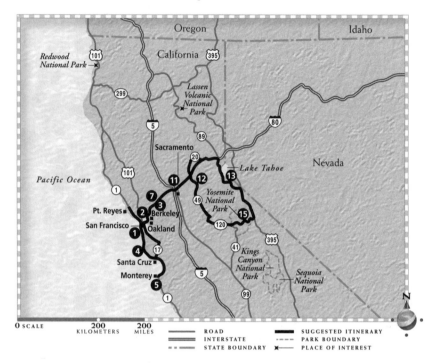

For a pleasant family trip, the key is to make sure the kids get hands-on fun, variety, and short drive times. Concentrate your trip in the crescent that runs from Monterey through San Francisco, Sacramento, the Gold Country, and Yosemite.

⑤ Monterey Peninsula (Monterey Bay Aquarium)
④ South Bay (Great America, Santa Cruz)
❶ San Francisco (Alcatraz, Exploratorium)
❷ Marin County (Bay Model, Point Reyes)
❸ East Bay (Lawrence Hall of Science)
❼ Wine Country (Marine World and Africa U.S.A.)
⑪ Sacramento (Old Sacramento, WaterWorld)
⑫ Gold Country (mines and caves)
⑬ Lake Tahoe (gondolas)
⑮ Yosemite

Time needed for this trip: 10 days

Best of the Bays Tour

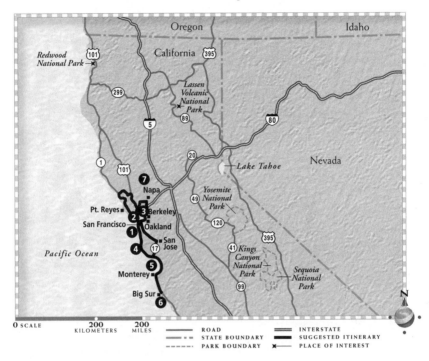

There's enough to keep anyone busy for weeks on California's central coast. Marine attractions include whale watching, kayaking, and observing elephant seals. The state's past is preserved in historic homes, missions, and museums. You can hike in redwood groves or immerse yourself in urban culture.

❻ Big Sur (Hearst Castle, parks, Point Lobos)
❺ Monterey Peninsula (Carmel, Monterey State Historic Park, Monterey Aquarium)
❹ South Bay (Año Nuevo, Stanford University, San Jose, Santa Cruz)
❶ San Francisco (Alcatraz, Chinatown, Golden Gate)
❷ Marin County (Headlands, Sausalito, Point Reyes)
❸ East Bay (Berkeley, Oakland, Mt. Diablo)
❼ Wine Country (Sonoma, Napa Valley, Calistoga)

Time needed for this trip: 1 to 2 weeks

High Sierras Tour

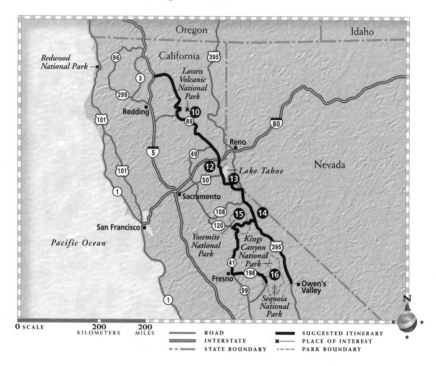

You can avoid the cities altogether and enjoy some of the nation's most spectacular places by staying in the high country. To the east and north, stay close
to U.S. 395 and CA 89. To connect Yosemite and Lake Tahoe, meander
through Gold Country on historic CA 49. Beautiful roads cross the range at
several points, including CA 120 in Yosemite, CA 88 south of Tahoe, and CA
70 through the Feather River canyon.

⑩ **Volcanoes** (Lassen Volcanic National Park)
⑫ **Gold Country**
⑬ **Lake Tahoe** (D. L. Bliss State Park, Emerald Bay)
⑭ **Mono Lake and Owens Valley** (ancient bristlecone forest)
⑮ **Yosemite National Park**
⑯ **Sequoia and Kings Canyon National Parks**

Time needed: 10 days

USING THE PLANNING MAP

A major aspect of itinerary planning is determining your mode of transportation and the route you will follow as you travel from destination to destination. The Planning Map on the following pages will allow you to do just that.

First, read through the destination chapters carefully and note the sights that intrigue you. Then, photocopy the Planning Map so you can try out several different routes that will take you to these destinations. (The mileage chart that follows will allow you to calculate your travel distances.) Decide where you will be starting your tour of Northern California. Will you fly into San Francisco, Oakland, or Sacramento, or will you start from somewhere else? Will you be driving from place to place or flying into major transportation hubs and renting a car for day trips? The answers to these questions will form the basis for your travel route design.

Once you have a firm idea of where your travels will take you, copy your route onto the additional Planning Map in the Appendix. You won't have to worry about where your map is, and the information you need on each destination will always be close at hand.

Robert Holmes

Planning Map: Northern California

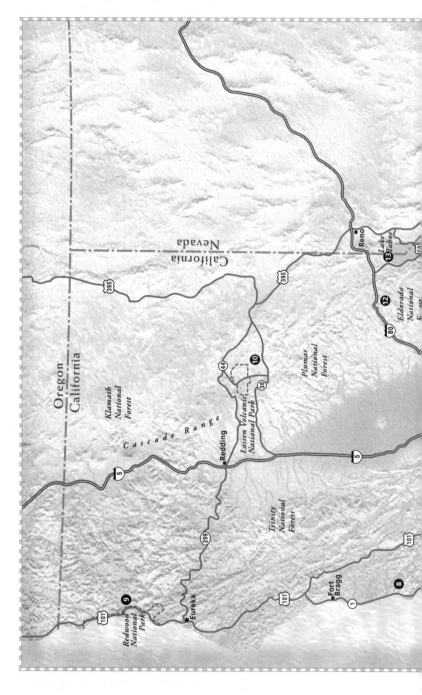

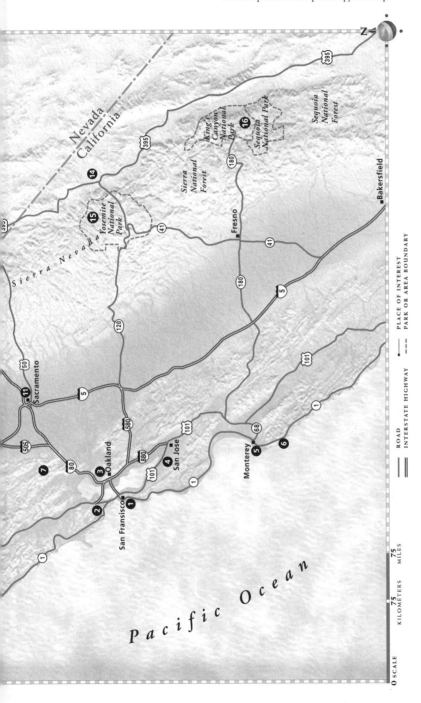

NORTHERN CALIFORNIA MILEAGE CHART

	Alturas	Chico	Crescent City	Eureka	Fresno	Lake Tahoe	Modesto	Monterey	Oakland	Red Bluff	Redding	Sacramento	San Francisco	San Jose	Santa Cruz	Sequoia N.P.	Stockton	Susanville	Ukiah
Chico	216																		
Crescent City	375	292																	
Eureka	301	228	84																
Fresno	471	267	542	448															
Lake Tahoe	265	155	461	395	291														
Modesto	377	173	448	364	94	197													
Monterey	517	329	476	392	177	346	180												
Oakland	404	195	371	287	160	198	66	113											
Red Bluff	176	41	251	187	245	210	201	357	192										
Redding	145	72	220	156	326	241	232	388	223	31									
Sacramento	307	103	382	294	164	120	70	226	92	131	162								
San Francisco	392	188	360	276	196	204	77	118	11	216	247	85							
San Jose	448	232	407	323	149	233	110	69	44	288	319	136	47						
Santa Cruz	478	269	437	353	177	255	140	41	74	318	349	166	77	30					
Sequoia N.P.	554	350	615	531	83	367	177	243	378	409	164	247	279	253	260				
Stockton	347	143	418	334	124	160	30	195	73	171	202	40	84	117	147	207			
Susanville	110	106	356	292	373	160	279	414	313	105	136	209	294	345	375	456	309		
Ukiah	327	166	240	156	302	258	208	236	131	156	187	138	120	167	197	385	62	178	
Yosemite Village	399	280	548	484	97	231	107	226	166	297	328	166	184	137	228	180	253	126	300

WHY VISIT NORTHERN CALIFORNIA?

Northern California is a land of superlatives. You'll find the world's tallest, oldest, and most massive living things in the wonderful forests of this state. The High Sierras boast the tallest mountain in the lower 48, visible from a highway through the nation's deepest valley. The country's most spectacular seacoast stretches for 80 miles south of Monterey. Great lava plateaus cover the northeast, guarded by Mount Shasta—the second tallest volcano in the contiguous United States.

The region's two premier vacation spots are located above a foothills region imbued with the history of the gold rush. Yosemite Valley in Yosemite National Park draws over 3 million visitors annually. To the north, the clear blue waters and forested mountains of the Lake Tahoe basin attract skiers in the winter and outdoor enthusiasts the rest of the year.

Capital city Sacramento anchors the huge Central Valley, the source of most of California's nation-leading agricultural production. The major rivers of the Sierra feed thousands of miles of canals and aqueducts to sustain the acres of pasture, grains, cotton, fruits, nuts, and vegetables. Wildlife refuges dot the valley, like islands along the Pacific flyway.

Northern California's heart is the San Francisco Bay Area, home to 6 million people. The East and South Bay regions support two premier universities, the cities of Oakland and San Jose, and the high tech Silicon Valley. To the north, Marin County is home to the active, wealthy, and politically correct—and possibly more therapists per capita then anywhere else in the world. The Wine Country, North Coast, and Monterey Peninsula surround the bay with a reservoir of scenic beauty, arts, culture, and cuisine.

The center of it all is the incomparable city of San Francisco. No trip to California is complete without a stroll through Chinatown, a trip to Alcatraz, and a walk on the Golden Gate Bridge—and there is so much more! Don't miss what venerable columnist Herb Caen calls the "Baghdad by the bay."

You will taste the blended spirit of Northern Californians as you explore. It's a region that's close in time to its roots, close geologically to both splendor and destruction, close technologically to the cutting edge, and close culturally to just about everything.

HISTORY

Before European explorers arrived, perhaps some 250,000 Indians inhabited California, living in small, hunter-gatherer tribes. They spoke many different dialects, which prevented extensive interaction. Most subsisted on the natural bounty of their home and migratory territories—fish, shellfish, and birds along the coast; acorn meal, deer, and small game farther inland.

In 1542, Juan Rodríquez Cabrillo and his crew were the first Europeans to see what would become the western United States, as they sailed north along the coast from Spanish-ruled Mexico. Though Cabrillo died on the way, his crew mapped the coast and claimed it for Spain. The claim changed hands when English pirate Sir Francis Drake sailed into a coastal bay for repairs—probably Drakes Bay south of Point Reyes—and claimed the area for Queen Elizabeth. The Spanish returned in 1602, landing in Monterey and reasserting sovereignty.

Settlement began in 1769 when Father Junipero Serra and Gaspar de Portola led an expedition to found missions along the coast. By 1823, twenty-one missions had been established, most separated by " . . . a hard day's travel . . . " along *El Camino Real* (the King's Highway). Military garrisons, or *presidios*, were created to secure Spanish control. Ultimately, the missions brought more death than salvation by introducing disease to the Indian population.

In 1833, thirteen years after Mexico's independence from Spain, state support for the missions ended and they fell into disuse. To encourage settlement, Mexico issued huge land grants to ranchers who produced hides and tallow for export. In the same period, American opportunity seekers trickled in by sea, and Russian sea otter hunters operated along the northern coast.

In the 1840s, American settlers began arriving over land via routes devised by Captain John C. Fremont, Kit Carson, and others. In 1846, hearing that the U.S. had declared war on Mexico, settlers in Sonoma staged the Bear Flag Revolt. They seized the home of a cooperative General M. G. Vallejo, raised the Bear Flag over the square, and created the California Republic. The republic was soon disestablished and the Bear Flag exchanged for the Stars and Stripes. U.S. troops occupied the presidios, and California became an American territory.

On January 24, 1848, James Marshall was working on John Sutter's sawmill in the Sierra foothills when he discovered gold in the millrace. Within two years, California's population swelled from 15,000 to 100,000—the gold rush was on. San Francisco blossomed as a center of trade, wealth, and power. California gained statehood in 1850 and, through political power plays, divided up many land grant rancheros, making them available to speculators. The boom faded as the easy gold and silver disappeared, though by now, California was well established. Agriculture picked up where precious metals left off. The Civil War had little impact on the state, save to encourage economic self-reliance.

High hopes following the completion of the transcontinental railroad in 1869 were dashed in the 1870s. Inflated land prices, cheap eastern goods, and an oversupply of labor led to the "Black Friday" of April 26, 1875, when the Bank of California shut its doors to stop a run. Recovery was gradual, but the rich resources of the state fueled continuing expansion. By the dawn of the twentieth century, San Francisco had risen to a peak of wealth and gilded corruption.

All the glory of San Francisco came crashing down at 5:12 a.m. on April 18, 1906, when the first "Big One" hit. A devastating earthquake led to fires that destroyed about three-fourths of the buildings in the city. San Franciscans still live with the heritage of community and industry that rebuilt the city, knowing all along that another "Big One" will come some day. The Panama Pacific International Exposition of 1915 celebrated the return of San Francisco, grander than ever.

Several waves of immigration swelled California's population. From 1910 to 1920, Mexicans fleeing revolution moved to the state in large numbers. The depression years brought refugees from dust bowl states. During World War II, thousands of defense workers came to the Bay Area and stayed. After the war, thousands of soldiers elected to remain as well.

Recent history is as complex as 10 million people living in such a diverse region might produce. San Francisco has welcomed Beat poets, flower children, immigrants, and gays. Berkeley has hosted the Free Speech Movement, anti-war protests, and social reform activism. Silicon Valley has grown into the world's high tech leader. Cesar Chavez led farm worker unionization in the Salinas Valley. Environmentalists have battled farmers over water rights issues and loggers over forest preservation. Suburban sprawl has eaten up rural land while creating traffic nightmares. And still, Northern California grows, struggles, and triumphs.

ARTS AND CULTURE

From afar, the Northern California culture seems singular and distinctive. The image of laid-back, post-hippie liberals sipping wine and lattes in the "land of fruits and nuts" is a widespread caricature. The truth, of course, is far more complex—though, thankfully, those who feed the stereotype can be found in relative abundance.

San Francisco is undoubtedly the capital of "culture." High society money and taste sustain the excellent symphony, ballet, opera, and fine arts museums. The newspaper still runs a society column with photos showing who's who chatting with who-else-is-who at fundraiser socials. In and around the city, there is no shortage of wealth, along with its antiquated habits and its thoroughly posh lifestyle.

The gay community in San Francisco, though not a monolithic culture, explodes the blandness of stodgy old money with huge, wild, costumed celebrations. Few can experience a Gay Pride parade without gaining respect for the extremes of personal expression. The ongoing fight of gays and lesbians for equal rights, acceptance, and an end to AIDS shows in the efforts of independent film makers, writers, and artists.

Many in the largely Hispanic Mission District have lived close to political and economic struggle for years. The Mission is also a hip area to live for the young and visionary—hip with an edge. Political sentiment is left-leaning, and the art, poetry, and theater born in the area often express that sentiment. The city's best and most passionate murals are found on Mission walls.

In general, the Bay Area integrates a rich variety of arts and cultures with great aplomb. Black-tied connoisseurs, beer-bellied bigots, green-haired skaters, politically correct vegans, Harley riding dykes, pocket protector nerds, Beemer cruising homeys, baggy pants grungers, tie-dyed freaks, and just plain folks rub elbows daily—and they like it that way.

Move away from the city scene, and the arts and culture sort themselves out a bit. Artistic centers like Carmel and Mendocino yield works that are calmer and inspired by nature. Popular music shifts from heady and angst-draining to friendly, lyric, and folksy.

Small, rural communities far from San Francisco resent their dependency on distant politics and economics. The outward friendliness of a culture may hide much, as in Humboldt County, where the two main sources of income—marijuana growing and logging—are both under constant pressure. Yet some of the most spiritually centered art comes from more isolated regions of the state. Of course, so do chainsaw-carved redwood bears.

CUISINE

As a whole, Californians consume as many Big Macs and Diet Pepsis as people anywhere else in the nation—perhaps more. Northern California's cities and suburbs are home to the same fast-food joints, strip malls, and convenience stores that we all know and love. The region is firmly in the grip of '90s pop cuisine. However . . .

When you step above the standard fare, the picture is bright indeed! The region is blessed with three key elements of fine cuisine—great seafood, excellent wines, and the best produce around. When these ingredients are provided to a thoroughly international cadre of chefs and restaurateurs, the results range from darn good to spectacular. San Francisco, Berkeley, Oakland, Marin County, Wine Country, North Coast, and Monterey Peninsula are all rich in quality eating opportunities, ranging from fine to funky.

The most interesting restaurants and cafés offer a marvelous synthesis of styles unique to the region. Sometimes, the best you can do in categorizing a menu is to apply terms such as "mixed grill," "eclectic cuisine," or "fusion cooking." A budget lunch at Berkeley's hole-in-the-wall Meal Ticket may feature Chinese pasta salad with a French baguette and tropical "house juice," or grilled Alaskan salmon with south-of-the-border cilantro salsa.

At Chez Panisse, in Berkeley's "Gourmet Ghetto," chef Alice Waters pioneered "California cuisine," an ideal blend of French basics, international contributions, health consciousness, and inspiration. Individual dishes may have various ethnic roots, but are generally on the lighter side, featuring liberal use of fresh produce, which is often locally grown or regionally authentic. Vegetarian alternatives are strongly represented on many menus, and artful presentation is stressed.

The influence of California cuisine has spread to most non-ethnic and non-traditional menus in the state. You'll often find Euro-style or Asian treatments of meat, seafood, and pasta, along with a rice or exotic grain side dish, multi-grain bread, and designer salad. Marvelous omelet and frittata breakfasts feature ingredients you simply can't find in Kansas. Lunch sandwiches and salads are the greenest anywhere.

Competition is stiff enough up and down the coast that Denny's grade food can only be found at Denny's. The rest of the state is less enlightened, although islands of creativity can be found everywhere.

FLORA AND FAUNA

Since the end of unregulated exploitation, California sea mammals have enjoyed a vigorous recovery. Gray whales migrate south in December and January, returning north from February through April. The beach at Año Nuevo is empty of elephant seals only in the summer, with peak concentrations present during mating and calving from mid-December into March. Seals and sea lions congregate on rocks or isolated beaches along the coast. South of Santa Cruz, sea otters can be seen floating beyond the surf, preening and cracking shellfish.

Ocean fisheries are struggling, but several sea life reserves protect rich ecosystems. At low tide, you can find starfish and anemones in tide pools, as divers search for abalone in the shallows.

On shore, beach grasses and dune land creepers give way to coastal meadows and shrubby scrub. On the central coast, Monterey cypress and pine shape themselves to shed the wind. Jackrabbits, mice, and ground birds hide from searching coyotes and soaring raptors. In coastal wetlands, algae and eelgrass yield to cordgrass, pickleweed, and heath. Shorebirds are plentiful.

The "fog fence" divides the moisture-loving coastal forest from the drier interior ecosystems. Redwood-dominated, mixed-evergreen forest thrives in the wet north. As you move south, the redwoods concentrate into cooler valleys while the coverage of pine, oak, and madrone increases. Deer are plentiful, as are raccoon, skunk, fox, and other small mammals.

Inland from the coast, oak-dotted, grassy hills ring the Central Valley. Fields of California poppy, goldfields, and lupines paint the hillsides in spring, while summer turns all to brown and gold. Thick oak and chaparral concentrate into steep defiles, defended by poison oak, while shiny leafed manzanita blends into the mountain forests above. Mountain lions stalk their prey in the remote high country.

In the Central Valley, the sea of grass that once hosted antelope and herds of tule elk is long gone. Native species have been displaced by aggressive alien species, overgrazing, and cultivation. Tule reed wetlands have been drained, and rivers diked and channeled. Only isolated areas resemble what once was, though the valley plays host to thousands of resident and migratory birds. Egrets, herons, cranes, ducks, swans, and geese frequent wildlife refuges, wetlands, and the Sacramento delta.

Ponderosa pine dominates lower Sierra slopes, with sugar pine, incense cedar, and fir growing higher up. Sequoia groves are found between 5000 and 7500 feet. While the grizzly bear displayed on the state flag is now extinct in California, black bears are numerous. They forage through the woods seeking plants, berries, small animals, and carrion. Higher still, a subalpine forest of red fir and lodgepole pine climbs toward the tree line where gnarled foxtail pines cling to life. Above this, marmots whistle among the lichen-covered granite while hikers photograph the diverse wildflowers and tundra-like vegetation of alpine meadows.

White fir, Jeffrey pine, and quaking aspen are common on the dry, eastern slopes of the Sierras and Cascades. Pinyon-juniper forests appear in the middle elevations, while pungent sagebrush spreads throughout the semi-arid eastern basins. Above it all, herds of bighorn sheep graze the high vales.

Forests of redwood and Douglas fir grow in the wet and mountainous northwest. Remnant herds of Roosevelt elk can be found grazing in national park lands. Moving eastward, the land dries in stages. The forest changes to pine and pinyon-juniper, and then into range land, sagebrush basins, and barren alkali flats.

THE LAY OF THE LAND

Northern California offers distinct landforms on a scale you won't find elsewhere. Dominating the state is the vast pairing of the Sierra Nevada mountain range with the great Central Valley at its feet. Together they are almost 400 miles long and over 100 miles wide—a geologically simple range and valley combination as large as the state of Pennsylvania!

The Sierras rise gradually from the Central Valley up to the high peaks on the eastern side of the range. From there, the mountains drop sharply into valleys and basins. In the Owens Valley, the elevation drops 2 vertical miles, from 14,495-foot Mount Whitney to the valley floor. To the east, the White Mountains with their sparse crown of ancient bristlecone pines reach to over 14,000 feet themselves, adding to the spectacular scale of the valley below.

The high elevations of the western Sierras feature U-shaped, glacier-cut valleys. The most famous are Kern Canyon in the wilderness of Sequoia National Park, Kings Canyon (the nation's deepest) in Kings Canyon National Park, and Yosemite Valley. As the mountains fall westward, the valleys sort themselves into deep-cut watersheds with long gradual ridges in between.

The Sierra rivers drain into the Sacramento River in the north and the San Juaquin in the south, both of which flow through the Central Valley and into the Sacramento delta. Here, sluggish waters pass through a thousand miles of canals and sloughs, eventually emptying into San Francisco Bay, then flowing through the Golden Gate and into the Pacific.

The mountains of the Coast Range are lower than the Sierras, rising to forested heights of 6000 feet or more in a few spots, but generally running in long north-south ridges with 1000- to 3000-foot summits. The valleys provide warm homes for towns, farms, and vineyards, while hillside pastures host sheep and cattle.

Moving northward, the peaks of the Sierras dwindle, those of the Coast Range rise, and the southern reaches of the Klamath and Cascade ranges intrude. The landscape becomes rugged and confused, rivers cut tortuous paths to the Pacific, and forest covers all. The land is wet and wild, drying in steps as you move eastward, with successive peaks and ranges blocking the flow of moisture.

The northeastern corner of the state is a land of volcanic cones, broad plateaus with exposed lava fields, and the beginnings of the basin and range landform which dominates Nevada. Mount Shasta rises like a glacier-capped sentinel. Mount Lassen—which blew its top in 1915— marks the southern end of the Cascade Range. The northeast offers wide forests, broad valleys, lonely lakes, and primeval geology to the intrepid traveler.

OUTDOOR ACTIVITIES

California's extensive public lands offer great hiking opportunities. Day hike destinations include the summit of Mount Lassen, the passes and summits above Lake Tahoe, the Methuselah Trail in the Ancient Bristlecone Pine Forest, the Redwood Mountain Grove Trail in Sequoia National Park, Paradise Valley in Kings Canyon National Park, Mono Pass in the Yosemite high country, Yosemite Falls and the north rim of the valley, and Calaveras Big Trees State Park. In the west, many good hikes are found in the coastal Marin wildlands, Tomales Point in Point Reyes National Seashore, several state parks on the North Coast,

Punta Gorda Lighthouse on the Lost Coast, the Bull Creek Trail in Humboldt Redwoods State Park, Redwood Creek Trail in Redwood National Park, and Fern Canyon in Prairie Creek Redwoods State Park. There are many others of merit. In coastal and foothill areas, follow tick prevention advice and watch out for poison oak!

Extended backpacking and horse pack trips can be enjoyed in several areas, the most spectacular being the High Sierras. Together with some smaller protected areas, the Golden Trout Wilderness, Sequoia National Park, Kings Canyon National Park, John Muir Wilderness, Ansel Adams Wilderness, and the southern half of Yosemite National Park preserve the lower 48's largest contiguous roadless area. North of Yosemite, great wilderness areas include the Desolation Wilderness and the lake and granite country of the Emigrant Wilderness. The Trinity Alps Wilderness and Marble Mountain Wilderness are the best of the northern mountains. At the crest of the Coast Range, east of Big Sur, the Ventana Wilderness features highland forest hiking with volcanic summits. The Pacific Crest Trail runs the length of the Sierras, crosses west to the Klamath Mountains, and then turns east again to the southern Cascades.

Mountain biking was invented in Marin County and is immensely popular throughout the region. Areas featuring miles of marked and mapped trails, good rental shops, and lots of riders include the west Marin wildlands, the East Bay hills above Berkeley and Oakland, the peninsula hills from Santa Cruz to San Francisco, the Lake Tahoe basin, and the Mammoth Lakes region. Road biking is also popular in the state. Backroads and minor highways in the southern Coast Range and Sierra foothills offer great rides through open rolling country.

Climbing options abound in the Sierras. While the faces of Yosemite are legendary, the same hard granite appears throughout the range. Other popular destinations include Castle Crags State Park and Pinnacles National Monument. Mountaineers enjoy various routes in the Sierras and the Trinity Alps, and Mount Shasta attracts fans of glaciers and exposed summits.

Rafting and kayaking are particularly popular in the rivers that drain the Sierras. The various forks of the Feather, Yuba, American, and Stanislaus rivers are well served by rental shops and guide outfits. For a one-stop inquiry, call Whitewater Voyages, a large company that offers a variety of trips on several rivers, (800) 488-7238. Canoeing is popular on quiet segments of rivers such as the Russian and Eel, as well as in the calm waters of lakes and estuaries.

Ocean sports are enjoyed up and down the coast, though cold water and rough surf offer stiff challenges along many stretches. Surfers frequent several areas along the peninsula between Santa Cruz and San Francisco and also in Humboldt County on the North Coast. Windsurfers enjoy the stiff breezes and modest swells on San Francisco Bay. Sea kayaking is newly popular in the region. Diving locations, instruction, and equipment rental shops can be found in Monterey and on the North Coast.

Soaring and hot air balloon trips can be enjoyed in the Napa Valley and elsewhere. Tahoe is a good location for both paragliding and parasailing. Certain bluffs on the peninsula coast are popular with hang gliders.

Rivers and lakes in the northern mountains offer the best trout and steelhead fishing. Wild populations are strong above the dams in the Sierras and in some coastal rivers. Stocked waters are options elsewhere. The salmon situation is grim. A California fishing license can be purchased for $23 at California Fish and Game offices or fishing stores.

PRACTICAL TIPS

HOW MUCH WILL IT COST?

Travel in Northern California tends to be more expensive than other areas. Gasoline prices are generally higher than much of the rest of the nation because of strict emissions laws, high state gas taxes, and specially formulated gasolines. Also, the popularity of several areas means inflated prices for food and lodging.

In late spring, there is always a rise in gas prices, ostensibly due to increased demand. In 1996, low supplies and reformulated gas costs were added to the list, allowing for the justification of price hikes up to 50 percent. Remote locations saw prices close to $2 per gallon while in the Bay Area, name-brand gas broke $1.60. Typically, prices drop slowly as the summer progresses. It's tempting to believe that companies create the initial spike to blunt consumers' anger over the more general rise that persists through the season. At $1.50 per gallon, in a vehicle getting 20 mpg, a 2,000-mile state tour will cost $150. In a 5-mpg motor home, the same trip comes to $600.

Expensive lodging can be found almost anywhere, but even budget prices are inflated in certain areas. Wine Country, the Russian River Valley, the coasts of Mendocino and Sonoma, Lake Tahoe, parts of Gold Country, Big Sur, the Monterey Peninsula, and San Francisco are all on the list. In vacation areas, prices climb between 10 and 30 percent in the summer and between 20 and 50 percent on summer weekends. Inns and bed and breakfasts will often have two-day minimum stays for Friday and Saturday nights during the months of May through September. Private campgrounds may show similar changes. All of this is possible because in these peak periods and locations accommodations are generally booked solid, often well in advance.

Basic campsites generally range from $9 to $16; sites with hookups from $15 to $30. Motel 6 style and private budget motels list double occupancy rates from $25 to $45. The range for mid-grade places is broader, but expect to pay from $40 to $90 in the off season or off the beaten track, $60 to $150 otherwise. In popular areas, the nice inns, bed and breakfasts, and hotels with history or character usually range from $80 to $140. Spa suites with views can climb toward $250, while Euro-style rooms with a shared bath may be bargains at as low as $50. Fine hotels range from $130 to outer space. Note, too, that most counties have some variation of a bed tax that adds about ten percent to the bill.

Dining costs are also somewhat inflated in the popular destinations, although stiff competition and consistently hungry locals assure that good budget choices are generally available everywhere. The egg, potato, burger, fries, and pasta style budget traveler, who opts to eat every meal out, will spend about $30 to $40 dollars a day, per person, tax and tip included. Switch to an omelet breakfast, lunch special, and fish dinner with wine, and you're talking $40 to $60. Clearly, free or light breakfasts and picnic lunches will save you money while fine dining blowouts have the opposite effect.

In sum, two people—driving about 150 miles per day in an average car, mixing camping with average lodging and the occasional charming inn, blending average meals with picnics and the occasional splurge, paying admission fees at various sites, and buying the odd souvenir—will spend about $1,000 per week. You'll have to determine your own niche—it's probably somewhere in between eating cheese sandwiches as you search for free campsites in your Geo Metro and hopping between four-star resorts in your Mercedes 500L.

CLIMATE

For the most part, Northern California offers pleasant weather throughout the year, particularly in the coastal regions south of Eureka. Rain amounts rise and fall in a steady bell curve, peaking in December and January while leaving most of the region bone dry in July. Extended rain periods are possible any time from October through March.

The Bay Area enjoys a remarkable and complex system of microclimates. Prevailing westerly winds send cool air flowing through the Golden Gate on most days of the year. This air chills the tip of the city, then flows across the bay, and washes up onto the hills above Berkeley and Oakland. Move up or down the bay away from this tongue of air, and the temperature rises dramatically. When it's 68° F. on Alcatraz, it can be 85° F. in San Jose.

Fog and low rain clouds follow similar patterns. Fog occurs year-round along the coast, though it is particularly common through the nights and mornings of the summer, burning off briefly in the afternoons. One thing to remember is that fog banks always have tops and fronts. Thus, by choosing an inn a little higher on the hill or a campsite on the inland side of the ridge, you might enjoy a beautiful sunset or dry tent instead of a dank sea of gray. In San Francisco, someone in the fog zone might experience hundreds of more hours of fog in a year than a friend over the hill, just ten blocks away!

Cross over the last ridge east of the coast, and you enter the Central Valley. Here, it is notoriously hot in the summer, as are several other inland valleys with low elevation. While San Francisco is balmy, the San Jose basin and the Napa Valley can be oppressive, simply because coastal mountains block ocean-cooled air from moderating the temperature. Though it's milder in the winter, the Central Valley often experiences "Tule fog"—a thick-as-pea-soup blanket that causes serious, chain reaction car wrecks every year.

Heavy snows close several main roads through the Sierras all winter long, though Yosemite Valley and the highways to Lake Tahoe are open year-round. Anyone traveling the mountainous areas of California in winter is required by law to carry chains or to drive a four-wheel-drive vehicle with snow tires. High mountain weather is generally mild in the summer, though occasional storms can cause delays and road problems. The lower slopes and foothills can be almost as hot as the Central Valley

The far northwest approaches rainforest conditions in certain coastal areas. Moisture that amounts to little more than a half-day fog in Monterey gathers into persistent, drizzly masses around Eureka. These conditions, however, are natural for the magnificent redwood groves. At the cost of wearing a rain jacket, you will enjoy the forest at its finest.

In the northeast, it's dry, though rain or snow falls with fair frequency on the high western slopes of the mountain ridges that march eastward into the basin and range country of Nevada.

WHEN TO GO

With the variety of destination and activity choices available in Northern California, there's a case to be made for visiting at any time of the year.

In the winter, rain is more frequent, but it follows the vagaries of the jet stream and can be absent for weeks at a time. Unlike most areas of the country, California begins to "green up" as soon as the rains come. The coastal hills are particularly beautiful when the new grass pushes through the old—something that can begin to happen in December! Winter sports are an obvious option in the mountains, and you can count on easy traveling in cool to mild temperatures everywhere else.

Spring can bring the best of all possible worlds. The coastal hills are lush and green, rain frequency diminishes, the summer fogs haven't arrived, nor have the crowds of vacationers that arrive with them. Water from melting snow gushes over waterfalls and provides peak thrills to rafters. Spring skiers can enjoy a day on the slopes above Tahoe, then sit by the lake in shorts and watch the sailboats. You'll enjoy off-season lodging prices and availability, but beginning as early as mid-April things begin to tighten up.

In the summer, the rains are gone, the hills turn gold, the beaches are warm (though the water stays cold!), and the tourists arrive. One of the season's best features is that the high mountain areas open up for exploration. Spring conditions come late to the high country so that hikers and bikers are greeted by fresh growth and wildflowers. If your visit must be in summer, focus on coastal and high mountain areas and save the valleys and foothills for another time. Plan on doing more advance work reserving rooms and campsites—and plan on spending

NORTHERN CALIFORNIA CLIMATE

Average daily high and low temperatures in degrees Fahrenheit, plus monthly precipitation in inches.

	San Francisco	Sacramento	Truckee	Eureka
Jan.	55/42 4.5	53/39 3.8	38/16 5.6	54/41 6
Mar.	62/45 3	65/44 2.8	46/21 4.3	55/43 5.3
May	67/50 .5	80/52 .3	60/36 1.2	58/48 1.4
July	72/54 .1	95/59 .1	81/43 .4	61/52 .1
Sept.	74/54 .3	90/57 .4	73/37 .9	62/51 .9
Nov.	64/46 2.5	65/44 3	52/24 4.4	58/45 6.4

more money. Note also that traffic floods out of urban areas on Friday afternoons and then floods back in again when the weekend is done.

Things quiet down again after Labor Day. Cooler days and crisper nights return, prices drop, availability rises, and travelers go back to work or school. The mountains offer ideal conditions for backpacking since passes are open and streams are low and easy to cross. Fall colors are particularly enticing along the eastern slope of the High Sierras, and in the aspen tree zones high up on the western slope.

TRANSPORTATION

Car Travel

Three key highway corridors provide access to the best sights of Northern California with the least amount of extraneous driving: CA 1 with U.S. 101, CA 49, and CA 89 with U.S. 395.

CA 1 and **U.S. 101**: These two highways parallel each other through coastal California, from below Big Sur until they merge near Eureka. The Coast Highway, CA 1, is a slow, winding, sometimes tortuous two-lane road that hugs the edge of the continent. But this is the route for enjoying the spectacular California coastline. U.S. 101 parallels the coast, about 20 miles or so inland, until it becomes the coast highway north of Eureka. It provides the most direct access to the Bay Area, Wine Country, and redwood parks.

If time is tight and you'll pass through the coastal region only once, drive the Big Sur Coast on CA 1 from San Luis Obispo to Monterey. Cut in to U.S. 101 to see San Francisco and the Wine Country, then take CA 128 through Anderson Valley and back out to CA 1 for the Mendocino Coast.

CA 49: Numbered in honor of the forty-niners of gold rush days, CA 49 runs through the Sierra foothills from Oakhurst, south of Yosemite, to Nevada City. It then heads up the Yuba River Valley and over the mountains toward Nevada. The road passes through numerous historic towns that are well worth a look. Several gold rush related parks and attractions are just off the road.

Many good loops incorporating CA 49 are possible. All three western access roads to Yosemite cross CA 49, as do four High Sierra pass roads, Interstate 80, and CA 89. From Oakhurst at the southern end of CA 49, Fresno and the access to Sequoia and Kings Canyon National Parks are temptingly close. If time is short and history is not

a priority, skip CA 49 as a general route and head for the high mountains. You can use information in the "Gold Country" chapter to
choose a spot or two to visit near your route through the foothills.

CA 89 and **U.S. 395**: This route is to the mountains what CA 1
is to the coast, though it is generally much faster. CA 89 starts at the
foot of Mount Shasta, runs south through lonely forest country, and
reaches an altitude of 8000 feet as it winds through Lassen Volcanic
National Park. Continuing past big Lake Almanor, it passes through
lovely high valleys, along the scenic western shore of Lake Tahoe, and
through gorgeous Sierra passes before it meets U.S. 395 and ends.
Continuing south, U.S. 395 passes through jumbled volcanic terrain,
past amazing Mono Lake, on through hot springs country near
Mammoth, and down into the spectacular Owens Valley.

Except for the Tahoe area, this corridor is relatively lightly trav-
eled. Side roads take you to lovely High Sierra valleys, Yosemite
National Park, the Ancient Bristlecone Pine Forest, and Bodie State
Historic Park. Loops are hard south of Yosemite, but easy to the north.

Air Travel

San Francisco, San Jose, Sacramento, and Oakland are all busy hubs of
interstate travel. Most major airlines have long distance routes to San
Francisco. Several, including Alaska, American, Reno Air, Southwest,
and United Shuttle, offer frequent discount flights to a variety of western cities.

While San Francisco International provides the most direct access to
the city, the Oakland airport is one of the best options for flying into the
Bay Area. Though growing rapidly, the airport is more relaxed and easier
to navigate than San Francisco International. A 20-minute, $2-shuttle
takes passengers to the BART (Bay Area Rapid Transit) station. Staying in
Berkeley can be easier and a bit cheaper than San Francisco.

Rail Travel

Though the heyday of passenger trains is long past, there's still nothing
that can compare to the relaxed magic of rail travel. Imagine sipping a
cool drink in the dome car as you gaze into a canyon, or dining on fresh
eggs and toast as Mount Shasta slides slowly by.

Two great Amtrak trains make daily runs through California. The
California Zephyr leaves Oakland for Chicago in the morning, winding

along the edge of the American River Canyon and climbing over Donner Pass to arrive in Reno in the early evening. The westbound trip arrives in Reno in the morning, Oakland in the afternoon. The *Coast Starlight* goes from Los Angeles to Oakland during the day, runs through the Central Valley at night, passes Mount Shasta in the morning, and travels on to Seattle. Southbound, it's Mount Shasta in the evening and Oakland in the morning. The timing is right on both of these runs for optimal daylight scenery viewing (though short daylight hours in the winter trim viewing hours).

Amtrak also has shorter, more frequent runs with stops in the Central Valley, as well as private connector bus service that will take you to such places as Yosemite and Sequoia National Parks. Travelers to the Bay Area can transfer directly to BART (see below) at the Richmond station. Call (800) 872-7245 for reservations.

Urban Transit

San Francisco, Berkeley, Oakland, and several other communities are linked by the excellent BART (Bay Area Rapid Transit) system. In San Francisco, you can step off the BART and onto a cable car at the Embarcadero or Powell Street stations.

The MUNI bus and trolley systems in San Francisco cover the city like a blanket. AC Transit in the East Bay, SAMTRANS on the peninsula, and Golden Gate Transit in Marin County are all very good. Several ferry companies travel to San Francisco from Oakland and Marin County. CalTrain has frequent commuter train service on the peninsula between San Jose and San Francisco. In the Bay Area, parking can be expensive and the traffic, nightmarish. Consider a BART-based mass transit day of exploration.

San Jose and Sacramento both have light rail and bus systems, though they are of more use to commuters than travelers. Attractions in these cities are generally in the central downtown area.

CAMPING, LODGING, AND DINING

With over half of Northern California protected in public lands of one kind or another, there is no shortage of good quality campgrounds. U.S. National Forest campgrounds are renowned for providing beautiful, private sites for about $9 to $12 dollars. National and state park sites are often as good at an average price of $14 to

$16. Private camping is much more varied in quality—you can find bad sites for $30 and great ones for $10—but RV and fifth-wheel campers will find hookups and pull-through sites more consistently available at private campgrounds.

The common problem of low availability on weekends and during peak season is magnified in the Northern California region. Mild year-round weather encourages weekenders to camp when the sun is out, even in the off season. In late spring and summer, Californians fleeing the city quickly jam campgrounds in popular areas. When possible, call the park in which you hope to stay and ask if there are likely to be sites open at your arrival time and date. If not, use a reservation system to secure a spot. The reservation numbers for the most frequently used campsites are listed on the "Resources" pages of this chapter.

Reservation fees are in addition to campground fees. National Forest sites are reservable only at certain popular campgrounds. Some sites are always left for first-come, first-served use.

Free camping is legal in dispersed campsites on Bureau of Land Management and Forest Service lands, as well as at certain highway pull-outs. It's also fairly common wherever hidden turnouts on unused roads suggest that a quiet sleep from dusk to dawn won't ruffle any feathers.

Northern California is blessed with scores of wonderful lodging options. B&Bs and charming inns abound, particularly in Wine Country and along the North Coast. Nineteenth and early twenti-eth-century historic hotels have been lovingly restored in many towns. Modern resorts and hotels, chain motels, and mom-and-pop options fill out the list nicely. The same availability suggestions apply to any and all lodging alternatives in popular areas: *check ahead and reserve when advised*.

This guide features a varied lodging list, giving special attention to unique, historic, outstanding, or necessary alternatives. In areas where one type of lodging dominates—expensive, romantic getaway inns on the North Coast for example—effort is made to list types appropriate to other budgets and travel styles. All prices listed are for double occu-pancy. Price ranges reflect basic room to luxury suite differences as well as seasonal variations. Those interested in thorough listings of one type of lodging should consult sources such as a B&B guide or Best Western directory. Suggestions, along with national reservation numbers, are listed in the "Recommended Reading" pages.

With the ocean nearby, the best wines in the country, the finest produce available, and a cuisine all its own, California is a fine diner's paradise. Even budget travel couples should try to reserve an extra $100 (or more) for a one-time splurge. Many fine restaurants are quite casual so dusty walking shoes and a worn polo shirt won't cause a stir. Listings are usually lunch and dinner places unless specifically noted as breakfast spots. Many restaurants are closed one or two days a week, often Sunday, Monday, and/or Tuesday. This is not specified in the listings, so call ahead.

RECOMMENDED READING

Backroad Wineries of Northern California by Bill Gleeson—good guide with information on tours and tasting.

Bed & Breakfast California by Linda Kay Bristow—scores of options for those interested in the B&B circuit.

Birder's Guide to Northern California by Lolo & Jim Westrich—has great suggestions for bird watching locations.

California Historical Landmarks (California Office of Historic Preservation)—records the writing of every historic plaque in the state. It's good as a rough historic guide for choosing stops and routes.

The Celebrated Jumping Frog of Calaveras County and Other Sketches by Mark Twain—Twain spent a number of years in California.

The Grapes of Wrath; *Cannery Row*; *East of Eden* by John Steinbeck—Several of Steinbeck's works are set in California.

Ishi in Two Worlds: A Biography of the Last Wild Indian in North America by Theodora Kroeber—tells the story of Ishi, last of the Yahi Indians, who wandered into the town of Oroville seeking help in 1911.

The Luck of Roaring Camp and Other Sketches (1870) by Bret Harte—Harte romanticized the gold rush days in several works.

My First Summer in the Sierra (1869), *The Mountains of California* (1894), and *Steep Trails* (1918) by John Muir—Muir led the battle for preservation of Yosemite and other areas.

On the Road by Jack Kerouac—a classic of the beat generation.

Pacific Coast Tree Finder by Tom Watts—a simple, clear guide for determining what kind of tree you've found. It's typically available in park shops.

The Valley of the Moon by Jack London—set in the Sonoma Valley. London grew up in Oakland, later working in canneries and on the docks. He lived the last years of his life with his wife near Glen Ellen.

RESOURCES

American Automobile Association: (800) 222-4357, for emergencies only

California Division of Tourism: (800) 862-2543, P.O. Box 1499, Sacramento, CA 95812-1499

California Highway Patrol Road Information: (800) 427-7623

California State Parks: (916) 653-6995, 1416 Ninth Street, Sacramento, CA 95814

Campground Reservation Numbers
    California State Parks: (800) 444-7275
    National Forests: (800) 280-2267
    National Parks & Monuments: (800) 365-2267
    Yosemite National Park: (800) 436-7275

Lodging Chain Reservation Numbers
    Best Western: 800-528-1234
    Clarion Inn: 800-CLARION
    Comfort Inn: 800-228-5150
    Days Inn: 800-325-2525
    Econolodge: 800-55-ECONO
    Hilton: 800-HILTON-7
    Holiday Inn: 800-465-4329
    Marriott: 800-228-9290
    Motel 6: 800-4-MOTEL-6
    Quality Suites: 800-228-5151
    Ramada Inns: 800-2-RAMADA
    Red Lion: 800-RED-LION
    Sheraton: 800-325-3535
    Sleep Inn: 800-SLEEP-IN
    Super 8: 800-800-8000
    Travelodge: 800-578-7878

National Forest Service: (415) 705-2874, 630 Sansome Street, San Francisco, CA 94111

National Park Service Western Region Information Center: (415) 556-0560, Fort Mason Building 201, San Francisco, CA 94123

Web Listings (all begin with http://)
    California State Home Page: www.ca.gov (many links)
    California State Parks: ceres.ca.gov/dpr
    National Parks: www.nps.gov/parks.html

1

SAN FRANCISCO

Hong Kong offers more glitter and steeper hills. New York possesses more urban muscle. Paris is grander, Prague more magical, Cairo more ancient, and Venice more romantic. Peoria has less traffic. Every city can claim to have something on San Francisco, but very few can claim, like San Francisco, to have it all.

The "City by the Bay" is both an experiment and a museum. Strong curbs on development make the city appear to stand still, but ideas, art, and culture spin about the place like a cyclone. People come from around the world to reinvent themselves. Only intolerance is not tolerated by the body politic—San Francisco is as much a home to the socially wayward as to the socialites.

Above all, the city is beautiful. Despite the wounds and scars that urban and geological troubles have produced, San Francisco feels balanced and whole. No matter where you go, beauty is always only a glance away. Amazing bridges soar to wild headlands and harbor isles. Artful people stroll past splendid architecture. Fine parks, plazas, and promenades provide space for thought and exercise. The fog plays about the Golden Gate and breaks gently over the hills. Fresh Pacific air wipes the sky clean.

The original San Franciscans were the farthest flung of the pioneers—people who didn't park their wagon or hop off the boat until there was nowhere left to go. They came to the edge to find gold, glory, and freedom, and they stayed. Today, that same spirit is what makes this fabulous city America's favorite. ◼

SAN FRANCISCO

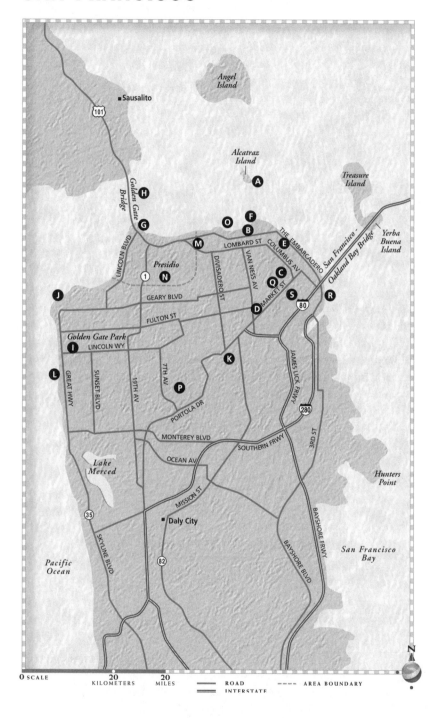

Sausalito

Angel
Island

Alcatraz
Island

Treasure
Island

Golden Gate
Bridge

Yerba
Buena
Island

San Francisco -
Oakland Bay Bridge

THE EMBARCADERO

LOMBARD ST

COLUMBUS AV

Presidio

DIVISADERO ST

VAN NESS AV

MARKET ST

GEARY BLVD

FULTON ST

Golden Gate Park

LINCOLN WY

LINCOLN BLVD

GREAT HWY

SUNSET BLVD

19TH AV

7TH AV

PORTOLA DR

JAMES LICK FRWY

MONTEREY BLVD

SOUTHERN FRWY

3RD ST

Lake
Merced

OCEAN AV

Hunters
Point

MISSION ST

Daly City

SKYLINE BLVD

BAYSHORE BLVD

BAYSHORE FRWY

Pacific
Ocean

San Francisco
Bay

0 SCALE   **20 KILOMETERS**   **20 MILES**   ——— **ROAD**   – – – **AREA BOUNDARY**
                                                   INTERSTATE

N

Sightseeing Highlights

A Alcatraz

B Cable Cars

C Chinatown

D Civic Center

E Coit Tower

F Fisherman's Wharf

G Fort Point

H Golden Gate Bridge

I Golden Gate Park

J Lands End

K Mission Dolores

L Ocean Beach

M Palace of Fine Arts

N Presidio

O San Francisco Maritime National Historical Park

P Twin Peaks

Q Union Square

R U.S.S. *Jeremiah O'Brien*

S Yerba Buena Gardens and San Francisco Museum of Modern Art

A PERFECT DAY IN SAN FRANCISCO

Park near Union Square and start walking. Information, transit passes, and city maps are available at the visitor center above Powell on Market. See Union Square, then walk down Grant Street through Chinatown. Enjoy the mix of Beat history, Chinatown, North Beach, and the red-light strip where Columbus meets Broadway. Follow Grant through North Beach, then up to Coit Tower. Hit the waterfront via Filbert and Washington Square. Gaze up Lombard to see the "crookedest street in the world" (walk it or drive it if you wish).

Buy tickets for the Alcatraz boat immediately. Before or after Alcatraz, browse Pier 39, Fisherman's Wharf, Hyde Street Pier, Ghirardelli Square, and the Municipal Pier in Aquatic Park. Catch a cable car at the Hyde Street turnaround and ride it back to Union Square. Visit Yerba Buena Gardens at Mission and Fourth if you have the time.

Pick up your car for an evening tour. Take Geary to Franklin, then Franklin to Bay Street. A left on Bay and a right on Laguna Street take you past Fort Mason and down to the Marina district. Enjoy the homes and views along Marina Boulevard. Turn left on Baker for a look at the Palace of Fine Arts. Back on Marina, bear left to the Golden Gate Bridge. Take the last exit before the toll plaza to reach the viewpoint for a bridge walk. Follow Lincoln west to 25th Avenue and Geary Boulevard, turning right to reach Point Lobos Boulevard and the ruins of the Sutro Baths. A sunset walk on Ocean Beach followed by drinks and dinner at the Cliff House complete the day.

Follow Fulton to Stanyan for a nighttime drive through the Haight. Turn right on Divisadero to the Castro, then up Market and Twin Peaks Boulevard for an unforgettable city lights view from Twin Peaks. If you have energy left, pick a nightlife zone from the listings and enjoy.

SAN FRANCISCO NEIGHBORHOODS

For the most part, San Francisco is divided into fairly distinct districts, each of which has a focal area where lodging, restaurants, and nightlife options are centered. In the "Food" and "Lodging" sections of this chapter, listings will be arranged by neighborhood. The resident can spend a lifetime discovering places in obscure locations, but the short-term explorer is wise to head to the centers.

SIGHTSEEING HIGHLIGHTS

★★★ **Alcatraz**—The word "Alcatraz" comes from the Spanish word for pelican—a bird that had this rock to itself for years uncounted. Around the time of the gold rush, a military garrison was stationed on Alcatraz to guard the bay. Military prisoners were held here because of the security provided by the cold, powerful tides. Later, in 1933, Alcatraz became a federal prison that hosted the likes of Al Capone. The prison was closed in 1963 due to the high cost of service and maintenance. The ruins are now maintained and administered by the National Park Service.

You'll be given a personal walkman for an excellent tape-guided tour of the prison. Outside, the island is alive with native plants and birds. Good walks take you to quiet spots with spectacular views of San Francisco, the Golden Gate Bridge, Marin Headlands, and Angel Island. It is the island's location as much as its history that makes it a three-star sight.

The Red & White Fleet is the only company offering trips to Alcatraz. The Blue & Gold Fleet offers scenic bay tours that pass near the island. Reserve your boat in advance if at all possible. Details: Alcatraz Island, San Francisco Bay; (415) 556-0560; round trip boat fare is $6; audio tape tours are $3; exploring without a tape is free. Red & White Fleet, Pier 41; (415) 546-2700 or (800) 229-2784; Blue & Gold Fleet, Pier 39; (415) 705-5444. Boats depart daily from 9:30 a.m. to 4:30 p.m. (2½ hours)

★★★ **Chinatown**—Grant Street between Bush and Broadway is the tourist's Chinatown and should not be missed. Walk along the narrow, crowded street, stepping into shops to search among the tacky souvenirs, intricate artworks, or unfathomable concoctions. Duck up Jackson, Washington, or Clay to explore the maze of alleys and the less touristy Stockton Street. Pick a restaurant at random and plunge in to enjoy tea, dim sum, and the music of the language. Everything is compressed in Chinatown—slow down to see it well. Details: Grant Street, San Francisco. (1½ hours)

★★★ **Golden Gate Bridge**—Rarely are grace and power blended so perfectly as they are in the magnificent Golden Gate Bridge. Opened in 1937, it has stood as the symbol of the city and the West Coast equivalent of the Statue of Liberty ever since. From all angles it is a wonder. Enjoy it from below at Fort Point or on a boat tour. Enjoy it from above with a drive onto the Marin Headlands. Walk out onto it, perhaps all the way across (a distance of 6450 feet), to feel its scale and to wonder at the views.

Fort Point and the bridge walk can be reached via the southern view area. Take the last, small exit from U.S. 101 about 500 feet before the tollbooths, or approach via Lincoln Boulevard in the Presidio. The northern viewpoint is at the first exit at the north end of the bridge. Take the second exit, at Alexander Avenue, and loop under the highway to reach the headlands road and viewpoints. Details: Golden Gate Bridge, San Francisco; open for walking (eastside) and biking (westside) daily from 5 a.m. to 9 p.m. (1 hour)

✰✰ **Cable Cars**—Cable cars operate by clamping on to a continuously moving steel cable that runs under the street. To stop, the operator releases the clutch lever while applying the brake. In their heyday, hundreds of cable cars operated along 100 miles of routes through the city. After the 1906 earthquake, the severely damaged system never recovered, and, by the middle of the century, they had all but disappeared. Citizens fought for their survival, and today you can ride the recently refurbished system through much of historic San Francisco.

You can buy tickets at the turnarounds or just board the car and pay the conductor. The longest lines are at Union Square and at the Hyde Street and Mason Street turnarounds near Fisherman's Wharf. The Embarcadero Station at the bottom of California Street is usually uncrowded.

The **Cable Car Museum** features San Francisco's first cable car, built in 1873, along with other transit history displays. You can observe the power plant that drives the cables for all three lines in the basement. Details: 1201 Mason Street, San Francisco; (415) 474-1887; open daily from 10 a.m. to 6 p.m. (until 5 p.m. in the winter). Donations are accepted. (½ hour)

✰✰ **Civic Center**—The **San Francisco City Hall**, built in 1914, is the centerpiece of this compact zone of government and fine arts buildings. If earthquake retrofitting has been completed, climb the Polk Street steps from the **Civic Center Plaza** for a look inside at the magnificent rotunda. Across the plaza on Larkin Street is the brand new **San Francisco Public Library**. Enter the library for a look at why the critics are raving.

Opposite City Hall, on Van Ness, are three outstanding fine arts performance halls. The opulent **War Memorial Opera House**, built in 1932, holds over 3,000 people. It too should be open after earthquake retrofitting. Next door, the **Veterans Building** holds the smaller **Herbst Auditorium**. Across Grove Street, the **Louise M. Davies Symphony Hall** is home to the San Francisco Symphony.

It should be noted that the Civic Center rubs elbows with the **Tenderloin**, a concentrated area of cheap hotels, porn shops, and the homeless. Though the area is basically safe, a daytime visit to the Civic Center may seem prudent. Details: The Civic Center is bounded by Market, Van Ness, and McAllister Streets, San Francisco. (1 hour)

★★ **Coit Tower**—Perched above North Beach on top of Telegraph Hill, Coit Tower is another enduring symbol of San Francisco. It was built by Lillie Coit in 1934 to honor her husband and his fellow firefighters. The top of the 210-foot tower is reached by elevator, and the views are splendid. Inside are wonderful murals painted by local artists when the structure was new.

A small park surrounds the tower, affording pleasant views and a place to relax. It's worth the walk here from North Beach since tourist traffic moves at a snail's pace up the entry road. You can walk up from the corner of Kearney and Filbert, or up the pretty **Filbert Steps** from Sansome Street to the east. Details: The auto entrance is via Lombard east of Grant, San Francisco; (415) 362-0808, tower open daily from 10 a.m. to 7:30 p.m. Admission is $3. (½ hour)

★★ **Fort Point**—Completed in 1861 to defend the entrance to the bay, Fort Point (the name of both the fort and the point) is now a military museum. The southern arch of the Golden Gate Bridge was designed to preserve the structure. Today, Fort Point is a popular place to get close to the bridge and to the surging tidal flows of the Golden Gate. There's a wave break around the point that attracts surfers. Joggers and walkers favor the 3½-mile promenade along the bay to the Marina Green. Details: Access is via Long Avenue from Lincoln Boulevard in the Presidio, San Francisco; fort open daily from 10 a.m. to 5 p.m. Admission is free. (1 hour)

★★ **Golden Gate Park**—This thousand-acre park stretches halfway across the city, from Stanyan Street to the sea. Created largely on reclaimed dune lands, it is a popular destination for residents and tourists alike. Sunday is a great day to visit since the inner half of John F. Kennedy Drive is closed to traffic. Walkers, cyclists, and skaters cruise the road and a festive atmosphere prevails.

Numerous sights within the park stand as one and two-star attractions on their own. The graceful **Conservatory of Flowers** was built in Britain, shipped around Cape Horn, and assembled here in 1878. The gardens inside and out are lovely. Renovation is in progress and may be complete by the time of your visit. Details: Golden Gate Park, San Francisco; (415) 666-7017; open daily from 9 a.m. to 5 p.m. Admission is $2.50. (½ hour)

The **California Academy of Sciences** is a museum of natural history that includes the excellent **Steinhart Aquarium** and **Morrison Planetarium**. It's a great option for families. Details: Golden Gate Park, San Francisco; (415) 750-7145; open daily from 10 a.m. to 5 p.m. (9 a.m. to 6 p.m. in July and August). Admission is $7. (2 hours)

Concerts and ceremonies of various sorts are scheduled in the **Music Concourse** in front of the California Academy. Across the concourse is the **M. H. de Young Memorial Museum**, San Francisco's finest art museum. You'll find the biggest touring exhibits here, as well as an outstanding permanent collection featuring Renaissance and medieval paintings, tapestries, and sculpture, (415) 863-3330. The **Asian Art Museum** is associated with the De Young. It features selections from the 10,000-item Avery Brundage collection, (415) 668-8921. Details: Golden Gate Park, San Francisco; both museums open Tuesday through Sunday from 10 a.m. to 5 p.m. Admission is $5 (allows entry to both). (2 hours)

Just southwest of the museums are two beautiful outdoor attractions. The **Japanese Tea Garden** features lovely, sculpted grounds with pools and bridges. All is balanced and serene. Have tea and cookies at the tea house where fortune cookies were invented in 1909. Details: Golden Gate Park, San Francisco; (415) 666-7200; open weekdays from 8 a.m. to 4:30 p.m.; weekends and holidays from 10 a.m. to 5 p.m. Admission is free. (45 minutes)

Across Martin Luther King Jr. Drive is the **Strybing Arboretum and Botanical Gardens**, a wonderful place to stroll among exotic plants or bask on a lawn. Details: Golden Gate Park, San Francisco; (415) 661-1316; open weekdays from 8 a.m. to 4:30 p.m., weekends and holidays from10 a.m. to 5 p.m. Admission is free. (1½ hours)

Farther down, you can rent a paddle boat or canoe to circumnavigate **Strawberry Hill** on **Stow Lake**, check out the bison at the

Buffalo Enclosure, or play some par-3 golf at the **Golden Gate Municipal Golf Course**. There are frequent concerts at the **Polo Field**, next to the **Fly Casting Pools**. Sports fields, picnic areas, and barbecue pits are scattered about.

✯✯ **Lands End**—At the northwest tip of the city, Lincoln Park and the Golden Gate National Recreation Area preserve a headland area that includes Point Lobos and Lands End Point. Point Lobos Avenue becomes the Great Highway as it swings past the ruins of the **Sutro Baths,** the site of a huge complex of indoor pools and baths built in 1886 that burned down 30 years ago. Next door is the **Cliff House**, (415) 386-3330, where you can dine or drink at the edge of the continent. The sunset views will make you smile—assuming the fog hasn't blanketed the windows. The building has burned and has been rebuilt twice since the original was constructed in 1863. On the terrace below the Cliff House is the **Camera Obscura**, the biggest camera in the world; you can even step inside. Details: (415) 750-0415. Admission is $1. (½ hour)

    Lincoln Park preserves most of Lands End. Trails provide access to the park, including a stretch along an abandoned headlands road that didn't stand the test of time. The **Lincoln Park Memorial Golf Course** is a public course with some of the best views around and reasonable green fees to boot. At the end of Legion of Honor Drive is the **Palace of the Legion of Honor**. This newly renovated museum has an outstanding collection of European art and is one of the city's finest. Details: Legion of Honor Drive, San Francisco; (415) 863-3330; open Tuesday through Sunday from 10 a.m. to 5 p.m. Admission is $6. (2 hours)

✯✯ **Palace of Fine Arts**—Built for the 1915 Panama Pacific International Exposition that celebrated the city's rise from the ashes of 1906, this ornate dome-and-pillar structure was never intended to last. Saved from the wrecking ball by adoring citizens and strengthened in the sixties, it is an enduring symbol of the city's sentiment. Take Baker Street from Richardson Street or Marina Boulevard, walk about, and enjoy the swans in the reflecting pool.

    Various performances are given at one end of the actual "palace," the curved building behind the rotunda. At the other end, families should check out the **Exploratorium**. This hands-on science museum is one of the best of its kind in the country, featuring scores of fun and educational displays. Don't miss the crawl-through "Tactile Dome." Details: Palace of Fine Arts, San Francisco; (415) 561-0360; open daily from 10 a.m. to 5 p.m. (until 6 p.m. in the summer and until 9:30 p.m. every Wednesday). Admission is $9. (2 hours)

✭✭ **San Francisco Maritime National Historical Park**—Located by Fisherman's Wharf, at the bottom of Hyde Street, the park is a great place to catch the spirit of the city. Ferries once plied the waters of San Francisco Bay in large numbers, serving Marin County and the East Bay before the bridges were built. Some of them docked at **Hyde Street Historic Ships Pier**, which now serves as home for several historic vessels, including a side-wheeler ferry and an iron-hulled square rigger. Details: Hyde Street, San Francisco; (415) 556-3002; pier open daily from 10 a.m. to 6 p.m. (9:30 a.m. to 5 p.m. in winter). Admission is $2. (1 hour)

At the bottom of Polk Street, the art deco **San Francisco National Maritime Museum** has a good nautical history collection. Details: Polk Street, San Francisco; (415) 556-8177; open daily from 10 a.m. to 5 p.m. Admission is free. (1 hour)

The green surrounding the park and the gracefully curved Municipal Pier are great places to stroll, relax, and people watch. The turnaround for the Hyde Street cable car is at the edge of the park— just look for the long line of tourists waiting for a ride.

✭ **Fisherman's Wharf**—As an *area*, Fisherman's Wharf has a lot to offer, but the wharf itself is basically a pier with restaurants and fish companies. It's a great place to get a simple and tasty crab salad, a crab sandwich, or crab legs. Enjoy them with a glass of wine and some genuine sourdough bread.

Along the three blocks of Jefferson Street, between the wharf and **Aquatic Park**, you'll find tourist heaven. **The Cannery** and **The Anchorage** are shopping and eating complexes fronting the street. Visit the **Wax Museum, Ripley's Believe It or Not! Museum**, or the **Medieval Dungeon** where torture is on display. When you've bought your T-shirts and postcards, move quickly on to Hyde Street Pier or the boat to Alcatraz.

To the west, above the Maritime Museum on Beach Street, is **Ghirardelli Square**. Once home to the Ghirardelli Chocolate Factory, this one-square-block, historic brick complex now hosts upscale shops, galleries, and tourist boutiques. It's a good spot to enjoy lunch with a view or to buy a fancier gift than what you'd find near the wharf. Tasty Ghirardelli chocolate is, of course, available.

Five hundred yards east of the wharf, **Pier 39** is basically a tacky tourist attraction lined with souvenir shops and eateries. One feature of interest is the section of floating docks that has been taken over by fat, boisterous sea lions looking for a free lunch—follow the barking. Another feature is the brand new **UnderWater World**, a long acrylic tunnel that runs through an aquarium beneath the waters of the bay. A tape-guided tour is available. Details: Pier 39, San Francisco; (415) 623-5300; open daily from 10 a.m. to 8:30 p.m. Admission is $13. (1 hour)

✯ **Ocean Beach**—Stretching broad, straight, and smooth along San Francisco's western edge, this wonderful beach attracts everyone who needs a dose of salt air and soothing waves. Kids play in the sand, frisbees and kites color the air, sitters sit, joggers jog, and strollers stroll. The water is too cold for all but the briefly brave and the wetsuit set. The advantage is that it's never crowded, and there are no concessionaires providing excess litter. At night, groups gather here and there around perfectly legal beach fires.

✯ **Presidio**—The nation's newest national park is in the midst of a transition. After decades of occupancy, the military is gone. Various factions have fought their way to a tenuous agreement on public and private use of the many buildings and facilities. It remains to be seen what the future will bring.

Lincoln Boulevard winds through the grounds, providing access to **Baker Beach**, the **World War II Memorial**, **Fort Point National Historic Site**, **San Francisco National Cemetery**, the parade ground, and the old Letterman Hospital complex. Details: The main entrances are via Lombard Street to the east (don't turn onto Richardson for the bridge) and Lincoln Boulevard from 25th Avenue to the west. CA 1 and U.S. 101 fly over and through the Presidio as they approach the Golden Gate Bridge. If you're on these arteries or the bridge, stay to the right and get off at the bridge viewpoint just south of the tollbooths.

✯ **Union Square**—This is where the chauffeur brings whoever is in the back of the limo to shop. Posh stores and fine hotels surround the square. If you are in the city at Christmas, be sure to come in the evening to see the displays. East of the square, the two-block-long **Maiden Lane** extends the chic shopping zone. The city's only Frank Lloyd Wright designed building is at 140 Maiden Lane. San Francisco's small Theater District is clustered around Geary just southwest of the square. The Powell Street cable car stops at Union Square and ends at Market Street.

☆ **Yerba Buena Gardens and San Francisco Museum of Modern Art (SFMOMA)**—The wondrous new San Francisco Museum of Modern Art has drawn much praise and some criticism for its unique architecture. Located across from Yerba Buena Gardens, it is a key element in the revitalization of the city's South of Market district. The permanent collection struggles just a bit to match its new home, but the touring exhibits are top notch. Details: 151 3rd Street, San Francisco; (415) 357-4000; open Tuesday through Sunday from 11 a.m. to 6 p.m. (until 9 p.m. on Thursdays). Admission is $7.

Across 3rd Street, the lawns and terraces of Yerba Buena Gardens are more of a gathering place than a botanical display. They are quite lovely, however, and provide a place to converse and relax. The **Center for the Arts** is at one end of the garden and the **Moscone Convention Center** is located across Howard Street. (1 hour)

☆ **Twin Peaks**—At Castro Street, arrow-straight Market Street begins to climb and curve as it winds up onto a series of hills in the center of the city. Near the top, Twin Peaks Boulevard cuts sharply off to the right, twisting around until it splits into a one-way road that shapes a figure eight around the two summits of Twin Peaks. On the east side of the north summit, an extended parking area gives access to one of the best nighttime views of any city, anywhere.

☆ **U.S.S. *Jeremiah O'Brien***—This last of the liberty ships spends most of its time moored at Pier 32, just south of the Bay Bridge on the Embarcadero. Hundreds of these transport ships were built in the bay during World War II—only the *O'Brien* remains. If you don't see the gray hulk docked at the broad pier, it might be out on a goodwill mission of some sort. Recently, it sailed around the world to join in the D-Day anniversary events. There are great views of the Bay Bridge from both the ship and pier. Details: Pier 32, San Francisco; (415) 441-3101; ship tours given weekdays from 9 a.m. to 3 p.m., and until 4 p.m. on weekends. Admission is $5. (1 hour)

Mission Dolores—Less than a week after this mission was founded, the Declaration of Independence was signed in Philadelphia. It is the oldest site in San Francisco. The permanent structure was completed in 1783, and the large basilica next door in 1913. Of particular interest is the mission cemetery where the graves of Indians and early pioneers can be found. Details: The basilica is at the corner of Dolores Street and 16th Street, the mission is next door, San Francisco; (415) 621-8203; open daily from 9 a.m. to 4 p.m. Admission is $1. (1 hour)

FITNESS AND RECREATION

San Francisco is a city for walking. Walk the 3½-mile promenade from the Marina Green to Fort Point. Enjoy the pounding surf as you walk up and down the miles-long Ocean Beach. Consider a loop through Golden Gate Park with a side trip along Haight Street. You won't move fast down Grant Street in Chinatown, but the diversions make up for the pace. The Embarcadero is particularly nice along the open area between the Bay Bridge and the Ferry Building. A walk down Mission between 16th and 24th gives you a taste of culture and commerce while connecting the BART stations.

FOOD

It has been said that there are enough restaurants in San Francisco to seat the city's entire population at one time. Explore the city for a while, and you'll be tempted to believe the claim. More importantly, should the experiment ever be undertaken, the great majority would be well fed indeed. With more restaurants per capita than any other city in the nation, San Francisco is a diner's paradise.

The city's cuisine is so rich and varied that it defies simplification. You'll find Chinese food in Chinatown, Italian in North Beach, seafood at Fisherman's Wharf, various Latin American options in the Mission, Japanese in Japantown, and California cuisine at hip spots everywhere. There are eateries featuring Russian, Filipino, Vietnamese, Ethiopian, Irish, and Greek foods. Great dim sum and Thai restaurants abound. There are all-American burger joints, cheese-steak shops, and biscuit-and-gravy diners. Don't come to San Francisco to lose weight! The pages that follow highlight just a few of the excellent restaurants. Sections are arranged by neighborhood.

The Castro—The corner of Market and Noe Streets is the center of the thoroughly gay Castro District. **Café Flore** is a good place to have

SAN FRANCISCO

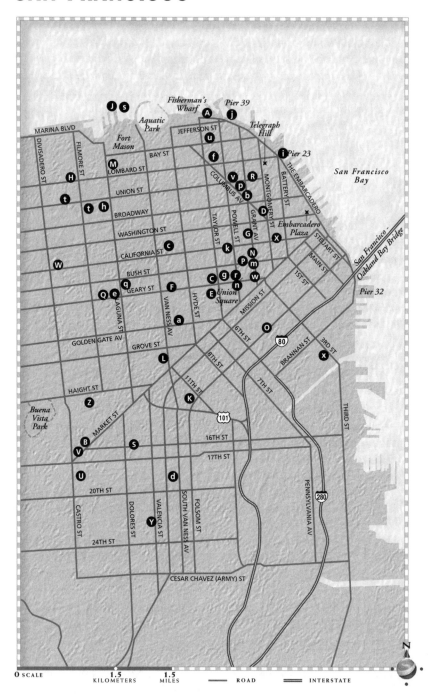

Food

- (A) Alioto's
- (B) Café Flore
- (C) China Moon Café
- (D) Cypress Club
- (E) Dottie's True Blue Café
- (F) Edinburgh Castle Pub
- (G) Empress of China
- (H) Flying Kamikazes
- (I) Fog City Diner
- (J) Green's
- (K) Hamburger Mary's
- (L) Hayes Street Grill
- (M) Irawaddy
- (N) The Lotus Garden
- (O) LuLu
- (P) Masa's
- (Q) Mifune
- (R) North Beach Pizza
- (S) Paella La Movida
- (T) Pane e Vino
- (U) Patio Café
- (V) Pozole
- (W) Rasselas
- (X) Rubicon
- (Y) Saigon Saigon
- (Z) Spaghetti Western
- (a) Stars
- (b) The Stinking Rose
- (c) Swan Oyster Depot
- (d) Taqueria Cancun
- (e) YoYo
- (f) Zax

Lodging

- (g) Adelaide Hotel
- (h) The Bed and Breakfast Inn
- (j) Dockside Boat and Bed
- (k) Fairmont Hotel
- (m) Grant Plaza
- (n) Hostel at Union Square
- (p) Hotel Bohème
- (e) Miyako Hotel
- (q) Queen Anne Hotel
- (r) Raphael Hotel
- (s) San Francisco International Hostel
- (t) The Sherman House
- (u) Tuscan Inn
- (v) The Washington Square Inn
- (w) Westin St. Francis Hotel

Camping

- (x) San Francisco RV Park

Note: Items with the same letter are located in the same area.

coffee and people watch in this lively area, 1815 Market, (415) 621-8579. Enjoy a retreat into the recesses of Castro society on the crowded patio of the **Patio Café**, 531 Castro, (415) 621-4640. While strolling the Castro, stop at **Pozole** for a tasty Mexican meal that will delight your appetite while sparing your purse, 2337 Market Street, (415) 626-2666.

Chinatown—There is plenty to eat on and around Grant Street and Stockton Street, and most restaurants are reasonably priced. **The Lotus Garden** serves vegetarian dishes below a Taoist temple, 532 Grant Street, (415) 397-0707, and fine Chinese dining in the heart of Chinatown doesn't get any better than the **Empress of China**, 838 Grant Street, (415) 434-1345.

Civic Center and Tenderloin—The famous **Stars** does, in fact, attract stars and wannabes for its "New American" cuisine. Reservations are wise, two entrances, at 555 Golden Gate Avenue and at 150 Redwood Alley, (415) 861-7827. You can't do better than **Dottie's True Blue Café** for hearty American breakfast and lunch fare. Nothing too fancy here, but everything is big and tasty, 522 Jones Street, (415) 885-2767. Whether it's the symphony or the opera after-wards, the seafood at **Hayes Street Grill** will whet your appetite for art, 320 Hayes Street, (415) 863-5545. For fish, chips, and pints of bit-ters in a very British setting, hit the **Edinburgh Castle Pub**, 950 Geary, (415) 885-4074.

The Financial District—The **Rubicon** is another option for the well-heeled. With backers like Francis Ford Coppola (whose wines are on the wine list), Robert DeNiro, and Robin Williams, how could the fabulous French fare miss? Bring the gold card, 558 Sacramento Street, (415) 434-4100. The **Fog City Diner** has been in a Visa commercial so it must be good. International options surround the classed-up diner fare. If you can get in, you can say you've been there, 1300 Battery Street, (415) 982-2000. Step into the **Cypress Club**, and you'll look around for the stage crew. This place is almost a scenic attraction on its own. The diverse menu is tops, as are the prices, 500 Jackson Street, (415) 296-8555.

Fisherman's Wharf—Down on the wharf are several touristy places to enjoy seafood, especially crab, right off the dock, including **Alioto's**. The Alioto name is famous in city politics as well as in feeding tourists,

8 Fisherman's Wharf, (415) 673-0183. The finest in vegetarian California cuisine is found at **Green's**, operated by the Zen Center in a thoroughly redone barracks building at Fort Mason. A meal here is a must for veggie connoisseurs. Located in Building A of the Fort Mason Center, the entrance is at the base of Buchanon Street, (415) 771-6222.

Japantown—Many restaurants are located within the Japan Trade and Cultural Center buildings. So if you find yourself staring at a mall-like wall where an address is supposed to be, look inside. **Mifune** has wonderful noodle-based dishes at good prices, 1737 Post Street, (415) 922-0337. Perhaps the best seafood restaurant in town is **YoYo**, which offers Japanese cooking with a French twist, 1625 Post Street, (415) 922-7788.

Lower Haight—Located where Haight Street meets Fillmore Street, the Lower Haight scene is young and lively. Breakfasts are huge in a sub-casual setting at **Spaghetti Western**, 576 Haight Street, (415) 864-8461.

Marina—For some rock 'n' roll with very good sushi, try the **Flying Kamikazes**, 3339 Steiner, (415) 567-4903. The **Irawaddy** at 1769 Lombard Street has unusual but excellent Burmese cuisine. Settle into your pillows and enjoy, (415) 931-2830.

Mission—There's no shortage of Latin American food in the Mission, and it's hard to go too far wrong. The **Taqueria Cancun** is tasty, fast, hearty, and cheap, 2288 Mission Street, (415) 252-9560. For great Spanish food, **Paella La Movida** can't be beat. Paella, of course, is the specialty, 3228 16th Street, (415) 552-3889. Proving the culinary diversity of the Mission, **Saigon Saigon** is the place to go for Vietnamese dining. Great service at good prices, 1132 Valencia, (415) 206-9635.

North Beach—**North Beach Pizza** is an area legend. The original location at 1499 Grant Street is a great place to grab a slice, day or night, (415) 433-2444. Garlic is the name of the game at The **Stinking Rose**, along with great Italian food at a fair price, 325 Columbus Street, (415) 781-7673. **Zax** at 2330 Taylor is a favorite bistro for those who love good fare.

Russian Hill, Pacific Heights, and Cow Hollow—The intimate **Pane e Vino** would be romantic if not for the vociferous bustle of the thoroughly Italian staff, 3011 Steiner Street, (415) 346-2111. For Ethiopian food with live jazz on the side, **Rasselas** has the goods, 2801 California, (415) 567-5010.

SoMa (South of Market)—A block from Yerba Buena Gardens, **LuLu** offers outstanding Mediterranean cuisine and features wood-burning-oven-roasted meats and great pizza, 816 Folsom, (415) 495-5775. For a beer and a bite—including worthy burgers—stop at **Hamburger Mary's**, a SoMa original at 1582 Folsom Street, (415) 626-1985.

Union Square and Nob Hill—Good places to eat abound in the area around Union Square and Nob Hill. The **China Moon Café** is pricey but worth it, 639 Post Street, (415) 775-4789. The most expensive restaurant in San Francisco is probably **Masa's**. The unique blending of French and California cuisine stresses artistic presentation. Make reservations before you leave home, 648 Bush Street, in the Hotel Vintage Court, (415) 989-7154. For an affordable, authentic San Francisco lunch, hit the **Swan Oyster Depot**, 1517 Polk Street, (415) 673-1101.

LODGING

The following listings focus on lodgings in San Francisco's central tourist area. Reservations are strongly recommended throughout the entire year.

San Francisco is awash with luxury hotels. The **Fairmont Hotel** features the wonderful Tonga Room, with its artificial tropical storm. The lobby is one of the most fabulous in the city. Rooms start at about $160 and climb rapidly, 950 Mason Street at California Street, (415) 772-5000 or (800) 527-4727.

The **Westin St. Francis Hotel** is a true city landmark. Large, at 1200 rooms, and stately, it has presided over Union Square for decades. Rooms start around $170, 335 Powell Street, (415) 397-7000 or (800) 228-3000.

Another hotel of particular note is **The Sherman House**. A four-story Victorian mansion and historical landmark with only 18 rooms, it was restored to its pre-1906 earthquake splendor in 1980. The original three-story recital hall, where Enrico Caruso once sang, has become the hotel's lobby. Rooms run from $250 to over $800!—a splendid place to stay for a select few, 2160 Green Street, (415) 563-3600.

In the budget and moderate range, a number of interesting hotels, inns, and B&Bs stand out. Several are in the close-to-Market Street zone that includes the Civic Center, Union Square, and Financial District. You can get a clean, decent room two blocks from Union Square for as little as $40 at the **Adelaide Hotel**. You'll have to share a bath, but you'll have friendly folks with which to share it, 5 Isadora Duncan Court (off Taylor between Geary and Post), (415) 441-2474. Old, elegant, and friendly, the **Raphael Hotel** has plenty of creature comforts as well as a personality. A good choice in the $100 and up range, 386 Geary Boulevard, (415) 986-2000 or (800) 821-5343,

Inexpensive to moderate options in the Japantown and Pacific Heights zone can also be found. San Francisco's first B&B, fittingly named **The Bed and Breakfast Inn**, is located on tiny Charlton off Union Street. Rooms start at $70 with shared bath, $115 with private bath, 4 Charlton Court, (415) 921-9784. The **Miyako Hotel**, next to the Japantown center, is well into the high-moderate range with rooms starting at $130, but you get simple Japanese elegance and quality for the price. The hotel is large and modern, 1625 Post Street, (415) 922-3200. Built in 1890, the elegant **Queen Anne Hotel** is a B&B bargain. Rooms start at $100, 1590 Sutter Street, (415) 441-2828 or (800) 227-3970.

In and around Chinatown, North Beach, and Russian Hill, you'll find even more options. For a cheap Chinatown room right on the strip, try the **Grant Plaza**. For $40, you get $40 worth, but it's well kept, 465 Grant Avenue, (415) 434-3883 or (800) 472-6899. To get a feel for the Beat era, stay at **Hotel Bohème**. Rooms run from $95 to $120, 444 Columbus, (415) 433-9111. For less than $100 (small room, shared bath), you can have continental breakfast, afternoon tea, and evening wine at **The Washington Square Inn**, a charming B&B in the heart of North Beach, 1660 Stockton Street, (415) 981-4220 or (800) 388-0220.

Budget chain motels and moderate independents are found in abundance near Fisherman's Wharf and on Lombard Street in the Marina District. How about staying on your own small boat at the **Dockside Boat and Bed**? You and your matey can ahoy for $95 and up, breakfast included. Individual boats are moored at Pier 39. Up into the high-moderate range is the **Tuscan Inn**, 425 North Point St., (415) 561-1100. Rooms in this luxurious hotel start around $120.

Hostels offer ultra-cheap accommodations. Two Hostelling International hostels are well located and inexpensive. The **Hostel at Union Square**, at 312 Mason Street, is indeed close to Union Square.

Beds are $15, (415) 788-5604. The **San Francisco International Hostel** is located in Building 240 at Fort Mason, (415) 771-7277, $15. Both have curfews and vacate times.

CAMPING

There is no camping in the city of San Francisco, but the **San Francisco RV Park** has 200 sites with full hookups, 250 King Street (between Third Street and Fourth Street), (415) 986-8730 or (800) 548-2425, $34.

NIGHTLIFE

Nightlife options are as diverse as the culinary offerings of the region. You can stop at an Irish pub after an evening at the opera, then dance to techno music until dawn. If you simply get to the core areas of the neighborhoods, you can soak in the street scene as you browse, trying a few different nightspots on for size. Things can get a little iffy around the SoMa, Mission, and Haight zones as the night grows old, though the happy crowds in the centers are generally safe and fun.

Castro—On Castro Street and Market Street, near their junction, the strolling and people watching is tops—a thoroughly gay scene. The **Twin Peaks Tavern** is a great place to people watch as you sip, 401 Castro Street, (415) 864-9470. The jazz and blues ambiance of the **Café du Nord** makes for a fun, mixed scene, 2170 Market Street, (415) 861-5016.

The Financial District—You can dine in the revolving **Equinox** restaurant at the top of the Hyatt Regency, but you can do better for the same money. However, a drink while watching the towers of finance roll by is worth an hour, 5 Embarcadero Center (bottom of California Street), (415) 788-1234. For a happy crowd and danceable live music, drop in at the cramped **Pier 23**, (415) 362-5125. When the press of bodies becomes too much, step out onto the sprawling deck for a long look at the bay. Food is served through the early evening, located on Pier 23, at the Embarcadero. The **Gordon Biersch Brewery Restaurant** is a touch industrial in decor, but not enough to get your business suit dirty. The site-brewed beers are admired by many, loved by some. There's classy pub grub upstairs, 2 Harrison Street, (415) 243-8246.

Fisherman's Wharf and Fort Mason—The street scene is found right at the Fisherman's Wharf, Pier 39, Jefferson Street, and Aquatic Park area, though the tourists and street performers begin to dissipate as the evening wanes. There's live music of the blues variety every night at **Lou's Pier 47**, 300 Jefferson Street, (415) 771-0377. Irish coffee allegedly arrived in San Francisco via the **Buena Vista Café**. In any case, it's still there, 2765 Hyde Street, (415) 474-5044. The **Eagle Café** on Pier 39 is a good place for a real drink amid the tourist schlock, (415) 433-3689.

Lower Haight—It's a compact and energetic scene that goes until the bars close, right on Haight around Fillmore. The **Mad Dog in the Fog** is a good place for pints and people. The energy is infectious, 530 Haight Street, (415) 626-7279. For a different perspective, cross the street to the **Noc Noc** for a quiet drink and a look at the weirdly sculpted interior, 557 Haight Street, (415) 861-5811. The nearby **Toronado** can be the third stop on your Lower Haight tour, 547 Haight Street, (415) 863-2276.

Mission—The action centers on 16th Street, between Mission and Valencia Streets, and spreads out from there. There's good live music upstairs and a noisy bar downstairs at the **Elbo Room**, 647 Valencia Street, (415) 552-7788. The bikes parked outside should give you a clue about trendy **Zeitgest**, 199 Valencia Street, (415) 255-7505. New bands tear it up at the **Kilowatt**, 3160 16th Street, (415) 861-2595.

North Beach—The intersection of Broadway and Columbus is the center of the very active North Beach scene. Head north on Grant or east on Broadway for some fascinating browsing. Four worthy nightspots cluster at the intersection of Columbus and Broadway. The compact, two-story **Vesuvio Café** is next to City Lights Books in the historic heart of the Beat District. Read your Jack Kerouac over beer or coffee here, 255 Columbus, (415) 362-3370. Across the street at the **Tosca Café**, listen to opera among jaded urbanites and other-worldly artists over coffee, 242 Columbus, (415) 391-1244. Next door, at historic **Specs**, the diverse crowd has an edge. Late night, the edge can crack, (415) 421-4112. North of Broadway, **Pearl's** offers free jazz nightly in a civil setting—good jazz, 256 Columbus, (415) 291-8255.

SAN FRANCISCO

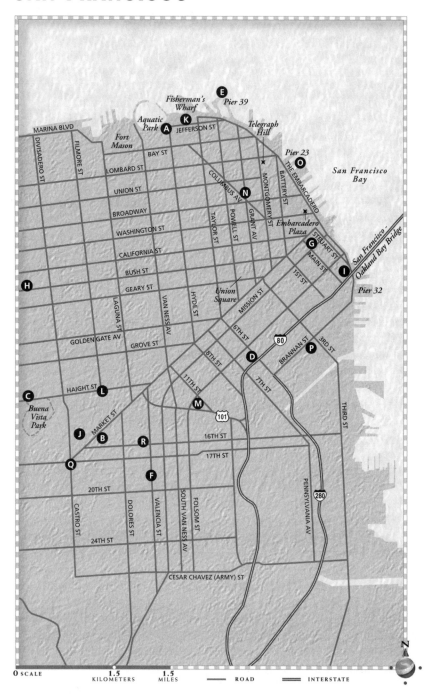

Nightlife

- **A** Buena Vista Café
- **B** Café du Nord
- **C** Club Boomerang
- **D** Club Dread
- **E** Eagle Café
- **F** Elbo Room
- **G** Equinox
- **H** Ireland's 32
- **I** Gordon Biersch Brewery Restaurant
- **J** Kilowatt
- **K** Lou's Pier 47
- **L** Mad Dog in the Fog
- **C** Nightbreak
- **L** Noc Noc
- **M** Paradise
- **N** Pearl's
- **C** Persian Aub Zam Zam
- **O** Pier 23
- **H** The Plough and Stars
- **N** Specs
- **L** Toranado
- **N** Tosca Café
- **P** Trocadero
- **M** 20 Tank Brewery
- **Q** Twin Peaks Tavern
- **N** Vesuvio Café
- **R** Zeitgest

Note: Items with the same letter are located in the same area.

The Richmond—There are pockets of interest on Geary, but the heart of the area is along Clement Street for several blocks west of Arguello. Stop in for a pint of stout at **Ireland's 32**, 3920 Geary Boulevard, (415) 386-6173. It's named after the number of counties that should be in the republic, so make sure you've got your politics straight before conversing. **The Plough and Stars** is a more popular Irish option, perhaps because it's less political, but also for the live Irish music that happens on occasion, 116 Clement Street, (415) 751-1122.

SoMa (South of Market)—Here's where it goes really late. Eleventh Street between Harrison and Folsom is the main zone, though other clubs in the big district are islands of action. **Club Dread** (The Endup) at Harrison and Sixth Street has deejays nightly, featuring reggae and world beat. For punk music, see what the lineup is at the **Trocadero**. It can get crazed, 520 Fourth Street, (415) 995-4600. At the corner of 11th and Folsom, the **Paradise** features three stages and a barroom where you can almost hear yourself. Enjoy performance art or poetry upstairs while the place rocks beneath you, 1501 Folsom Street, (415) 861-6906. The **20 Tank Brewery** offers a good range of site-brewed ales in a warehouse setting, 316 Eleventh Street, (415) 255-9455.

Upper Haight—This area gets a little sketchy as the night progresses, but there are plenty of folk about between Masonic and Golden Gate Park. A block from Golden Gate Park, the **Nightbreak** features thrashing rock bands in a featureless box.

If it's open, and if the bartender doesn't throw you out for no apparent reason, you can get a martini at the **Persian Aub Zam Zam**. Take a chance, 1633 Haight Street, (415) 861-2545. The **Club Boomerang** has live new bands nightly, 1840 Haight Street, (415) 387-2996.

2

MARIN COUNTY

Marin County is rich in many ways. Statistically, its residents top the income list of all Northern California counties. The fruits of wealth translate into safe and interesting towns with charming cafés and boutiques, all enjoyable for the visitor. Most of all, Marin is blessed with a system of local, county, state, and federal park lands that encompass about a third of the county and its most scenic areas.

Marin is also rich in a well-earned reputation. It seems that every trendy, new-age, self-improvement method or spirtual path finds a home in the county. No greater concentration of well-massaged, juice-drinking, hot-tub-soaking, spandex-suited joggers in therapy can be found anywhere else in the universe. Then again, the visitor will quickly note that the smiles per capita rate is on par with the sport utility vehicles per capita rate—a very high percentage indeed. Marin is the land of the happy yuppie. Of course, as with all such caricatures, the reality is much more complex.

The county is home to famous musicians such as Grace Slick, Bob Weir, and Carlos Santana. George Lucas has studios at Skywalker Ranch, and his Industrial Light and Magic facility is located in San Rafael. Pixar, the animation company that created the movie *Toy Story*, is next door. To the north, much of the county is still devoted to sheep and cattle grazing.

Access to Marin is via U.S. 101, CA 1, the Golden Gate Bridge, Interstate 580 and the Richmond-San Rafael Bridge, or CA 37 from the Wine Country. ◼

MARIN COUNTY

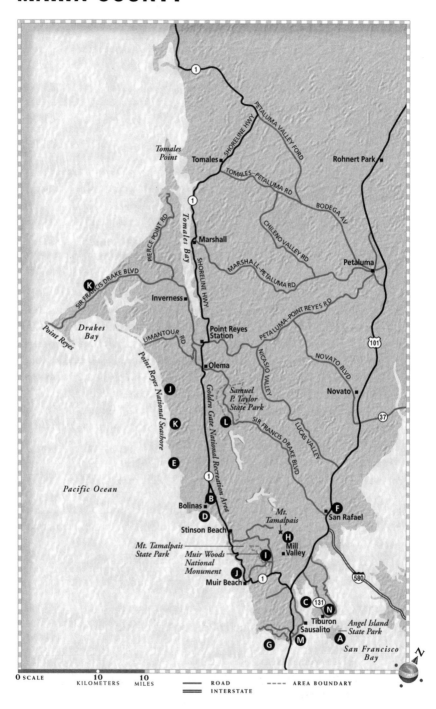

Tomales Point

Tomales

Rohnert Park

SHORELINE HWY

PETALUMA VALLEY FORD

TOMALES–PETALUMA RD

BODEGA AV

CHILENO VALLEY RD

MARSHALL–PETALUMA RD

Marshall

Petaluma

K

SIR FRANCIS DRAKE BLVD

PIERCE POINT RD

Tomales Bay

SHORELINE HWY

Inverness

Point Reyes

Drakes Bay

LIMANTOUR RD

Point Reyes National Seashore

Point Reyes Station

PETALUMA–POINT REYES RD

101

J

Olema

NOVATO BLVD

Samuel P. Taylor State Park

Novato

K

Nicasio Valley

L

SIR FRANCIS DRAKE BLVD

LUCAS VALLEY

37

E

Golden Gate National Recreation Area

Pacific Ocean

1

B

Bolinas

D

F

San Rafael

Stinson Beach

Mt. Tamalpais

Mt. Tamalpais State Park

H

Mill Valley

Muir Woods National Monument

I

J

Muir Beach

1

580

C

131

N

Tiburon

Angel Island State Park

Sausalito

G

M

A

San Francisco Bay

N

0 SCALE   **10** KILOMETERS   **10** MILES   ROAD   – – – – AREA BOUNDARY

INTERSTATE

Sightseeing Highlights

Ⓐ Angel Island

Ⓑ Audubon Canyon Ranch

Ⓒ Bay Model

Ⓓ Bolinas

Ⓔ Marin Coastal Wildlands

Ⓕ Marin County Civic Center

Ⓖ Marin Headlands

Ⓗ Mount Tamalpais State Park

Ⓘ Muir Woods National Monument

Ⓙ Nude Beaches

Ⓚ Point Reyes National Seashore

Ⓛ Samuel P. Taylor State Park

Ⓜ Sausalito

Ⓝ Tiburon

A PERFECT DAY IN MARIN COUNTY

Enjoy a bay view over breakfast in Tiburon. Take U.S. 101 north to downtown San Rafael and Fourth Street for a look at the town. Get on Sir Francis Drake Boulevard in San Anselmo and drive through the Samuel P. Taylor State Park to the coast. Choose between a hike on Tomales Point and a visit to Point Reyes Light Station with a walk on the beach. Hit Bolinas for a late lunch, followed by a drive up Mount Tamalpais or a visit to Muir Woods. Splurge on dinner at the

Casa Madrona in Sausalito. If it's not too late, follow Alexander
Avenue from town, under the freeway, and up onto the headlands for
a spectacular view.

SIGHTSEEING HIGHLIGHTS

★★★ **Marin Headlands**—Although much of the Marin coastline
features beautiful, protected headlands, the area at the southern tip
of the county is generally referred to as the "Marin Headlands." Two
of the three stars in this rating derive from the splendor of California
headlands in general. The third is earned by the world-class views of
San Francisco with the Golden Gate Bridge in the foreground.

Take the Alexander Avenue exit, the first exit north of the
Golden Gate Bridge after the vista point (or, if heading south, the
last exit before you reach it). Alexander Avenue from Sausalito cuts
under the freeway and climbs sharply up into the headlands, becom-
ing the Conzelman Road. About one quarter of a mile up is **Spencer
Battery**, just where the road takes a big swing to the right. A short
path next to an old gun emplacement leads to a great overlook.

Halfway to the top, you can turn on McCollough Road to reach
Rodeo Lagoon and Beach. Just north of the lagoon, the **California
Marine Mammal Center** works to save and rehabilitate injured sea
life. Details: (415) 289-7325; open daily from 10 a.m. to 4 p.m.
Admission is free. (1 hour)

At the top of Conzelman Road are long disused gun emplacements and magazines, along with what is possibly the best roadside
view of the Golden Gate Bridge and the surrounding city. The summit behind is called **Hawk Hill** in honor of the thousands of raptors
that migrate by here in the late summer and early fall. Continue
down a narrow, one-way road to Point Bonita and around into
Rodeo Valley. There are trailheads and a youth hostel in the valley.
The **Point Bonita Lighthouse** is open weekend afternoons only.
Details: At Rodeo Lagoon; (415) 331-1540; open daily from 9:30
a.m. to 4:30 p.m.

★★★ **Point Reyes National Seashore**—Point Reyes is a magnificent blend of forested hills, rugged headlands, rare wildlife, historic
ranches, rolling dunes, sandy beaches, golden sun, and blanketing
fog. The Point Reyes peninsula rides on the Pacific plate, separated
from the main North American land mass by the San Andreas Fault,

which runs directly under the Olema Valley and Tomales Bay. The park is slipping away northward at an average rate of 2 inches per year—though it jumped 20 feet in the 1906 earthquake! Details: Access is from CA 1 and Marin County's Sir Francis Drake Boulevard; (415) 663-1092. The Bear Valley Visitor Center, just west of Olema, is open daily from 9 a.m. to 5 p.m. Admission is free.

There are three broad areas to explore on Point Reyes. The **Philip Burton Wilderness Area** in the southern half of the park features numerous trails through forested hills, many of which lead to the coastal paths and provide access to wild cliffs and beaches. Trail access for good day hikes is easy from Limantour Road, Bear Valley Visitor Center and Five Brooks (all from CA 1), and the Palomarin Trailhead (via Mesa Road in Bolinas). Primitive camping is available in four hike-in areas. Free, first-come, first-served camping permits are available at the Bear Valley Visitor Center. (half day)

Sir Francis Drake Boulevard passes through open, non-wilderness land on its way out to **Drakes Estero** (or estuary), **Point Reyes Beaches**, **Drakes Beach**, and **Point Reyes Light Station**. The lighthouse and visitor center are definitely worth a visit, though frequent fog curtails views as it adds mystery. The beaches are sprawling and wild, though it does get crowded near the parking areas on hot summer days. Watch out for rip tides and rough surf! Drakes Estero is a good area for bird watching. The **Mount Vision Overlook** offers a great view of the entire park. It is reached via Mount Vision Road off of Sir Francis Drake Boulevard. (3 hours)

Pierce Point Road leads to **Tomales Point** and the **Tule Elk Range** at the northern end of Point Reyes. An easy 5-mile trail follows the crest of the peninsula from the parking area to the tip of Tomales Point, where Tomales Bay meets the Pacific. A sizable herd of Tule elk roams freely on the point and is easily viewed. Several kinds of hawks frequent the bluffs. At dusk, owls can be seen perching on small rock summits along the ridge. (3 hours)

✯✯ **Angel Island**—The island has been used for many purposes over the years, but it is now a state park with several miles of hiking trails and biking roads. Exploring the island offers fantastic views of San Francisco, Marin, and the East Bay. Walking and biking roads provide access to forts from the Civil and Spanish-American wars, as well as old missile and gun emplacements. Near the northeastern point of the island is an immigration station that served as San

Francisco's "Ellis Island" for a time before being converted to a
World War II internment camp for Japanese citizens.
   Details: The park can be reached on weekends by ferry from San
Francisco via the Red & White Fleet, (415) 546-2896, $9 round-trip.
Better still are the frequent daily ferries from the waterfront in
Tiburon, (415) 435-2131, $5 round-trip. Several campsites on the
island can be reserved through Destinet, (800) 444-7275. (half day)

★★ **Marin Coastal Wildlands**—Through awareness and effort, the
people of Marin County and the Bay Area have succeeded in protecting large areas of coastal land from development. The result is that
access to a beautiful coastal wilderness is only ten minutes from downtown San Francisco. An extensive trail system links the contiguous
wildlands of **Golden Gate National Recreation Area, Mount
Tamalpais State Park, Muir Woods National Monument, Marin
Municipal Water District Watershed, Samuel P. Taylor State
Park,** and **Point Reyes National Seashore**.
   The **Coastal Trail** through the Golden Gate National Recreation
Area can be linked with the **Coast Trail** in Point Reyes' **Philip
Burton Wilderness** to make a 40-mile hiking, biking, and riding cor-
ridor with lots of side trails and alternate loops. Access to the wildlands
is available at many points, including: Marin Headlands roads, Rodeo
Valley, Tennessee Valley Road, CA 1 and the Panoramic Highway,
Muir Woods, Stinson Beach, Point Reyes trailheads, and Samuel P.
Taylor State Park, as well as from fire road trailheads in Mill Valley,
Kentfield, Ross, and San Anselmo.

★★ **Mount Tamalpais State Park**—Mount "Tam" reigns over Marin
County and the North Bay. The 360-degree views from the summit,
only a ten-minute hike from the parking area, are unforgettable. Access
is via the Panoramic Highway, which begins and ends at CA 1, running
from the ridge top above Mill Valley to Stinson Beach. Follow the signs
and take Ridgecrest Road to the top. Many well-loved hiking, biking,
and horse trails thread through the park and protected watershed lands
that surround the peak, including the bed of an old narrow gauge rail.
Details: (415) 388-2070; open dawn to dusk. Admission to the park is $5
for day use. (half day)

★★ **Muir Woods National Monument**—Nestled in a narrow, steep
valley, the relatively small Muir Woods preserves a grove of ancient

redwoods. With its proximity to San Francisco, it receives more visitors than all the other redwood parks combined. There is an easy loop path through the Grove along Redwood Creek. If your trip will not include a northward swing, Muir Woods is a three-star, must-see destination. On the other hand, if the North Coast national and state parks are on your itinerary, you might choose to pass up the difficult parking and noisy visitors.

Like most popular parks, however, solitude is just a walk away. Muir Woods is surrounded by public lands, linked together with an excellent trail system. Details: Take Muir Woods Road or the Panoramic Highway from CA 1 north of Mill Valley, (415) 388-2595; open daily from 8 a.m. to sunset. Admission is free. (1½ hours)

✰ **Audubon Canyon Ranch**—From mid-March through July, the ranch is open for walkers to observe herons and egrets in their nesting environment. As with most Audubon sites, the birds come first, so access is strictly limited and the ranch is closed at sensitive times. The canyon drains into Bolinas Lagoon and is accessible via CA 1. Details: Located 3½ miles north of Stinson Beach on CA 1; call for reservations; (415) 868-9244; open daily from 10 a.m. to 4 p.m. Donations accepted.

✰ **Bolinas**—This could be the town that time forgot. At the least, it's a town that many residents would like time and tourists to forget. The highway sign for the Bolinas turnoff from CA 1 mysteriously disappears every time a new one is erected. Turn west on the Olema-Bolinas Road just north of Bolinas Lagoon to reach this relaxed, communally spirited town that harkens to the sixties. Visit the **Point Reyes Bird Observatory** for a bird-banding demonstration, or continue to the **Palomarin Trailhead** for hikes into Point Reyes. Details: Mesa Road; (415) 868-0655.

✰ **Samuel P. Taylor State Park**—On Sir Francis Drake Boulevard, near the coast, this park preserves old-growth redwoods along Lagunitas Creek, as well as several square miles of Marin wildlands. You can stop at several points along the road to enjoy the trees and stream. The campground is one of the more pleasant places to camp within an hour of the city. Details: Take Sir Francis Drake Boulevard west from San Anselmo or east from CA 1; (415) 488-9897.

✰ **Sausalito**—Sausalito has an archetypal, Mediterranean waterfront charm. Fine homes climb the hills behind the bayside shops and restaurants. The boats sliding through the calm waters provide a foreground for the skyline of San Francisco. People stroll casually in the afternoon sun, stopping to enjoy a view or a cool drink.

Details: Take the Alexander Avenue or Marin City exit from U.S. 101. Traffic can be thick and slow on the weekends. Consider taking a Golden Gate Ferry, from the Ferry Building in San Francisco, (415) 332-6600, $4.25 one-way, or a Red & White Fleet boat, from Pier 43½, (415) 546-2896, $5.50 one-way. Both ferries run about every 1½ hours.

✩ **Tiburon**—Like Sausalito, Tiburon features bayside relaxation in a thoroughly comfortable setting. As you wait for your ferry to Angel Island, lunch on the deck at a bayside café, where warm sun and cool breezes are balanced to perfection and the burble of voices is interrupted only by the printing of credit card receipts. If you wish, climb the hill for better views and a look at **Old St. Hilary's Church**, built in 1888.

Details: Tiburon is reached via U.S. 101 to Tiburon Boulevard (CA 131). Just as for Sausalito, San Francisco ferry service is offered by Golden Gate Ferry, from the Ferry Building in San Francisco, (415) 332-6600, $4.25 one-way, or a Red & White Fleet boat, from Pier 43½, (415) 546-2896, $5.50 one-way. Both ferries run about every 1½ hours.

Bay Model—In 1954, the Army Corps of Engineers constructed a huge and topographically correct model of the San Francisco Bay in order to study the movement of tides and river flows. The model and visitor center are housed in a warehouse-like building a mile north of Sausalito. Call ahead to see when the model will be filled with water—the best time to see it. Details: 2100 Bridgeway Boulevard, Sausalito; (415) 332-3871; open Tuesday through Sunday from 9 a.m. to 4 p.m. (closed Sundays in winter). Admission is free. (1 hour)

Marin County Civic Center—Frank Lloyd Wright designed this seat of county government shortly before his death. The structure incorporates arched and curved elements in a hillside setting. Details: Look to the east as you drive by on U.S. 101, or take a closer look by exiting 2 miles north of San Rafael, (415) 499-7407; open Monday through Friday, from 8:30 a.m. to 4:30 p.m.; tours by arrangement. (1 hour)

Nude Beaches—Sunbathing in the buff is moderately popular in and around the bay. **Red Rocks Nudist Beach** is more or less officially clothing free. It's located less than a mile south of Stinson Beach. Some out-thrust rocks break up **Muir Beach** into southern and northern sections—on the northern half, clothing is traditionally considered optional.

FITNESS AND RECREATION

Marin County is where Gary Fisher invented the mountain bike, and Mount Tam has always been Fisher's proving ground for new models. The **Marin Coastal Wildlands** are a great place for a ride. For the most part, bikers are limited to fire roads and must stay off of single-track footpaths. Fortunately, there are plenty of fire roads in the fire-prone Bay Area. Rentals, maps, and good advice are available at several excellent outlets throughout Marin County.

Hiking is also a great option in Marin. For an easy, outstanding hike, walk the ridge path that runs the length of **Tomales Point** at the northern end of Point Reyes. Closer to the city, a loop between **Tennessee Valley** and **Rodeo Valley** provides access to a great stretch of roadless coast. To have some company and a steady climb, hike the **Old Railroad Grade** from the end of Summit Avenue in Mill Valley (via East Blithedale Avenue and Throckmorton Avenue) to the summit of Mount Tam. Whether biking or hiking, watch out for poison oak throughout the area and take tick precautions, especially from October through April.

FOOD

In Sausalito, the **Casa Madrona** offers a bay view with lunch and dinner dining at its finest. The menu features California cuisine with an international twist, 801 Bridgeway Boulevard, (415) 332-0502. **Sushi Ran** is tucked away on a side street above the bay. You won't find better sushi and sake in Marin, 107 Caledonia Street, (415) 332-3620.

Tiburon has several good eateries. **Sam's Anchor Café** is a popular bayside option with a great deck, 27 Main Street, (415) 435-4527.

The **Buckeye Roadhouse**, right on CA 1 in Mill Valley, features eclectic dining in bold surrounds. There's a good bar too, 15 Shoreline Highway, (415) 331-2600. Up in Mill Valley proper, **Piazza D'Angelo** serves great Italian food—the calzones are yummy!—22 Miller Avenue, (415) 388-2000.

In Larkspur, the **Lark Creek Inn** is certainly among the best. The "American" cuisine is stretched well away from the traditional

MARIN COUNTY

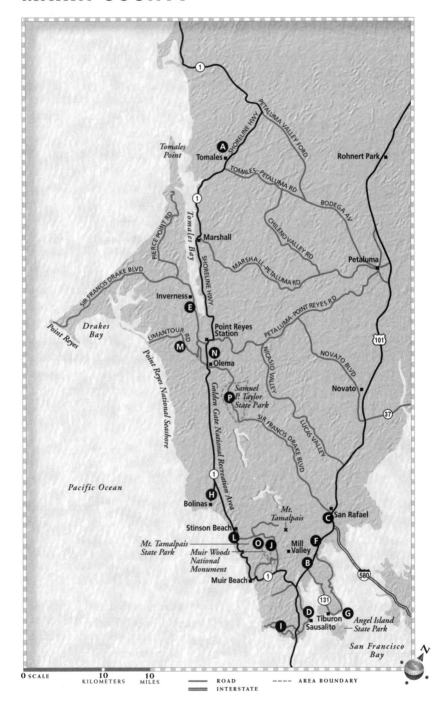

Tomales Point

Tomales ■ 🅐

Pierce Point Rd

Sir Francis Drake Blvd

Tomales Bay

Marshall ■

Shoreline Hwy

Petaluma Valley Ford

Tomales–Petaluma Rd

Chileno Valley Rd

Bodega Av

Marshall–Petaluma Rd

Rohnert Park ■

Petaluma ■

Inverness ■ 🅔

Drakes Bay

Point Reyes

Limantour Rd

🅜

Point Reyes National Seashore

Point Reyes Station ■

🅝

Olema ■

Petaluma–Point Reyes Rd

Nicasio Valley

Novato Blvd

101

Novato ■

37

Golden Gate National Recreation Area

Samuel P. Taylor State Park

🅟

Sir Francis Drake Blvd

Lucas Valley

Pacific Ocean

1

🅗

Bolinas ■

Mt. Tamalpais ✦

Stinson Beach ■

🅛

San Rafael ■ 🅒

Mt. Tamalpais State Park

Muir Woods National Monument

🅞 🅙

Mill Valley ■

🅕

🅑

Muir Beach ■

1

580

131

🅓

🅖

Tiburon ■

Sausalito ■

Angel Island — State Park

🅘

San Francisco Bay

N

0 SCALE

10
KILOMETERS

10
MILES

━━━ ROAD

━━━ INTERSTATE

--- AREA BOUNDARY

Food

Ⓐ Angel's Café

Ⓑ Buckeye Roadhouse

Ⓒ Carlo's

Ⓓ Casa Madrona

Ⓔ Gray Whale Pizza

Ⓕ Lark Creek Inn

Ⓒ Las Camelias

Ⓒ Milly's

Ⓔ Parkside Café

Ⓕ Piazza D'Angelo

Ⓒ Royal Thai

Ⓖ Sam's Anchor Café

Ⓗ Shop Café

Ⓓ Sushi Ran

Lodging

Ⓓ Alta Mira

Ⓔ Blackthorne Inn

Ⓓ Casa Madrona

Ⓘ Marin Headlands Hostel

Ⓙ Mountain Home Inn

Ⓒ Panama Hotel

Ⓚ Point Reyes Hostel

Ⓛ Redwoods Haus B&B

Ⓜ Roundstone Farm

Camping

Ⓝ Olema Ranch Campground

Ⓞ Pantoll Station

Ⓟ Samuel P. Taylor State Park

Ⓛ Steep Ravine

Note: Items with the same letter are located in the same town or area.

with great success. Service is excellent and the prices are high. Sunday
brunch is splendid, 234 Magnolia Avenue, (415) 924-7766.

San Rafael has several good restaurants on or near Fourth Street.
For great Thai, hit **Royal Thai** at 610 Third Street, (415) 386-1795.
Carlo's is authentic Italian at its best, 1700 Fourth Street, (415) 457-
6252. For high-end, vegan cuisine, nothing compares to **Milly's**.
Carnivores and even casual vegetarians may be baffled by the taste and
appearance of many dishes, but aficionados promise me it's the "bee's
knees," 1613 Fourth Street, (415) 459-1601. **Las Camelias** gets the
nod as the Mexican restaurant of choice, 912 Lincoln Avenue, (415)
453-5850.

Try the **Parkside Café** in Stinson Beach for breakfast or lunch,
43 Arenal (off of CA 1), (415) 868-1272. In Bolinas, the **Shop Café** is a
rustic and friendly place to eavesdrop on the town news, 46 Wharf
Road, (415) 868-9984. **Gray Whale Pizza** in Inverness is a good place
to stop and feed the family on your Point Reyes excursion.

If you're heading north on CA 1, stop at **Angel's Café** in charming Tomales for breakfast. The tasty fare is reasonably priced at $5 to
$7 a meal. Kathy, the owner, has been collecting ceramic angel fig-
urines for over 20 years. They watch over you as you dine.

LODGING

Freeway chain motels and budget independents can be found along
U.S. 101 from Mill Valley north. Use the phone numbers on the
"Resources" page to contact any of them.

In Sausalito, the **Casa Madrona** is the plush choice with rooms
and cottages between $125 and $200. A hot tub and beautiful views
are included, 801 Bridgeway Boulevard, (415) 332-0502 or (800) 288-
0502. The **Alta Mira** also has a great view and a restaurant. Basic
rooms are $70, view rooms are much more, 125 Buckley Avenue,
(415) 332-1350.

At the edge of the wildlands, high above Mill Valley, is the wonderful **Mountain Home Inn**. Rooms are high at $130 to $250 (includes
breakfast), but the views alone are worth the price. Trailheads are right
out the door. Hikers and mountain bikers commonly stop for refresh-
ment during the day. At night, the lights of the bay twinkle below. If
you're going to splurge near the city, this is a great choice, 810
Panoramic Highway, (415) 381-9000.

In San Rafael, the **Panama Hotel** has class and character.

Interesting and occasionally famous people stay here—a good story might be yours. With shared-bath rooms starting at $50, it can be a real bargain (private bath, $90 and up), 4 Bayview Street, (415) 457-3993.

Along the coast, Stinson Beach has several motels, including the **Redwoods Haus B&B**. Rooms at this thoroughly Euro-style inn range from $60 to $80, 1 Belvedere Avenue, (415) 868-1034. Olema boasts the **Roundstone Farm**, a lovely B&B with a ranch setting, views of Tomales Bay, and great breakfasts, 9940 Sir Francis Drake Boulevard, (415) 663-1020. In Inverness, try the wonderfully constructed **Blackthorne Inn**. Plan on spending $120 or more, 266 Vallejo, (415) 553-8621.

On a loop above the main road in Rodeo Valley is the **Marin Headlands Hostel**, a Hostelling International facility. The location is a perfect base for exploring the city and the headlands. Beds are $11 a night, (415) 331-2777. The **Point Reyes Hostel** is a couple hundred yards off Limantour Road, in the heart of Point Reyes National Seashore. Beds are $10, (415) 663-8811.

CAMPING

There are two walk-in campgrounds with a total of only 22 sites in Mount Tamalpais State Park. One is just next to **Pantoll Station** at the junction of Panoramic Highway and Ridgecrest Road. The other is at **Steep Ravine**, 1 mile south of Stinson Beach. Fees for both are $10 to $11. Steep Ravine also has cabins for $30, (415) 388-2070 for information and reservations.

Samuel P. Taylor State Park is a great place to camp. Trailers up to 27 feet long can be accommodated. Sites are $11 to $15, and are located west of Lagunitas on Sir Francis Drake Boulevard. Call (415) 488-9897 for information, (800) 444-7275 for reservations. There is a $6.75 fee per reservation. The **Olema Ranch Campground** down the road is pleasant enough. There are hookups, store, café, and more at the junction of Sir Francis Drake Boulevard and CA 1, (415) 663-8001 or (800) 655-2267. Point Reyes National Seashore has only hike-in sites, (415) 663-1092 for reservations and information.

NIGHTLIFE

Marin is pretty quiet in the evenings. The main action is on Fourth Street in San Rafael. **New Georges** is a great place to see live music. With the concentration of musicians in Marin County, the caliber at this club runs from above average to exceptional, 842 Fourth Street, (415) 457-8424. Nearby are a few quiet spots for a break and a chat.

In Mill Valley, the oh-so-tiny **Sweetwater** is the place to see the truly famous sitting in with a local favorite. The big shots appreciate the hassle-free fit into the jaded crowd. Get there early, or you'll have to listen to the rock, blues, and jazz through the wall, 153 Throckmorton, (415) 388-2880.

For a good, site-brewed ale and a game of pool, stop in at the **Marin Brewing Company**. The beer may not be as good as the Triple Rock in Berkeley, but second place in this brewpub happy region is very good indeed, 1809 Larkspur Landing Circle, near the ferry terminal on Sir Francis Drake Boulevard, (415) 462-4677.

3
THE EAST BAY:
BERKELEY AND OAKLAND

Berkeley and Oakland rise from the East Bay "flats" to the crest of the hills. They enjoy the bay's best weather, receiving the cool, clean air that flows through the Golden Gate while avoiding the fog and chills of San Francisco. Area residents enjoy thousands of acres of recreational lands in their own backyards.

Oakland gained prominence in 1869 as the terminus of the transcontinental railroad and grew into a center of trade and industry. Today, despite a good economic base, the city struggles with issues of crime and poverty. The traveler need not rub elbows with problem areas, however; much of Oakland is quite wonderful.

The city of Berkeley exists in a love-hate relationship with the renowned University of California at Berkeley. Some 30,000 students enroll at "Cal" each fall, flooding the city with energy and potential. Intellectually inflated and politically left-leaning, Berkeley is a hotbed of activism—a circus of tie-dyed freaks, espresso yuppies, used-book hounds, pesto critics, street preachers, brewpub bums, rallying students, smoky poets, homeless hustlers, and nobel laureates.

The rest of the East Bay consists largely of bedroom communities. Richmond gets a nod as a past powerhouse of industry—scores of liberty ships were built here in World War II. Walnut Creek, Concord, and Livermore are suburbia at its best and worst. Mount Diablo rises above it all, unconcerned by the housing tracts that nibble at its skirts. ◧

BERKELEY

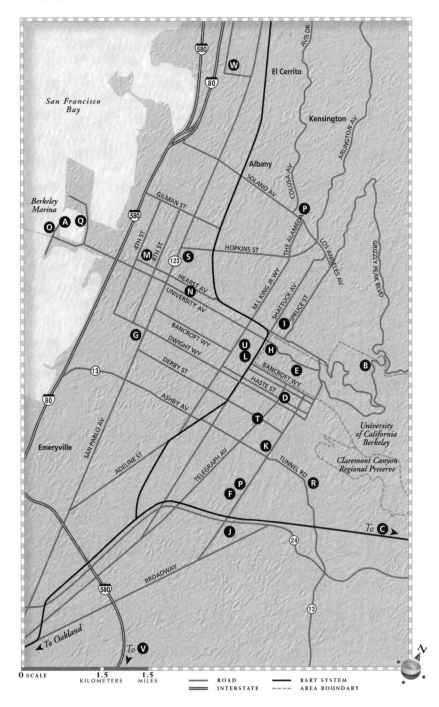

San Francisco Bay

Berkeley Marina

Berkeley

El Cerrito

Kensington

Albany

Emeryville

University of California Berkeley

Claremont Canyon Regional Preserve

To Oakland

To C

To V

AVIS DR

COLUSA AV

SOLANO AV

THE ALAMEDA

ARLINGTON AV

LOS ANGELES AV

GRIZZLY PEAK BLVD

SPRUCE ST

M L KING JR WY

SHATTUCK AV

GILMAN ST

HOPKINS ST

HEARST AV

UNIVERSITY AV

BANCROFT WY

DWIGHT WY

DERBY ST

ASHBY AV

BANCROFT WY

HASTE ST

TELEGRAPH AV

TUNNEL RD

SAN PABLO AV

ADELINE ST

BROADWAY

4TH ST

8TH ST

580

80

580

80

13

13

13

123

24

O SCALE 1.5 KILOMETERS 1.5 MILES

ROAD — BART SYSTEM

INTERSTATE --- AREA BOUNDARY

Sightseeing Highlights

A Berkeley Marina

B Lawrence Hall of Science

C Mount Diablo

D Telegraph Avenue and Sproul Plaza

E University of California at Berkeley

Food

F Barney's Gourmet Hamburgers

D Blue Nile

G Brick Hut

D Café Intermezzo

H Cambodiana's

I Chez Panisse

J Citron

K La Mediterranée

L Mel's Diner

M O Chané

N Santa Fe Bar & Grill

O Skates On the Bay

P Zachary's Chicago Style Pizza

Lodging

Q Berkeley Marina Mariott

R Claremont Resort, Spa & Tennis Club

S Golden Bear Motel

T Gramma's Rose Garden Inn

D Hotel Durant

L Shattuck Hotel

U YMCA

Camping

V Anthony Chabot Regional Park

W Audiss RV Park

C Mount Diablo State Park

Note: Items with the same letter are located in the same area.

A PERFECT DAY IN THE EAST BAY

After breakfast at The Brick Hut in Berkeley, drive to the Ashby BART station (at Ashby and Adeline Streets in Berkeley), then "BART" (also works as a verb) to 12th Street Station in Oakland. Walk up Broadway to see the city hall and the heart of town, then down 14th to Lake Merritt. Enjoy a lakeshore stroll and a look at the Camron-Stanford House. Visit the excellent Oakland Museum, then catch the Richmond BART to Berkeley. Take a walking tour of the campus and then a ride to the top of Sather Tower. Experience Telegraph Avenue and "Berserkeley," then BART back to Ashby Station. Enjoy sunset on the Berkeley Pier and dinner with a view at Skates on the Bay.

SIGHTSEEING HIGHLIGHTS

✮✮ **Oakland Museum of California**—Just west of Lake Merritt, this outstanding museum is a great place to get a rich overview of the Golden State. The three main sections of the museum present California art, history, and ecology in a way that gives the visitor a clear sense of the flow, scope, and relationship of the area's culture. It is perhaps the best museum of its kind in the state. Details: 1001 Oak Street, Oakland; (510) 238-3401; open Wednesday through Saturday from 10 a.m. to 5 p.m., Sunday noon to 7 p.m. Admission is $4. (2 hours)

✮✮ **Telegraph Avenue and Sproul Plaza**—Students of human behavior should consider this a three-star destination. Telegraph Avenue links downtown Oakland to the University of California, ending at the entrance to Sproul Plaza. The administration building and student union glare at each other across the plaza, as activists stir lunchtime crowds with speeches on the issue of the day. Jazz bands play below in front of Zellerbach Auditorium as impromptu bucket drummers beat above.

The five blocks of Telegraph just south of campus are a circus of humanity. Shy, schoolgirl-dressed freshmen from Japan stroll past studded and pierced skaters. Pipe-smoking profs buy espresso, ignoring a request for spare change. Cadres of well-groomed jocks push past clusters of grubby gypsy kids. Street vendors line the avenue, selling batik baby clothes, hand-crafted jewelry, pro-pot T-shirts, and anti-cop bumper stickers.

The shops on Telegraph are equally attractive. Nearly 40 cafés and coffeehouses line the row, selling an ethnically wide-ranging array of dishes at wonderfully affordable prices. **Cody's**, **Moe's**, **Shakespeare**, **Shambala**, and **Half Price** team up in a block-and-a-half long strip to provide the most concentrated selection of new, used, discount, and spiritual books anywhere.

Just above Telegraph, between Haste Street and Dwight Way, are the trees, vegetable gardens, basketball courts, and lawn of **People's Park**. The park is university owned land that was confiscated by local citizens in 1969. The university put up a fence, but the outcry after deadly riots led to its removal. The park has since been a jealously guarded symbol and a site for several protests. The movement, however, is showing signs of fatigue, and the university has recovered authority over part of the parcel.

✯ **University of California at Berkeley**—The beautiful "Cal" campus is great for relaxed strolling and offers a number of attractions to the visitor. **Strawberry Creek** flows down from the hills and through the campus. Alongside the creek are lovely paths, redwood trees, a eucalyptus grove, charming bridges, and interesting sculpture. Above campus, Strawberry Creek flows through the beautiful **Botanical Gardens**. Details: Centennial Road, Berkeley; (510) 642-3343; open daily from 9 a.m. to 4:45 p.m. Admission is free. (1½ hours)

Several campus museums are worth noting. The **University Art Museum and Pacific Film Archive** features Asian and modern rotating exhibits, as well as various series of art films. Details: 2626 Bancroft Way, Berkeley; (510) 642-0808, or call (510) 642-1412 for film information; museum open Wednesday through Sunday from 11 a.m. to 5 p.m. (until 9 p.m. Thursday). Admission is $6 (free on Thursday evenings).

In Kroeber Hall, you'll find the **Museum of Anthropology**. Details: University of California, Berkeley; open weekdays from 10 a.m. to 4:30 p.m. (until 9 p.m. Thursday), and weekends from noon to 4:30 p.m. Admission is $2. (1 hour)

The **Museum of Paleontology**, in the Life Sciences Building, has skeletons, fossils, and more. Details: (510) 642-1821.

Sather Tower, the Campenile, is a 300-foot tall landmark, visible for miles. Those same miles of visibility can be enjoyed from the top of the tower for a small elevator fee. If you're lucky, you'll be there when the carillon is played at noon (or at 2 p.m., Saturday and Sunday). Details: University of California, Berkeley; elevator leaves every five minutes or so from 10 a.m. to 3:15 p.m. every day (closes at 1:30 p.m. Sunday). Admission is 50 cents. (1 hour)

✻ **Berkeley Marina**—The marina is a great place to spend an hour. The **Waterfront Walk** offers a 1¼-mile waterside path popular with walkers and joggers. A sunset stroll out onto the 600-yard long Berkeley Pier, the refurbished remnant of a much longer structure, yields a marvelous view of San Francisco and the Golden Gate. For obvious reasons the marina is a favored location for windsurfers and kite flyers. Details: Located on the bay at the end of University Avenue, Berkeley. Good lodging and dining are available.

✻ **Lake Merritt**—Without Lake Merritt, downtown Oakland might seem as drab as any city forced to face off against San Francisco. Instead, this urban saltwater lake provides a 3-mile stretch of water-front park land, affording recreational opportunities and splendid views of the skyline. At the western end of the lake, the **Camron-Stanford House** reminds strollers of the Victorian Oakland that once was. Details: 1418 Lakeside Drive; Oakland; (510) 835-1976; tours are offered Wednesday and Sunday afternoons.

In **Lakeside Park** you'll find **Children's Fairyland**, a glorified playground with a carousel, puppet shows, and farm animals—kids love it. The park also features a Japanese garden and boat rentals. The **Merritt Queen**, a small paddlewheeler, cruises the lake from the boathouse. Details: Lakeside Park, Oakland; (510) 444-3807; cruises given on weekends from 11 a.m. to 3 p.m. Admission is $1.50. (½ hour)

✻ **Mount Diablo**—You can see more of the earth's surface from the summit of Mount Diablo than from any other point on the planet except Mount Kilimanjaro (if the air is clear). The phenomenon is related to the shape of the Central Valley. As the world curves away, sphere that it is, the margins of the Central Valley rise toward the hills in compensation, exposing more land to the viewer upon Mount Diablo's summit. In addi-tion, the mountain is isolated at the center of the long valley. Take a look.

Mount Diablo State Park offers hiking and biking trails, rock climbing, and views galore. Details: For the north entrance, take the Ignacio Valley Road exit from Interstate 680. Follow Ignacio Valley Road east to a right on Walnut Avenue, which merges into Northgate, the entrance road. The south entrance road intersects Diablo Road east of Danville. Take the Diablo Road exit from Interstate 680.

✻ **Lawrence Hall of Science**—Located on Centennial Drive, high above the Berkeley campus, this hands-on museum features wonderful exhibits that can be enjoyed by both kids and parents (but mostly kids). Outside the unique concrete structure, children can climb on a full-size model of a whale, while the adults admire the panoramic view. Details: Take Hearst Avenue from Shattuck in downtown Berkeley. Turn right into the campus on Gayley Road, left above the stadium on Stadium Way, then left again on Centennial; (510) 642-5132; open daily from 10 a.m. to 4 p.m. Admission is $6. (2 hours)

Jack London Square—Where Broadway meets the Inner Harbor in downtown Oakland, this somewhat awkwardly laid out collection of waterfront restaurants, shops, and nightspots welcomes the visitor. Part of the ongoing revitalization of the city, the stretch (it's not really a square) features a relocated log cabin once lived in by Jack London. The place not to miss is London's one-time watering hole, **Heinhold's First and Last Chance Saloon**. Built in 1880, the place hasn't changed. Unfortunately, the ground has shifted substantially, leaving the pub with what might be the most steeply slanted floor of any commercial establishment in the known universe. Details: Heinhold's and the London cabin are toward the east end of the "square," where Webster meets the Embarcadero.

FITNESS AND RECREATION

The Bay Area is a place to be outdoors. The hills above Oakland and Berkeley are quite wild, protected by a series of regional parks, preserves, and watershed lands. Above Berkeley, **Tilden Regional Park** offers swimming in Lake Anza, strolling in the Botanical Gardens, golfing on a hilly course, and hiking and biking on several miles of trails. Take Centennial Way up through the Berkeley campus, or Claremont Avenue to Grizzly Peak Boulevard, then left to the park.

To reach **Robert Sibley Volcanic Regional Preserve** and **Redwood Regional Park**, take a right on Grizzly Peak from Claremont Avenue. Both have good hiking and biking trails. Sibley preserves a volcanic cone and other formations. The **East Bay Skyline National Recreation Trail** connects Tilden, Sibley, Redwood, and others, following the ridge crest. The trail is part of a larger system that circles the entire bay region.

Good jogging or walking loops include **Lake Merritt** (3.2 miles), **North Waterfront Park** at the Berkeley Marina (1.3 miles), and **Aquatic Park** at the bottom of Bancroft Way in Berkeley (2.2 miles).

FOOD

Several good spots are found in the downtown Oakland and Jack London Square vicinity. Have dim sum in the huge dining room at the **Lantern**, in Oakland's Chinatown, 814 Webster Street, (510) 451-0627. For authentic and inexpensive Vietnamese fare, **Vi's Restaurant** is the place—a diamond in the rough, 724 Webster Street, (510) 835-8375. Everyone loves **Zza's Trattoria**. The thin crust of the pizza crunches delicately before the toppings melt in your mouth. Aaahhh! 552 Grand Avenue, (510) 839-9124.

College Avenue through North Oakland is a great stretch for dining. **Citron** features intimate dining and top quality French cuisine, 5484 College Avenue, (510) 653-5484. Even with two locations, you may well have to wait in line for the pizza consistently voted the best of the East Bay at **Zachary's Chicago Style Pizza**. Their specialty is an amazing deep dish with a layer of crust baked in between filling and topping, 5801 College Avenue, (510) 655-6385, or 1853 Solano Avenue, (510) 525-5950. They don't make 'em any better than they do at **Barney's Gourmet Hamburgers**, 5819 College Avenue, (510) 601-0444. **La Mediterraneé** offers a Lebanese menu in a pleasant setting with good prices, 2936 College Avenue, (510) 540-7773.

On Telegraph Avenue, the **Café Intermezzo** serves insanely huge salads and sandwiches at great prices. Buy one and share, 2475 Telegraph Avenue, (510) 849-1128. The **Blue Nile** is one of the bay's top Ethiopian restaurants, with the bonus of exotic ambiance and good prices, 2525 Telegraph Avenue, (510) 540-6777.

Many good places to eat are located on Shattuck Avenue, which runs through downtown and north Berkeley. For a thick shake with your cheeseburger and fries, try **Mel's Diner**, 2240 Shattuck Avenue, (510) 540-6351. Above Shattuck, at 2156 University Avenue, **Cambodiana's** has unbeatable Cambodian fare. Reservations are advised, (510) 843-4630.

Where Shattuck meets Vine Street, Berkeley's "Gourmet Ghetto" is a center of eating and pantry stocking. Still the pinnacle of East Bay dining, **Chez Panisse** helped hatch California cuisine and then raised it to fine art. Bill Clinton always stops by when he's in town. Prix fixe in the downstairs dining room runs from $35 to $70. Upstairs, the café entrées are around $15, 1517 Shattuck Avenue, (510) 548-5525 (510-548-5049 for the café), lunch and dinner, closed Sunday.

OAKLAND

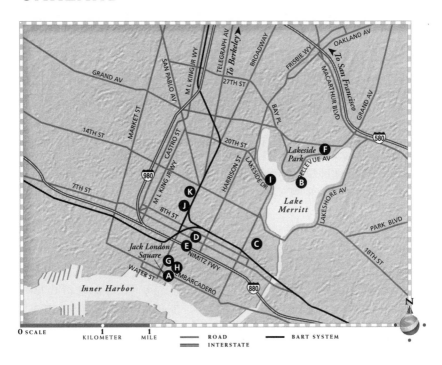

Sightseeing Highlights

- **Ⓐ** Jack London Square
- **Ⓑ** Lake Merritt
- **Ⓒ** Oakland Museum of CA

Food

- **Ⓓ** Lantern
- **Ⓔ** Vi's Restaurant
- **Ⓕ** Zza's Trattoria

Lodging

- **Ⓖ** Best Western Thunderbird Inn
- **Ⓗ** Jack London Inn
- **Ⓘ** Lake Merritt Hotel
- **Ⓙ** Marriot Park Oakland Hotel
- **Ⓚ** Washington Inn

Several places are near the bay, toward the bottom of University Avenue or around Fourth Street near Hearst. Located in an old train station, the **Santa Fe Bar & Grill** has been serving consistently good, high-end cuisine for years, 1310 University Avenue, (510) 841-4740. The **Brick Hut** serves excellent breakfasts and lunches with a distinctly feminist attitude, on San Pablo near Dwight. The inspiration at **Skates on the Bay** at the end of University Avenue by the Berkeley Pier is the marvelous view. Dinner from the varied menu ranges from $12 to $20, (510) 549-1900. **O Chamé** is a terrific, casual, and artful Japanese café—one of Berkeley's best, 1830 Fourth Street, (510) 841-8783.

LODGING

The **Claremont Resort, Spa, and Tennis Club** is *the* place to stay in the East Bay. Located in Oakland, right on the Berkeley border, this huge, white, Edwardian palace is visible for miles. The views of the bay from restaurant, bar, and bayside rooms are spectacular. Enjoy a massage, soak, and swim after a long day of walking through the city. Rooms start at $185, Ashby Avenue and Domingo Avenue (you can't miss it), (510) 843-3000. In downtown Oakland, the **Lake Merritt Hotel** offers bargain luxury with a lake view. Rooms range from $90 to $160. Continental breakfast is served in the Terrace Room, 1800 Madison Street, (510) 832-2300 or (800) 933-4683. Also in the city center is the **Washington Inn**, a small, restored hotel built before World War I. The $100 to $130 rooms are a bargain that includes breakfast, 495 10th Street, (510) 452-1776 or (800) 464-1776. Across the way is the huge **Marriott Park Oakland Hotel**. Rooms range from $115 to $150, some featuring terrific views, 1001 Broadway, (510) 451-4000 or (800) 338-1338.

At Jack London Square, the **Best Western Thunderbird Inn** has rooms from $65 to $80 and a pool, 233 Broadway, (510) 452-4565 or (800) 633-5973. Nearby, the **Jack London Inn** has clean, budget rooms for around $40, 444 Embarcadero West, (510) 444-2032.

The **Berkeley Marina Marriott** has a wonderful location at the Berkeley Marina. Rooms run from $100 to $140, 200 Marina Boulevard, (510) 548-7920 or (800) 228-9290. Just above Telegraph Avenue on Durant Street, is the **Hotel Durant**. Rooms start at $85 and offer great access to the campus, 2600 Durant Street, (510) 845-8981. **Gramma's Rose Garden Inn** is a pleasant B&B only three blocks from all the action on Telegraph Avenue. All rooms have a private bath, $85 to $150, 2740 Telegraph Avenue, (510) 549-2145. Downtown, you'll find the older, moderately elegant **Shattuck Hotel**. Rooms go from $70 to $80 and include a continental breakfast, 2086 Allston Way, (510) 845-7300 or (800) 742-8882. A good, clean budget alternative is the **Golden Bear Motel**, 1620 San Pablo Avenue, (510) 525-6770. Rooms are $49. True budgeteers can stay at the downtown **YMCA**. Tiny singles are $25, and you can use the facilities, 2001 Allston Way, (510) 848-6800.

CAMPING

There are three campgrounds in **Mount Diablo State Park**. Trailers are limited to 20 feet and motor homes to 24 feet, due to the narrow, winding roads. You must arrive before sunset when the park entrance roads close. Sites are from $12 to $15, (510) 837-2525. Make reservations through Destinet, (800) 444-7275, $6.75 per reservation.

    Anthony Chabot Regional Park has 31 sites for $13. Take Interstate 580 to the Estudillo Avenue exit in San Leandro. Head east into the park on Estudillo, which becomes Lake Chabot Road, (510) 635-0135.

    In El Cerrito, the **Audiss RV Park** has sites. Take the Central Avenue exit from Interstate 80, turn left on San Mateo Street, then right on El Dorado, 5828 El Dorado Avenue, (510) 525-3435.

NIGHTLIFE

Compared to the city, East Bay nightlife is pretty tame, ends early, and tends to favor coffee over beer. Several neighborhood zones are good for browsing, a bite, and a drink up until 11 p.m. or midnight. Bars and clubs close at 1 a.m. or 2 a.m. These same areas are more alive during the morning and afternoons.

    Near downtown Oakland, the only evening area of much activity is Jack London Square. Most are there to eat or see a film, but there are a couple of nightspots, including the tiny, ancient, and sinking **Heinhold's First and Last Chance Saloon**, (510) 839-6761. **Shenanigan's** has a good bar with its restaurant in the square, (510) 839-8333. Farther into town, the **Pacific Coast Brewing Company**, 906 Washington Street, has good brews, (510) 836-2739.

    On College Avenue, between Broadway and Alcatraz Avenue, the Rockridge and Lower Claremont neighborhoods have much to offer.

Toward Broadway, **Bill McNally's** is a fine Irish pub, 5352 College Avenue, (510) 654-9463. Near the BART station, the **Edible Complex** has pricey coffee but serves as a gathering place of good minds. The **E-Line Ale House** has a dozen taps, good pub grub, and Scott, the friendly bartender. It's a great place for conversation and camaraderie, 5612 College Avenue, (510) 547-8786.

Farther north, College Avenue and Ashby Avenue intersect at the center of Elmwood. At the corner, **Espresso Roma** has beer, coffee, pastries, and light entrées, as well as a room with wall plugs that laptop users treasure, 2960 College Avenue, (510) 644-3773.

Heading toward the Berkeley campus on Telegraph Avenue from Parker Street, you'll hit the **Bison Brewing Company**. The Bison is a great place to see light electric, jazz, and alternative new bands while enjoying (usually) a site-brewed or guest beer. A pool table, balcony, good grub, and weird architecture complete the picture, 2598 Telegraph Avenue, (510) 841-7734. Between Dwight Way and Haste Street, **Cody's** bookstore is open until 10 p.m., **Moe's Books** until 11 p.m., and the **Caffé Mediterraneum** until midnight—there's an evening right there. **Blake's**, 2367 Telegraph Avenue, (510) 848-0886, has good food and beer upstairs with live music or deejays downstairs. Monday night is a blues open mike night with occasional visits by the greats, 2367 Telegraph Avenue, (510) 848-0886. **Caffé Strada** at Bancroft and College is a big draw for students who need espresso (as are a dozen other places), 2300 College Avenue, (510) 843-5282.

The happening place is the **Jupiter**. Take a pint of good micro-brew into the splendid courtyard out back to enjoy top local bands, 2181 Shattuck Avenue, (510) 843-1761. The best of all spots is the **Triple Rock**. This brewpub consistently serves the finest site-brewed beer in the bay. Try the I.P.A., Tree Frog, Stonehenge Stout, or their classic Red Rock. It's a great place to relax and talk, 1920 Shattuck Avenue, (510) 843-2739.

Elsewhere, the **Albatross** (also the Bird) at 1822 San Pablo Avenue, Berkeley, was the first pub in town—and perhaps still the best. Bob, the Icelandic owner, doesn't tolerate rowdiness, but playing a board game by the fire or reading to classical music at the bar is welcomed. This is the best darts bar in town, (510) 849-4714. For live music, either Irish traditional or jamming electric, the **Starry Plough** is an excellent choice, 3101 Shattuck Avenue, Berkeley, (510) 841-2082.

4

THE SOUTH BAY AND THE PENINSULA COAST

The South Bay has, in recent decades, been a rapidly growing, economic success story. Silicon Valley (roughly, the flat lands from Palo Alto to San Jose and around toward Fremont) hosts corporate headquarters for such companies as Apple, Hewlett Packard, and Sun Microsystems. Stanford University has enjoyed a meteoric rise to rival Harvard as the nation's premier private school. At 840,000, San Jose is now the most populated city in Northern California.

The region around San Jose has been justly compared to Los Angeles—the South Bay hills can trap smog over the hot, sprawling, strip-malled suburbs and their maze of freeways. Fortunately, the region is much smaller than Los Angeles, and it is a safe and hospitable place to live. Though the area has several fine attractions, you may choose to breeze through the South Bay, stopping only for gas.

The hills and coast of the peninsula are a different story. Bitter battles between preservationists and developers have stalled subdivision of the headlands, perhaps permanently. Towns are still small and pleasant; CA 1 is still a winding two-lane road; and coastal vistas are uninterrupted by corporate towers and cookie-cutter housing. While touring the peninsula coast, it is entirely possible to forget that 6 million people are going about their business just over the hills.

Several good parks and public beaches line the coast, including a vital breeding ground for the once endangered elephant seal and the southernmost bastion of old-growth coastal redwoods. ◼

SOUTH BAY AND PENINSULA COAST

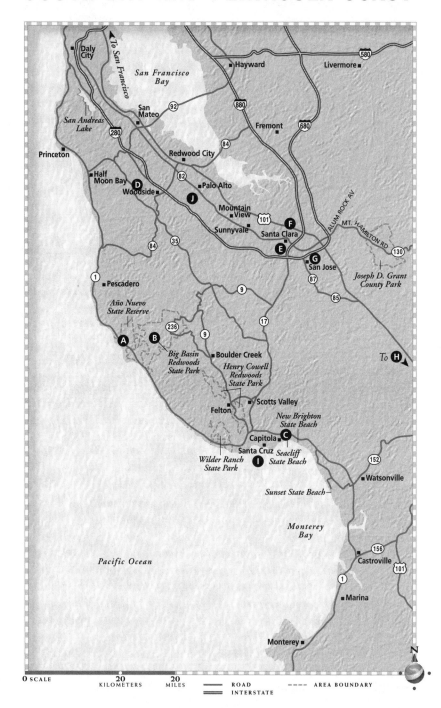

Sightseeing Highlights

Ⓐ Año Nuevo State Reserve

Ⓑ Big Basin Redwoods State Park

Ⓒ Capitola

Ⓓ Filoli

Ⓔ Mission Santa Clara de Asis

Ⓕ Paramount's Great America

Ⓖ Rosicrucian Egyptian Museum and Planetarium

Ⓖ San Jose City Center

Ⓗ San Juan Bautista

Ⓘ Santa Cruz

Ⓙ Stanford University

Ⓖ Winchester Mystery House

Note: Items with the same letter are located in the same town or area.

A PERFECT DAY ON THE PENINSULA

Spend the morning in Palo Alto, having breakfast on University Avenue and visiting the sights of the Stanford University campus. Hook up with CA 84 for a winding journey through the hills to the coast. Visit Año Nuevo State Reserve for a look at the elephant seals. If time allows, take a longer hike in Año Nuevo, along Waddell Creek in Big Basin Redwoods State Park, or on the headlands at Wilder Ranch State Park. Enjoy the Santa Cruz Beach Boardwalk late in the day, then retire to Capitola for an evening constitutional and bed.

SIGHTSEEING HIGHLIGHTS

✯✯✯ **Año Nuevo State Reserve**—Male elephant seals, with their bulbous prosci, are shameless when it comes to displaying mating behavior and violence in front of the gawking humans at Año Nuevo. From November through February, adult elephant seals arrive, males battle for dominance, and the females later give birth to and nurse their young. A month after the pups are born, males again mate with their harem while the lesser bulls watch from the sidelines. Elephant seals are present at other times of the year as well—juveniles stay through March and return in September, molting females are around in April and May, and molting males in July and August. Only in June are the beaches likely to be empty.

For the peak period from December 15 through March, you must make reservations for the popular seal viewing tour. At other times, you can just stop at the park. Only key seal areas have limited access, the rest of this large reserve is open for hiking and other activities. Details: The park entrance is 13 miles south of Pescadero on CA 1; call for current information, (415) 879-2025 for park information, (800) 444-7275 for reservations; open daily from 8 a.m. to dusk. Parking is $4, general entry is free, and guided walks are $4. (2½ hours)

✯✯ **Big Basin Redwoods State Park**—This large park in the hard-to-reach heart of the peninsula preserves some of the southernmost stands of old-growth redwoods. Wonderful hikes lead through groves to the summits or from the ridge to the sea. Two campgrounds are available. Access is via the twisting CA 236 from CA 9. A narrow finger of the park reaches the Pacific south of Año Nuevo via Waddell Creek. There's a trailhead here, though no road. Details: The headquarters are 9 miles northwest of Boulder Creek on CA 236; (408) 338-6132 for information; open daily from 8 a.m. to dusk. Day use parking is $4. (3 hours)

✯✯ **Santa Cruz**—This is a beach, boardwalk, and student town—not a place to get serious. The **Santa Cruz Beach Boardwalk** was constructed in 1904. It features a wonderful, old wooden roller coaster that provides a sense of danger not related to speed or height. Other attractions include a magnificent carousel and amusements housed in an elaborate old casino. Strolling, people watching, and ice cream consumption are standard practice. **Santa Cruz Beach**, immediately below the boardwalk, is one of many that line Monterey Bay.

The **Santa Cruz City Museum of Natural History** is worth a visit. Marine natural history is emphasized, though a special nod is given to the monarch butterflies, some of which winter in the trees on the museum grounds. Details: 1305 East Cliff Drive (across the river from the town center), Santa Cruz; (408) 429-3773; open Tuesday through Friday from 10 a.m. to 5 p.m. (1 a.m. to 5 p.m. on Saturday and Sunday). Admission is free. (1 hour)

Another museum of note is the **Surfing Museum**. You can imagine what's on display. It's in the lighthouse on Cliff Drive at Lighthouse Point. Down below is a favorite surfing break. Details: Cliff Drive at Lighthouse Point, Santa Cruz; (408) 429-3429; open Thursday through Monday from noon to 4 p.m. Admission is free. (½ hour)

For a real head shaker, check out the 3-D wax version of **DaVinci's Last Supper** at the Santa Cruz Memorial Park. Details: Ocean Street above CA 17, Santa Cruz; (408) 426-1601; open Monday through Saturday from 1 p.m. to 4 p.m. Admission is free. (15 minutes)

★★ **San Juan Bautista**—A few miles east of U.S. 101 on CA 156, this town of less than 2000 sits right on the San Andreas Fault. It was an unfortunate place to build the **Mission San Juan Bautista** in 1797, but they couldn't have guessed it at the time. The mission's outer walls came down in the 1906 quake, but the interior, dating to 1816, survived. Reconstruction restored the outer walls and opened up interior archways that had been blocked, returning the mission to its status as the largest in California. Details: (408) 623-4528; open daily from 9:30 a.m. to 4:30 p.m. A $1 donation is requested.

The mission sits in wonderful **Old Plaza**, surrounded by several historic, Spanish-colonial buildings—all part of the **San Juan Bautista State Historic Park**. The **Plaza Hotel**, built in 1858, once served as a major overnight stop on the stagecoach route. The nearby **Castro House** was built in 1840. These and other structures, including some replicas, combine successfully to create the feel of a bygone era. Details: Second and Mariposa Streets, San Juan Bautista; (408) 623-4881; open daily from 10 a.m. to 4:30 p.m. Admission is $2. (2 hours)

The modern town of **San Juan Bautista** is not particularly modern at all and is worth a look. There you'll find the **San Juan Bakery**, the oldest in the west.

⭐⭐ **Stanford University**—The campus of Stanford University is the largest in the world, thanks to the wealth and land holdings of its founder and prime benefactor, railroad baron Leland Stanford Jr. A campus tour is a pleasant choice for a morning. Take Palm Drive from the El Camino Real (CA 82) in Palo Alto. Details: Visitor Center is in the lobby of Memorial Hall; (415) 723-2560; open Monday through Friday, 8 a.m. to 5 p.m.; opens at 9 a.m. on weekends. Free tours daily at 11 a.m. and 3:15 p.m.

The heart of campus is the "Quad." The beautiful **Memorial Church** with its ornate, gilded facade and mosaic tiled mural presides over colonnaded stone walkways and red tile roofs. Nearby, the 285-foot **Hoover Tower** dominates the scene. A $2 elevator ride to the top affords great views of the campus and South Bay region.

A wonderful spot for peaceful contemplation is the **Rodin Sculpture Garden** outside of the earthquake-damaged and still closed **Museum of Art**, call (510) 723-3469 for updated information. Several rare castings are found in the garden, including the amazing *Gates of Hell*. The new **Papua New Guinea Sculpture Garden** in the Eucalyptus Grove at the corner of Santa Teresa and Lomita Drive features towering totems, one of which was carved on site during a special ceremony.

Other options include a visit to the **Hoover Institution on War, Revolution, and Peace**, a conservative think tank and site of research into international issues, and to the associated **Hoover Library**, repository of President Herbert Hoover's papers. The **Stanford Linear Accelerator**, a 2-mile long building that passes directly under Interstate 280, offers morning and afternoon tours. Details: 2575 Sand Hill Road, call (415) 926-2204 for dates and reservations. The tour is free. (1½ hours)

⭐ **Capitola**—This charming bayside town is just down the road from Santa Cruz. The narrow streets and Victorian summer homes blend perfectly with the small shops that cater to the vacationers and tourists. If the glitz of the boardwalk and energy of the students are too much in Santa Cruz, book a room in Capitola. An evening walk along the Esplanade is a pleasant way to end the day. Details: Take the Capitola exit from CA 1.

✯ **Filoli**—This historic mansion was the home of the exceedingly wealthy Mr. and Mrs. William B. Bourn II. Built from 1916–1919, the 654-acre estate features magnificent formal gardens, a 43-room mansion, and outbuildings. It was used as the mansion for the television program "Dynasty." You can reserve a spot on a two-hour morning or afternoon tour. Self-guiding tours are possible on weekends. Details: Take Cañada Road from Interstate 280 north of Woodside; (415) 364-2880; open Tuesday through Saturday during the months of February through November. Admission is $8. (2 hours)

✯ **Mission Santa Clara de Asis**—Located at the heart of the Santa Clara University campus, the present mission church was built in 1928 as a replica of the 1822 church. The plaza and gardens are original. Details: Take CA 82 from Interstate 880 to reach the campus in Santa Clara; (408) 554-4023; open Monday through Friday from 8 a.m. to 6 p.m. Admission is free. (1 hour)

✯ **Rosicrucian Egyptian Museum and Planetarium**—This unusual attraction features Egyptian and other ancient artifacts, as well as a replica of an Egyptian rock tomb. It is also the international headquarters of the Rosicrucian order, a group dedicated to philosophical inquiry and education. More people visit this interesting museum than any other attraction in San Jose. Details: 1342 Naglee Avenue, San Jose; (408) 947-3600; open daily from 9 a.m. to 5 p.m. Admission is $6. (2 hours)

✯ **San Jose City Center**—Downtown San Jose is on few tourist itineraries, but it has several points of interest. Though almost all of the oldest structures are gone, San Jose was established in 1777 as the "first civil settlement" in California. It served as the state capital from 1849–1851. The center of things is the **Plaza Park** on Market Street north of San Carlos Street (CA 82). Interstate 680, Interstate 880, Interstate 280, and U.S. 101 all get close to the city's center.

On St. John Street between Alameda Avenue and San Pedro Street, the **Peralta Adobe**, built in 1797, preserves the last vestiges of El Pueblo de San Jose de Guadalupe that covered much of what is now the city center. Across the street is the **Fallon House**, a fine home dating to 1854. Details: A visitor center for both sites is located at 175 West St. John Street, San Jose; (408) 993-8182; Fallon

House tours are Wednesday through Sunday from 11 a.m. to 4:30 p.m. Admission is $6. (1 hour)

The **Technology Museum of Innovation** has displays and interactive exhibits featuring, not surprisingly, innovations in technology! It's great for families with older kids. Details: 145 W. San Carlos Street, San Jose; (408) 279-7170; open Tuesday through Sunday from 10 a.m. to 5 p.m. Admission is $6.

Nearby, the **Children's Discovery Museum** makes technology friendly to the younger set. Details: 180 Woz Way, San Jose; (408) 279-7150; open Tuesday through Sunday from 10 a.m. to 5 p.m. (noon to 5 p.m. on Sunday). Admission is $6. (2 hours)

The work of contemporary artists is exhibited in the **San Jose Museum of Art**. Details: 110 South Market Street, at the north end of Plaza Park; San Jose; (408) 294-2787; open Tuesday through Sunday from 10 p.m. to 5 p.m. (until 8 p.m. on Thursdays). Admission is $6. (2 hours)

Just north of the museum is **St. Joseph's Cathedral**, built in 1875, replacing early versions that date back to 1803.

✯ **Scenic Railways**—The **Roaring Camp and Big Trees Railroad**, a narrow gauge line, takes an 1¼-hour roundtrip through the redwoods from Roaring Camp, near Felton. In the summer, there are four or five trips daily. Call for the schedule. (2 hours)

The **Santa Cruz**, **Big Trees, and Pacific Railway**, offers a 2½-hour roundtrip from the Felton Station, stopping at Roaring Camp and going right to the Boardwalk in Santa Cruz. Details: Take CA 17 to Mount Hermon Road, through Scott's Valley, to Felton. Turn left onto Graham Hill Road for Roaring Camp. (3 hours)

Call (408) 335-4400 for information on both trains. Trains depart from the old Southern Pacific Depot in Felton, but are scheduled out of Roaring Camp at 10:30 a.m. and 2:30 p.m. Trains run daily in the summer, weekends the rest of the year. Either trip is about $14.

✯ **Winchester Mystery House**—It's hard to know what to make of this spiritually guided obsession of Sarah Winchester, heir of the Winchester Rifle fortune. She was supposedly directed from beyond to continue adding rooms to her home. You'll shake your head at the tiny chambers, secret passages, and stairways to nowhere. Details: It's four miles west of town at 525 South Winchester Boulevard, San

Jose, just north of Interstate 280 (from Interstate 280 South, take the Winchester Boulevard exit; or from Interstate 880, take Stevens Creek Boulevard to Winchester Boulevard); (408) 247-2000; open daily with tours offered from 9 a.m. to 4 p.m. (later in the summer). Admission is $12.50. (1 hour)

Paramount's Great America—This is Northern California's Disneyland. Take the kids to the best amusement park in the bay and let them test their stomachs against the rides. Details: Take the Great America Parkway exit from either CA 101 or CA 237, Santa Clara; (408) 988-1800; summer hours are from 10 a.m. to 9 p.m., until 11 p.m. on Saturday (open weekends only in spring and fall and closed during winter). Admission is $28. (half day)

FITNESS AND RECREATION

The **Skyline to the Sea Trail** runs from the high ridges of Big Basin Redwoods State Park, down along West Waddell Creek to the Pacific. The hike can be done in a day, although you'll need two vehicles or good luck hitching to return to your car. Camping overnight and returning up the east fork makes a good loop.

Another long, gentle trail follows a fire road up into the hills of **The Forest of Nisene Marks State Park**. Land for the park was donated by the Marks family in 1963 and features second-growth redwoods. Take Aptos Creek Road to the north end of the town of Aptos. Rock climbers will enjoy the outcrops in **Castle Rock State Park**. Take CA 35 two-and-a-half miles south from the junction with CA 9 to reach the trailheads.

Santa Cruz is a center for outdoor enthusiasts. Surfing is popular at several spots around the upper Monterey Bay and Peninsula Coast. **Go Skate**, 601 Beach Street, is a good place to rent surf gear, as well as in-line skates and other equipment, (408) 425-8578. Mountain biking is popular in the hills above town, particularly in **Henry Cowell Redwoods State Park**.

FOOD

In Palo Alto, the area around University Avenue between Alma and Cowper is the place to browse. The **Gordon Biersch Brewery Restaurant** at 640 Emerson Street is a good place for easy eating

SOUTH BAY AND PENINSULA COAST

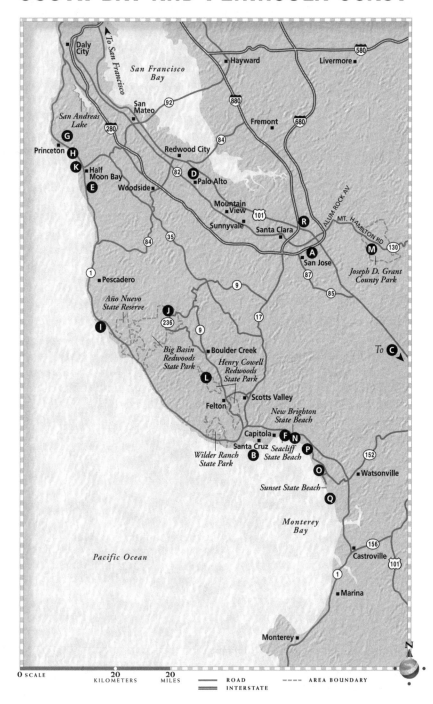

Food

- Ⓐ Bella Mia
- Ⓑ Café Bittersweet
- Ⓐ Casa Castillo
- Ⓐ Eulipia
- Ⓒ Faultline
- Ⓓ Gordon Biersch Brewery Restaurant
- Ⓓ L'Amie Donia
- Ⓐ Les Saisons
- Ⓑ Memphis Minnie's
- Ⓔ Pasta Moon
- Ⓓ Peninsula Creamery Fountain & Grill
- Ⓓ Pollo's
- Ⓑ Pontiac Grill
- Ⓕ Shadowbrook Restaurant
- Ⓖ The Shore Bird
- Ⓐ Tied House

Camping

- Ⓙ Big Basin Redwoods State Park
- Ⓚ Half Moon Bay State Beach
- Ⓛ Henry Cowell Redwoods State Park
- Ⓜ Joseph T. Grant County Park
- Ⓝ New Brighton State Beach
- Ⓔ Pelican Point RV Park
- Ⓞ Santa Cruz KOA
- Ⓟ Seacliff State Beach
- Ⓠ Sunset State Beach
- Ⓡ Trailer Tel

Lodging

- Ⓐ Best Western Inn
- Ⓓ Cardinal Hotel
- Ⓗ Cypress Inn on Miramar Beach
- Ⓑ Darling House
- Ⓐ Fairmont Hotel
- Ⓓ Garden Court Hotel
- Ⓖ Harbor View Inn
- Ⓓ Hidden Villa Hostel
- Ⓘ Pigeon Point Lighthouse Hostel
- Ⓒ Posada De San Juan
- Ⓒ San Juan Inn
- Ⓑ Santa Cruz Hostel
- Ⓑ Sea and Sand Inn

Note: Items with the same letter are located in the same town or area.

over a pint of ale, (415) 323-7723. Fine French fare can be had for a price at **L'Amie Donia**, 530 Bryant Street. A good wine list, nice patios, and an unusual zinc bar complement the great food, (415) 323-7614. Stop in at the **Peninsula Creamery Fountain & Grill** for a thoroughly American food fest at breakfast, lunch, or dinner, 566 Emerson Street, (415) 323-3131. **Pollo's** is the place for fast, cheap, and filling Mexican food, 543 Emerson Street, (415) 473-0212.

Downtown San Jose has many good places within four or five blocks of Plaza Park. The elegant **Les Saisons** in the Fairmont Hotel, 170 South Market Street, is a lovely place to go for continental cuisine if your suit isn't wrinkled and you have money to burn, (408) 998-3950. California cuisine with a good deal of international influence characterizes the understated fine dining at **Eulipia**, 374 South First Street, (408) 280-6161. For great Italian at more modest prices, head to **Bella Mia** at 58 South First Street, (408) 280-1993. For good Mexican food in a comfortable setting, **Casa Castillo** at 200 South First Street is a good choice, (408) 971-8132. Burgers and beer go hand-in-hand at the **Tied House**, a brewpub at 65 North San Pedro Street, (408) 295-2739.

In Santa Cruz, **Café Bittersweet** is a top choice for fine dining. The mixed menu leans a bit towards Mediterranean and the wine list is quite good, 2332 Mission Street, (408) 423-9999. **Memphis Minnie's** puts a Cajun twist to the sea's bounty, 1415 Santa Cruz Street, (408) 429-6464. Cheap eats can be had in many places, notably the **Pontiac Grill**, a diner that Elvis would have liked, 44 Front Street, (408) 427-2290.

Elsewhere, just north of Half Moon Bay in Princeton, enjoy outdoor dining on the water at **The Shore Bird**, a good steak and seafood place, 390 Capistrano Road, (415) 728-5541. **Pasta Moon** in Half Moon Bay offers fantastic Italian at mid-level prices. You'll find it in the Tin Palace at 315 Main Street, (415) 726-5125. In Capitola, don't miss the **Shadowbrook Restaurant**. To reach the lit and terraced restaurant from the parking lot, ride the funicular down past a waterfall. Get an outdoor table if the weather cooperates. The fresh seafood and other entrées are a match for the setting, 1750 Wharf Road, (408) 475-1511. The **Faultline** in San Juan Bautista has a valley view and fine continental cuisine for a price. It's near the mission at 11 Franklin Street, (408) 623-2117.

LODGING

Chain motels and hotels litter the stretch from San Mateo through San Jose. Use the numbers on the "Resources" page to locate many of them.

For plush in Palo Alto, the **Garden Court Hotel** fits the bill, and it's right in the center of things. Rooms start at $190, 520 Cowper Street, (415) 322-9000. Nearby, the **Cardinal Hotel** is an aging gem. Rooms with shared bath are as low as $55, with private bath, $65. South of campus in Los Altos Hills, the **Hidden Villa Hostel** has $9 beds, 26870 Moody Road, (415) 949-8648.

The **Fairmont Hotel** in downtown San Jose is the choice for modern luxury. Rooms start at $90 on the weekends, $155 week-days—a reflection of the fact that business guests are the main patrons, 170 South Market Street, (408) 998-1900. The **Best Western Inn**, at 455 South Second Street is an economical choice for downtown, with rooms from $50.

Four miles north of Half Moon Bay in El Granada, the **Harbor View Inn** is clean and reasonable with rooms for $65, 51 Avenue Alhambra, (415) 726-2329. Just south near Miramar, the **Cypress Inn on Miramar Beach** is on the water. Rooms range from $150 to $275, and all have a fireplace and ocean view, 407 Mirada Road, (415) 726-6002. The **Pigeon Point Lighthouse Hostel** is a great place to stay. There's an outdoor hot tub and the location is amazing. Beds are from $11 to $14, with private rooms going for $20 to $25. Reservations are essential in the summer. Special tickets and transportation to see the elephant seals are possible for hostel guests. It's at Pigeon Point, between Pescadero and Año Nuevo, (415) 879-0633.

Chain motels are common around Santa Cruz, especially along CA 1 (Mission Street). Other options are also available. On a cliff overlooking the bay, the **Sea and Sand Inn** has rooms from $80, $120 in the high season. The views are terrific, and a continental breakfast is served, 201 West Cliff Drive, (408) 427-3400. Walkers, bicyclists, and skaters enjoy the wide, paved, bayside path that runs along West Cliff Drive. A little farther out and a notch up the economic scale, the **Darling House** is a nice B&B with fabulous views. The Spanish-style house was built in 1910 as a summer home. The hot tub is a treat, and the breakfasts are wonderfully healthful, 314 West Cliff Drive, (408) 458-1958. The **Santa Cruz Hostel** is within two blocks of the ocean. Beds are from $12 to $14, 315 Main Street, (408) 423-8304.

In San Juan Bautista, the very nice **Posada De San Juan** has Spanish decor and rooms from $80, 310 Fourth Street, (408) 623-4030. Rooms at the **San Juan Inn** start at $50, 410 Alameda Road at CA 156, (408) 623-4380.

CAMPING

On CA 130, the road to Lick Observatory, **Joseph T. Grant County Park** has campsites. Just off U.S. 101, **Trailer Tel** has RV sites. Take the Oakland Road exit and go north, (408) 453-3535.

Half Moon Bay State Beach has OK sites for $12. Take Kelly Avenue from town; (415) 726-8820 for information, (800) 444-7275 for reservations. **Pelican Point RV Park** is at 1001 Miramontes Point Road, ¼ mile from the beach, (415) 726-9100.

There's good camping in **Big Basin Redwoods State Park**, including both walk-in and drive-in sites, as well as tent-cabins that are woodsy and peaceful. Sites are from $14 to $18. Take CA 9 to CA 236, (408) 338-6132 for information, (800) 444-7275 for reservations, and (800) 874-8368 for tent-cabin reservations. Just north of Santa Cruz on CA 9, **Henry Cowell Redwoods State Park** has nice sites from $14 to $18, (408) 438-2396 for information, (800) 444-7275 for reservations.

Along Monterey Bay, **New Brighton State Beach** east of Capitola, (408) 475-4850, and **Sunset State Beach** near Watsonville, (408) 724-1266, both have tent sites for $14. **Seacliff State Beach** has $25 sites for self-contained camper units only, (408) 688-3222. Call (800) 444-7275 for reservations for all three. The **Santa Cruz KOA** is 14 miles south of town. Take San Andreas Road west from CA 1, $32 and up, (408) 722-0551.

NIGHTLIFE

In Palo Alto, **The Edge** is the place for loud, young music, 260 California Avenue, (415) 324-3343. For a good game of pool, a beer, and Cajun food, visit the **Blue Chalk**, 630 Ramona Street, (415) 326-1020. The **Stanford Theatre** shows art films at 221 University Avenue, (415) 324-3700. A great place for coffee or beer is the **University Coffee Café** at 271 University Avenue, (415) 322-5301. Browse University Avenue for many other pleasant choices. **Stanford University** offers a fine performance schedule of music, dance, and theater. Call (415) 725-2787 for information.

San Jose's fine arts options are impressive. The primary performance venue is the **San Jose Center for the Performing Arts**, 255 Almaden Boulevard. Call (408) 453-7108 for information. For specific performance schedules, call **Opera San Jose** at (408) 283-4880, the **San Jose Symphony** at (408) 279-5949, or the **San Jose Cleveland**

Ballet at (408) 288-2800. For innovative, new theater productions, contact the **San Jose Repertory Theatre**, 1 North First Street, (408) 291-2255. More classic theater fare is produced by the **San Jose Stage Company**, 490 South First Street, (408) 283-7142. For musicals, call the **San Jose Civic Light Opera**, (408) 453-7108.

The area to browse in downtown San Jose is First Street around San Salvador Street and the general area east and north of Plaza Park. **Paddy's** is a good Irish pub with stout on tap at 31 East Santa Clara Street, (408) 293-1118. The cinema and coffeehouse scene is in the 200 and 300 blocks of South First, take your pick. A block further down, the **F/X** has live music at 400 South First, (408) 298-9796, as does the **Cactus Club** at 417 South First, (408) 280-0885. For a good pint of site-brewed beer, try the **Tied House**, 65 North San Pedro Street, (408) 295-2739.

In Santa Cruz, on Pacific Avenue and Front Street between Water and Laurel, you'll find many nightspots in this non-boardwalk heart of town, especially at the southern end of the zone. Browse the **Bookshop Santa Cruz** and enjoy an espresso within at **Georgiana's Café**, 1522 Pacific Avenue, (408) 427-9900. For house-brewed ales, stop at the **Front Street Pub**, 516 Front Street, (408) 429-8838. **Kuumbwa** features varied live music and dancing, 320–2 Cedar Street, (408) 427-2227. The **Catalyst** is a hopping, live music venue featuring occasional famous or soon-to-be famous bands, 1011 Pacific Avenue, (408) 423-1336.

5

MONTEREY PENINSULA

The Monterey Peninsula is a remarkable, squarish thumb of land that juts into the ocean at the southern end of Monterey Bay. The beautiful natural setting and concentration of attractions make it a very popular tourist destination.

The Spanish established a mission and presidio at Monterey in 1770 (though the mission was moved to Carmel a year later). The city became the capital of California in 1775, and a provincial capital for independent Mexico in 1821. After the gold rush, the city began to draw vacationers—a role interrupted by a 20-year stint as the "sardine capital of the world." Today, the face of Monterey reflects its colonial roots, its touristy present, and its Steinbeck-immortalized fishiness.

The Pebble Beach Land Company controls the southern two-thirds of the peninsula. Well-heeled residents can Lexus to any one of seven golf courses in about a dozen square miles. The estates and distractions of the well-to-do can be enjoyed via Seventeen-Mile Drive, a toll road through the property.

To the south, the town of Carmel-by-the-Sea is almost too nice a place to live. Long after the fading of the missions, Carmel was reborn as a resort town. It evolved, as so many places do, from artist's enclave to moneyed retreat. Despite a heavy burden of tourists, it is still a thoroughly charming place to live and visit.

Fortunately for those living in the easy, comfortable, and lovely town of Pacific Grove, few people bother to include it on a travel itinerary. I'm sure the residents don't mind at all.

A PERFECT DAY AROUND MONTEREY

You can do the whole peninsula in a day. Start in Monterey with an early morning walk on the historic plaza and Fisherman's Wharf. Arrive early at the Monterey Bay Aquarium (with your pre-purchased ticket) for a three-hour visit. Drive along Ocean View Boulevard and Sunset Drive around Pacific Grove, stopping to see the monarchs if in season. Get on Seventeen-Mile Drive at the Pacific Grove Gate to see the golf courses, mansions, and Lone Cypress tree. You end up in Carmel in time for dinner and strolling on Ocean Avenue. Enjoy sunset from Carmel Beach.

SIGHTSEEING HIGHLIGHTS

✯✯✯ **Monterey Bay Aquarium**—The Monterey Bay Aquarium is not a performance-oriented amusement attraction, but a premier marine life exhibit. It is devoted exclusively to the rich flora and fauna of Monterey Bay, presenting it with a devotion to ecological accuracy. This world-class attraction gives Cannery Row a shot of true class.

The aquarium features the Outer Bay—a new, million-gallon "indoor ocean" that is viewed through the largest window in the world. The kelp forest features a three-story view through 7-inch thick acrylic. Telescopes enable viewing of sea otters lounging offshore, while microscopes permit an up-close look at plankton swimming in a dish. Kids can pet bat rays or touch starfish in a tide pool exhibit.

With over 2 million visitors a year, waits can be long to get tickets at the door. Consider buying in advance from the aquarium, from a BASS ticket outlet, or from any of the many local hotels and motels that sell tickets. Details: 886 Cannery Row, Monterey; (800) 756-3737; open daily from 10 a.m. to 6 p.m. (opens at 9 a.m., June 15 through Labor Day). Admission is $11.75. (2½ hours)

✯✯ **Carmel-by-the-Sea**— . . . or just "Carmel" if you're not feeling poetic. This wonderful town has a long history. The **Mission San Carlos Borromeo Del Rio Carmelo** was built above the Carmel River in 1771 to replace the one established on a poor site in Monterey a year earlier. If you visit one mission on your trip, this should probably be it. Thanks to careful restoration begun in 1934, its size, layout, and buildings are close to the original. Junipero Serra, the main figure of the mission period, died here and is buried in the mission church.

MONTEREY PENINSULA

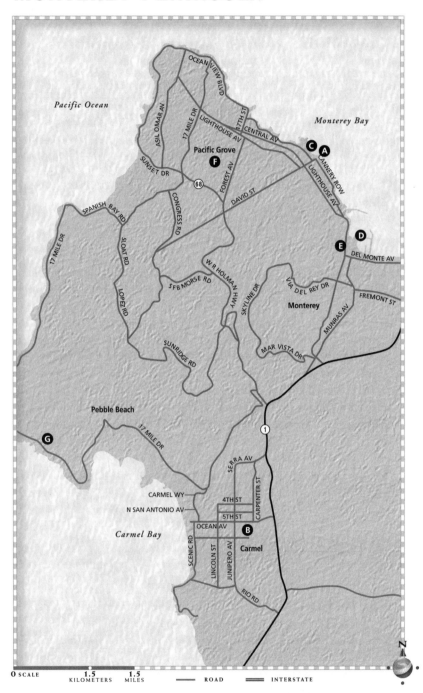

Pacific Ocean

Monterey Bay

OCEAN VIEW BLVD

ASIL OMAR AV

17 MILE DR

LIGHTHOUSE AV

17TH ST

CENTRAL AV

C **A**

CANNERY ROW

Pacific Grove

F

FOREST AV

LIGHTHOUSE AV

SUNSET DR

68

DAVID ST

SPANISH BAY RD

CONGRESS RD

D

E

DEL MONTE AV

17 MILE DR

SLOAT RD

W R HOLMAN HWY

SKYLINE DR

VIA DEL REY DR

FREMONT ST

S F B MORSE RD

LOPEZ RD

Monterey

MUNRAS AV

SUNRIDGE RD

MAR VISTA DR

Pebble Beach

G

17 MILE DR

1

SERRA AV

CARMEL WY

4TH ST

CARPENTER ST

N SAN ANTONIO AV

5TH ST

OCEAN AV

B

Carmel Bay

SCENIC RD

LINCOLN ST

JUNIPERO AV

Carmel

RIO RD

N

0 SCALE   1.5   1.5   ROAD   INTERSTATE
KILOMETERS   MILES

Sightseeing Highlights

🅐 Cannery Row

🅑 Carmel-by-the-Sea

🅒 Monterey Bay Aquarium

🅓 Monterey Fisherman's Wharf

🅔 Monterey State Historic Park

🅕 Pacific Grove

🅖 Seventeen-Mile Drive

Carmel can be thought of as a living laboratory of community spirit. All residents must visit the post office because there is no mail delivery. There are no billboards, neon signs, mortuaries, or jails, and sidewalks are only found on a couple of main streets. Trees have the right to grow unimpeded unless the city council approves their demise.

Ocean Avenue is Carmel's main street. Slightly bored residents browse the upscale shops and galleries, while visitors enjoy the ambiance of wealth and artistry. The **Carmel Art Association**, on Dolores between Fifth and Sixth, is perhaps the best known gallery in town. Owned and operated by artists, the gallery features works from local painters and sculptors. You can enjoy a stroll along Carmel Bay on the easy coast walk that runs along **Carmel Beach City Park**.

Just below Carmel Point, a mile south of the town center, Robinson Jeffers' **Tor House** sits in a residential neighborhood overlooking the bay. Jeffers ranks among the best American poets and is famous for works that evoke the spirit and mystery of the Big Sur and Monterey coasts. Tor House is a granite cottage named for the rugged knoll on which it is built. **Hawk Tower**, also on the grounds, was built by Jeffers, himself, as a retreat. You can take a look as you drive by above or below the property, or reserve one of the few tour slots available. Details: 26304 Ocean View Avenue, Carmel; call (408) 624-1813, or (408) 624-1840 on Friday and Saturday; six-person tours are scheduled hourly on Friday and Saturday from 10 a.m. to 4 p.m. The fee is $5.

☆☆ **Monterey State Historic Park**—The park preserves several homes and buildings from old Monterey. The main area is **Custom House Plaza**, next to Fisherman's Wharf. The **Custom House** has flown the flags of Spain (1814–1822), Mexico (1822–1846), and the U.S., and is the oldest government building on the Pacific Coast. Now a museum, it features historic trade goods. Also on the plaza, the 1847 **Pacific House** has served as a tavern, courthouse, newspaper office, church, and Army recreation hall. Monterey heritage items and Native American artifacts are on display. Details: Custom House Plaza, Monterey; both buildings open Wednesday through Sunday from 10 a.m. to 5 p.m. during the summer (10 a.m. to 4 p.m. the rest of the year). Admission is free. (2 hours)

The **Stevenson House**, where Robert Louis Stevenson is said to have written *Treasure Island*, features an outstanding Stevenson memorabilia collection. Details: 530 Houston St., Monterey; Tours begin hourly from 10 a.m. to 1 p.m. and at 3 p.m. and 4 p.m. (summer only) on Thursday through Tuesday. (½ hour)

Not actually a part of the park, but on the plaza is the **Maritime Museum of Monterey**, featuring a fine maritime collection, including a display of ship models. Details: 20 Custom House Plaza; (408) 649-7118; open Tuesday through Sunday from 10 a.m. to 5 p.m. (open Mondays on national holidays). Admission is $5. (45 minutes)

Information schedules for these and other park sites are available at the headquarters just off the plaza on Oliver Street. Pamphlets and books for the **Path of History**, a self-guided walking tour, are available here and elsewhere. The route is about 2 miles long and can take the better part of a morning if you do a few house tours. Various staff-guided walks tour the path, individual houses, or historic gardens.

☆☆ **Seventeen-Mile Drive**—Pebble Beach, essentially a huge gated community, will gladly take $6.50 per car at any one of four gates to allow you to drive through the area on this scenic toll road. The two main attractions are the fruits of wealth and the fruits of even more wealth. Stunning mansions litter Pebble Beach, particularly along the cliffs. You'll be hard pressed not to feel like one of the Beverly Hillbillies if you don't have a fat wallet yourself.

The drive passes through or near all seven of the golf courses, including private Cypress Point and barely public Pebble Beach, both of which run right to the water's edge. Stop for a look at the world-famous **Lone Cypress**, the best-loved example of the Monterey cypress trees that thrive on the peninsula as nowhere else. If your vision of scenic perfection blends magnificent homes and perfect fairways with nature's surf-chiseled bluffs and gnarled trees, then this is your road.

Details: The four gates are found two blocks north of Ocean Street in Carmel on North San Antonio Avenue; on CA 1 one mile north of Carmel; along CA 68 (Holman Highway) at the west end of the Monterey Presidio; and in Pacific Grove off CA 68 a quarter mile east of Asilomar. Admission is $6.50 per car. (2 hours)

✮ **Monterey Fisherman's Wharf**—Adjacent to the plaza and Historic Park, the Monterey Fisherman's Wharf thrusts its shop-lined expanse into the sea. Tackier even than Cannery Row, its advantage is its location, surrounded by the waters of the bay with the current, active fishing wharf in plain sight (Municipal Wharf). Fishing, whale watching, and glass-bottom boat excursions depart here as well. Details: Park near Del Monte and Pacifc Streets and walk to Customs House Plaza and the waterfront.

✮ **Pacific Grove**—This thoroughly underrated town is a great place to stay and relax on your Monterey Bay trip. The town occupies the northern point of the peninsula, and almost all the coastline around the town is preserved as park land. Sunset Drive and Ocean View Drive combine to provide a lovely shoreline route.

The lands and facilities of the **Asilomar Conference Center** are operated as a unit of the California State Park System. The center is reserved by groups for retreats and conferences, but rooms are available to overnight guests on the many nights the center is not fully booked. **Asilomar State Beach** is between the Asilomar Center and the ocean.

Point Piños Lighthouse is nestled among the fairways of the **Pacific Grove Municipal Golf Course**—a great choice for those who want to golf on the peninsula without taking out a second mortgage. Details: At the west end of Lighthouse Avenue; Pacific Grove; (408) 648-3116; the lighthouse is open Thursday through Sunday (and holidays) from 1 p.m. to 4 p.m. Admission is free. The **Lighthouse Reserve, Hays Perkins Park, Lovers Point Park**, and **Shoreline Park** wrap Point Piños and the north shore. The **Pacific Grove**

Marine Gardens Fish Preserve takes the protection out from the shore. (1 hour)

Cannery Row—This hokey tourist row milks John Steinbeck for all he's worth. If not for the Monterey Bay Aquarium and a few diving, snorkeling, and bay exploration opportunities, Cannery Row would be a must-miss for all but the worst souvenir and wax museum addicts. Having read that, you have to go and see it, don't you? I did. And, yes, I'd go back. There's something strangely enjoyable about browsing tacky shops in renovated cannery buildings and licking a frozen yogurt by the bust of an exploited author—and there are some nicer galleries and shops along the way. Details: Located along the waterfront north of the Presidio and Shoreline Park, downtown Monterey. (½ hour)

FITNESS AND RECREATION

The **Monterey Bay Recreation Trail** runs from Lovers Point Park and Beach in Pacific Grove, along the waterfront through Monterey, and beyond into Seaside and Fort Ord. This is a good path for cycling, jogging, or strolling. From a Pacific Grove B&B, a 4-mile roundtrip walk will take you to the aquarium, Cannery Row, the State Historic Park, and Fisherman's Wharf. Add another 1½ miles, and you can do the "Path of History" in Monterey.

For a good workout, visit the extensive **Monterey Sports Center** at 301 Franklin Street in downtown Monterey. They have a gym, two pools, various fitness and weight rooms, and child care services. Hours are Monday through Friday from 6 a.m. to 9:30 p.m., Saturday from 9 a.m. to 5 p.m., and Sunday from noon to 5 p.m., (408) 646-3700, $5.50 per day.

Adventures by the Sea rents bikes, kayaks, and in-line skates. Kayak tours of the bay with all-day rental are $45. There are three locations: 299 Cannery Row, 201 Alvarado Mall (at the Maritime Museum), and at Lovers Point Beach in Pacific Grove. Call (408) 372-1807 for reservations and information.

Diving equipment rental, tours, and classes are offered by the **Monterey Bay Dive Center**, 225 Cannery Row, (408) 656-0454, or 598 Foam Street, Monterey, (408) 655-1818. For deep sea fishing, try **Randy's Fishing Trips**, 66 Old Fisherman's Wharf, (408) 372-7440. Six-hour whale watching trips by **Monterey Bay Whale Watch** are guided by marine biologists. Trips leave from Sam's Fishing on Fisherman's Wharf, $40 to $45, (408) 375-4658.

FOOD

Lighthouse Avenue is the main drag in Pacific Grove. **Pasta Mia** is well loved for its Italian-just-like-mama-did-it fare. Prices are reasonable, 481 Lighthouse Avenue, (408) 375-7709. Elsewhere, **Gernot's Victoria House** is a splendid place to wine and dine. The setting is a huge mansion on the water at Lover's Point. The cuisine is European, and the prices are not far from Earth, 649 Lighthouse Avenue, (408) 646-1477. **The Fishwife** at 1996½ Sunset Drive is a great place for reasonably priced seafood, some of it with a Cajun twist, (408) 375-7107. Just off Cannery Row, try the **Sardine Factory** for good seafood at slightly inflated prices, 701 Wave Street, (408) 373-3775.

Fisherman's Wharf, Cannery Row, and downtown Monterey offer loads of restaurants. The top place is certainly **Fresh Cream**, in the Heritage Harbor complex, just across from Fisherman's Wharf. Enjoy thoroughly French cuisine at its best as you take in the beautiful harbor view. Entrées start at over $25, (408) 375-9798. At the other end, **Supremo** has hearty, reasonable Mexican fare at 500 Hartnell Street, (408) 373-3737. Fisherman's Wharf boasts **Café Fina**, where the pizza is good and the site-made pasta is even better, (408) 372-5200.

In Carmel, Ocean Avenue and the surrounding side streets feature dozens of eateries. **Caffé Napoli** on Ocean above Monte Verde has good Italian dishes at reasonable prices, (408) 625-4033. At Fifth Avenue and Junipero Street, you can sit next to a fire on the patio at the **General Store and Forge in the Forest**. The food is basic and tasty, (408) 624-2233. For an upscale treat, try the **Crème Carmel Restaurant**. The California cuisine is decidedly French at the roots, on San Carlos Street, between Ocean and Seventh Avenue, (408) 624-0444.

LODGING

The motel chains have dozens of outlets on the outskirts of Monterey and up the road in Seaside and Sand City, as well as clustered about the tourist centers. Use the numbers listed on the "Resources" page to contact the one of your choice.

In Pacific Grove, consider a night at the **Asilomar Conference**

Center. Depending on availability, you can choose a smaller, rustic room in a building designed by architect Julia Morgan for $71, or a newer, larger room in a "deluxe" building for $81. Another $7 gets you a fireplace. There are a large heated pool, social hall, general store, cafeteria-style dining hall, lovely grounds, and a private trail to Asilomar State Beach. A full breakfast is included, 800 Asilomar Boulevard, (408) 372-8016. The beautiful, Victorian **Green Gables Inn**, built in 1888, is a classic and elegant B&B. Somehow, English antiques, a teddy bear, and splendid views of the bay seem a great combination here. With wine and hors d'oeuvres, rooms range from $100 to $160, 104 Fifth Street, Pacific Grove, (408) 375-2095 or (800) 375-2095. Nearby, **The Martine Inn** is perhaps even more elegant than the Green Gables, though more spacious and less delicate. Perched right above Ocean View Boulevard, the views are unbeatable, 255 Ocean View Boulevard, (408) 373-3388. A stay at the **Butterfly Grove Inn** in the winter gives you a chance to view one of the few gathering spots for Monarch butterflies, right on the property! Rooms run from about $45 to $65, 1073 Lighthouse Avenue, (408) 373-4921.

Right on Cannery Row in Monterey, the **Spindrift Inn** is a luxurious choice. Prices vary widely, with rooms starting at $100 in the winter and $180 on summer weekends, 652 Cannery Row, (408) 646-8900 or (800) 841-1879. The **Old Monterey Inn** is a classy B&B set amid the oaks and above the bustle of town. Rooms run from $170 to $240 and are worth it, 500 Martin Street, (408) 375-8284 or (800) 350-2344. A budget choice is the **Del Monte Beach Inn**, 1110 Del Monte Avenue. Shared-bath rooms can be as low as $45, and it's close to the action, (408) 649-4410. The venerable **Monterey Hotel** in downtown has rooms ranging from $90 to $160. Breakfast and afternoon refreshments are included, 406 Alvarado Street, (408) 375-3184 or (800) 727-0960 for reservations.

In Carmel, the historic **Pine Inn** is a landmark structure in the heart of town. Rooms start at $85, rising to $220 for a king suite. It's on Ocean Avenue at Monte Verde, (408) 624-3851 or (800) 228-3851. Close to the center, the **Adobe Inn** has a pool, sauna, and full-featured rooms with wood-burning fireplaces. Rooms range from $95 to $200, Dolores Street and Eighth Avenue, (408) 624-3933. The **Best Western Town House Lodge** is also close to town center. It has good, basic rooms from $65 to $100, Fifth Avenue and San Carlos Street, (408) 624-3933. At the corner of Mission Street and

MONTEREY PENINSULA

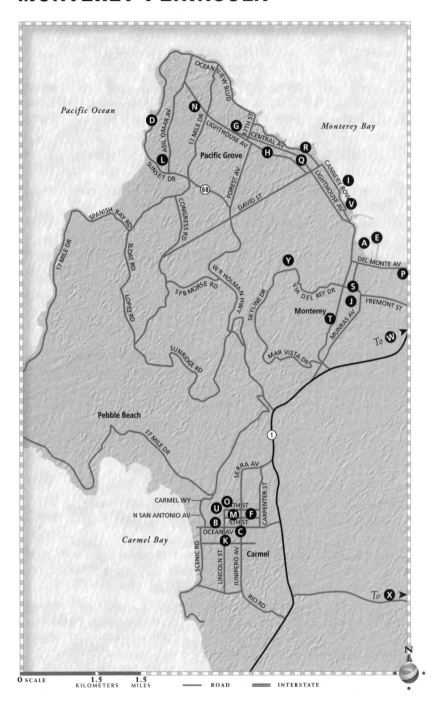

Food

Ⓐ Café Fina

Ⓑ Caffé Napoli

Ⓒ Crème Carmel Restaurant

Ⓓ The Fishwife

Ⓔ Fresh Cream

Ⓕ General Store and Forge in the Forest

Ⓖ Gernot's Victoria House

Ⓗ Pasta Mia

Ⓘ Sardine Factory

Ⓙ Supremo

Lodging

Ⓚ Adobe Inn

Ⓛ Asilomar Conference Center

Ⓜ Best Western Town House Lodge

Ⓝ Butterfly Grove Inn

Ⓞ Carmel Wayfarer Inn

Ⓟ Del Monte Beach Inn

Ⓠ Green Gables Inn

Ⓡ The Martine Inn

Ⓢ Monterey Hotel

Ⓣ Old Monterey Inn

Ⓤ Pine Inn

Ⓥ Spindrift Inn

Camping

Ⓦ Laguna Seca Recreation Area

Ⓧ Saddle Mountain Recreation Park

Ⓨ Veterans Memorial Park

Fourth Avenue, the **Carmel Wayfarer Inn** has rooms from $80 to
$100. Carmel is not a cheap place to stay.

CAMPING

Tent and RV sites are available at **Laguna Seca Recreation Area**, 9
miles east of Monterey on CA 218, (408) 758-3185. Right above
Monterey, **Veterans Memorial Park** has 40 sites with no hookups.
Take Jefferson Street west from Pacific Street, (408) 646-3865.
Saddle Mountain Recreation Park, a private facility, has tent and
RV sites, a game room, and hiking trails. Take Carmel Valley Road
east from CA 1 for 5 miles. Turn right on Schulte Road and continue
on to 27625 Schulte, (408) 624-1617.

NIGHTLIFE

The **Monterey Jazz Festival** brings together world-renowned musicians for a long weekend of splendid entertainment. If you'll be in
the area in late September, try to fit it in. Events take place on several stages at the Monterey Fairgrounds. Call (800) 307-3378 for
information. At other times, Cannery Row stays alive into the night.
Try **Doc Rickett's Lab** at 95 Prescott Avenue for live music on
weekends, (408) 649-4241. At the corner of Prescott and Wave
Street, **O'Kanes Irish Pub** is just that, (408) 375-7564. On the top
floor at 625 Cannery Row is **Planet Gemini**, which offers live music
on weekdays and comedy on the weekends, (408) 373-1449.

6
BIG SUR

The coastline from Carmel south to San Simeon is an American treasure. Big Sur (meaning "big south") was named by early Monterey settlers in reference to the large rugged land down the coast—and rugged it is. From the 5000-foot heights of the Santa Lucia mountains, the land drops steeply to the angry Pacific far below. Waves beat at the huge headlands, slowly eating away at the mountain's feet. Isolated sea stacks litter the shallows. Calmer coves, often invisible from the road above, host sea lions, their barking calls echoing weirdly among the cliffs. Always, the roar of the gray-green Pacific fills the air.

In the lonely southern reaches, no human habitation interrupts the national forest lands that run to the sea. Further north, there are gentler stretches, private lands, state parks, and a few tiny towns and resorts. Throughout, the age-long battle of patient mountain versus eager ocean dominates all.

The Coast Highway provides the only access to this long, remote stretch. Completed in the 1930s and little changed since then, the road is a marvel of engineering. Graceful arched bridges cross steep canyons, while across the faces of the headlands, the road climbs and winds, a tenacious snake clinging to survival. Plan on the better part of a day to cover the 80 miles from Carmel to San Simeon. The average speed on the road is around 35 mph—less on summer weekends when you're nine cars behind a trundling RV. This is no place to be in a hurry. Take your time and stop often. Big Sur, after all, is some of the best the planet has to offer. ◼

BIG SUR

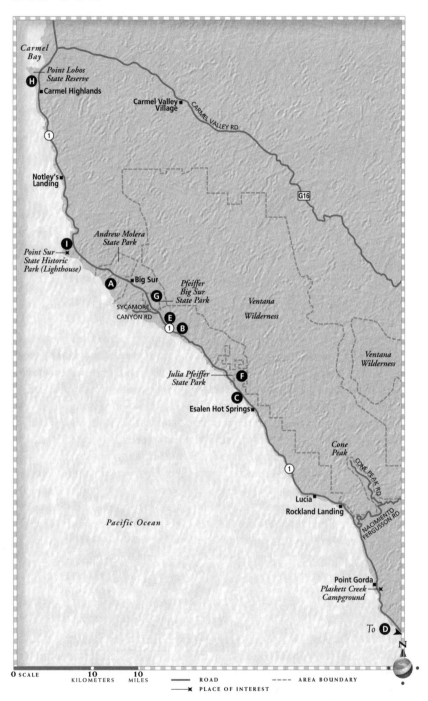

Carmel
Bay

*Point Lobos
State Reserve*
H
■ Carmel Highlands

Carmel Valley
Village ■

CARMEL VALLEY RD

①

Notley's
Landing ■

G16

*Andrew Molera
State Park*

I

Point Sur
State Historic
Park (Lighthouse)

A
■ Big Sur

Pfeiffer
Big Sur
State Park

G

SYCAMORE
CANYON RD

E
① **B**

Ventana

Wilderness

Ventana
Wilderness

Julia Pfeiffer
State Park

F

C

Esalen Hot Springs ■

Cone
Peak

CONE PEAK RD

①

Pacific Ocean

Lucia ■
Rockland Landing ■

NACIMIENTO
FERGUSSON RD

Point Gorda ■
Plaskett Creek
Campground

To **D**

N

0 SCALE	10	10	
	KILOMETERS	MILES	——— ROAD

- - - AREA BOUNDARY

✕ PLACE OF INTEREST

Sightseeing Highlights

Ⓐ Andrew Molera State Park

Ⓑ Coast Gallery

Ⓒ Esalen Institute

Ⓓ Hearst Castle

Ⓔ Henry Miller Memorial Library

Ⓕ Julia Pfieffer Burns State Park

Ⓖ Pfieffer Big Sur State Park

Ⓗ Point Lobos State Reserve

Ⓘ Point Sur State Historic Park and Light Station

A PERFECT DAY ON THE BIG SUR COAST

Enjoy the contrast between human opulence and natural spectacle. In the morning, tour the fabulous Hearst Castle and peer into the wealth and life of publishing magnate William Randolph Hearst. Drive north along the Big Sur Coast, stopping anywhere and everywhere. The Lucia Lodge is a good spot for lunch on the deck. Consider a tour up the Nacimiento Road and a hike to Cone Peak. Stop in at the Henry Miller Library or Coast Gallery to rest your eyes from the big vistas outside. An easy hike at Andrew Molera gives you sunset on the beach with just enough time to find campsite or car before nightfall.

SIGHTSEEING HIGHLIGHTS

✪✪✪ **Hearst Castle**—With 165 rooms and 127 acres of gardens, pools, and patios, William Randolph Hearst's *La Cuesta Encantada*, the Enchanted Hill, is a glorious example of self-indulgence. Julia Morgan designed much of the castle, responding with plans to suit Hearst's ongoing purchases of art and architectural artifacts. The result is a glorious but almost bizarre blend of classic European

styles. When Hearst died in 1951, it still wasn't finished—even after
30 years of construction. Since no one could afford to move in, the
State of California took over the complex and added it to the State
Park system.

You can choose from four different tours, each of which takes
approximately one hour and 45 minutes. Tour #1 is a good choice for
your first visit. All tours leave by shuttle bus from the visitor center
above CA 1. Details: The castle is in the hills overlooking San Simeon,
8 miles north of Cambria; call Destinet at (800) 444-4445, reservations
are advised; the visitor center and ticket office are open from 8 a.m. to
4 p.m. Admission is $14. (2 hours)

✪✪✪ **Point Lobos State Reserve**—At the south end of Carmel Bay,
Point Lobos is a rugged promontory with numerous coves and headlands along a heavily eroded shoreline. The waters surrounding the
point are also protected in a special underwater reserve. Wonderful
short hikes lead to several great spots, including **Devil's Cauldron**, a
churning pool with a high tide blowhole. **Sea Lion Point** hosts
California and Stellar sea lions. Diving and snorkeling are possible, but
camping is not permitted. Details: (408) 624-4909; open from 9 a.m. to
4 p.m. Admission is $7 for day use. (1 hour)

✪✪ **Julia Pfeiffer Burns State Park**—This park encompasses a good
stretch of spectacular coastline, though much of the 3,580 acres is
above the road. At the north edge of the park, a dirt road descends to
Partington Cove where the remains of a wooden bridge built in 1870
recall the cove's one time use as a boat landing for bootleggers. At
McWay Canyon, a trail leads from the parking area, under the highway, and down to the observation point for **McWay Falls**. This gorgeous waterfall drops 80 feet straight to the beach. Two very special
walk-in campsites on the headlands are available to reservation hold-
ers. Details: 15 miles south of the town of Big Sur on CA 1; call (408)
667-2315 for information.

✪✪ **Point Sur State Historic Park and Light Station**—You can't
miss Point Sur, a volcanic hill attached to the coast with a gracefully
curving sand bar. The lighthouse, built in 1899, sits 361 feet above the
surf on the outer crest of the rock. Access is possible only at limited
times—the land between the highway and lighthouse is private.
Details: Call (408) 625-4419 for information and tour reservations.

Wednesdays and weekends are the reported times for access, but they are not posted and there is no visitor facility. The tour is free. (1½ hours)

☆ **Andrew Molera State Park**—The Big Sur River meets the ocean after passing through the gentle valley and low hills of this pleasant, lightly used, 4,800-acre park. Several easy hiking and riding trails thread through the park, and beach combing is easy south of the river mouth. The park features a nice walk-in campground with good, open sites. Details: 2 miles north of the town of Big Sur; (408) 627-2315. The **Molera Educational Sanctuary and Ornithology Center** is open during business hours. Admission is $5 for day use.

☆ **Henry Miller Memorial Library**—South of Pfeiffer Big Sur near the unincorporated "town" of Nepenthe, Henry Miller's writings and paintings are preserved at this small library. Miller was one of several artists who lived a rough-edged, bohemian existence for a time on the Big Sur Coast. Details: Located 3 miles south of Pfeiffer Big Sur State Park on CA 1; (408) 667-2574; summer hours are daily from 11 a.m. to 5 p.m. (open weekends only in winter). Admission is $1. (½ hour)

☆ **Pfeiffer Big Sur State Park**—CA 1 loops inland, following the Big Sur River upstream through a forested valley, past the few businesses of the town of Big Sur, and into Pfeiffer Big Sur State Park. The 800-acre park is quite popular, featuring trails through stands of redwood, conifers, and oaks. A large campground and lodge accommodate visitors. There is access by trail to the **Ventana Wilderness** in Los Padres National Forest. Details: Located 3 miles south of the town of Big Sur; (408) 667-2315. Day use parking is $6.

You can reach **Pfeiffer Beach** by turning down Sycamore Canyon Road at the southern edge of the park, just north of the Big Sur Ranger Station. The narrow, 2-mile road winds down to day use parking and beach access.

Coast Gallery—Just south of Nepenthe, the lovely Coast Gallery appears at a bend in the road. Artworks for sale include many by local artists. The café upstairs sells light snacks and beverages. The building and grounds themselves are interesting. It's a great place to take a break from driving. Details: Located 3 miles south of Pfeiffer Big Sur State Park on CA 1; (408) 667-2574; open daily, 9 a.m. to 5 p.m. (½ hour)

Esalen Institute—At the mouth of Hot Springs Creek, 3 miles south of McWay Canyon, the Esalen Institute serves as a retreat for people seeking relaxation and enlightenment. All visits are by reservation only, and most involve participation in group seminars and activities. Accommodations and hot tub soaking are open to individuals on a space-available basis. Details: 4 miles south of Julia Pfeiffer Burns State Park; call (408) 667-3047 for information and reservations.

FITNESS AND RECREATION

Coastal trails in the state parks and Los Padres National Forest provide numerous options for hiking, biking, and riding, though paths can be steep. **Andrew Molera State Park** is the best for easy loops of 2 to 5 miles. **Molera Horseback Tours** operates from a building at the park headquarters. Their offerings include one to two-and-a-half-hour trips, (408) 625-5486 or (800) 942-5486. Fees range from $25 to $55.

The **Ventana Wilderness** has a good network of trails. The terrain is steep and dry, and most loop possibilities are better done as an overnight. Consult the rangers and maps at the ranger station just south of Pfeiffer Big Sur State Park.

Paul Otteson

FOOD

For a drink and a hearty, budget bite with the locals, try the **Village Pub** in the Village Shops at the River Inn near the town of Big Sur, (408) 667-2355. Also in the Big Sur town area, the **Ripplewood Café** offers good, basic breakfast and lunch fare, (408) 667-2242.

A long drive leads down to the splendid **Nepenthe**, a bar and restaurant by the sea. The dining is fine, but so too is gazing over the waves from the terrace. The restaurant is "in" Nepenthe, 3 miles south of Pfeiffer Big Sur State Park, (408) 667-2345.

The **Lucia Lodge** in Lucia is a marvelous place for a meal. It offers the only outdoor dining over the water anywhere on the Big Sur coast. Morning coffee as the fog begins to break is magical, (408) 667-2391.

Above San Simeon in the tiny town of Gorda, the **Whalewatcher Café** offers California cuisine by the sea and wonderful homemade desserts, (805) 927-3918.

LODGING

In Pfeiffer Big Sur State Park, the **Big Sur Lodge** has basic rooms, the Trail Head Café, and a heated pool. Rates are from $80 for a basic room in the winter to $180 for a fireplace and kitchen unit in the summer, (408) 667-3100 or (800) 424-4787.

For money-is-no-object, romantic, private, luxury lounging with a loved one, the **Ventana Big Sur Country Inn Resort** is the place for you. Rooms start at $200 and climb to a cool $1000. It's above the road near Nepenthe, (408) 667-2331 or (800) 628-6500.

Deetjen's Big Sur Inn was started by Norwegian Helmuth Deetjen. Over the years he created a marvelous, rustic inn with single-wall construction, hand-hewn doors, and wood-burning stoves. There are no phones or TVs—perfect. It's just north of the Coast Gallery near Nepenthe. Rooms range from $70 to $150, (408) 667-2377.

You can stay at the **Esalen Institute** when beds aren't needed for seminar participants. Beds are sold as "room and board," featuring three full meals and use of grounds, baths, and massage services. A bunk is $85 per person, a double room is $125 each person. Reserve by calling (408) 667-3000.

The **Lucia Lodge** in Lucia is an oasis on the lonely southern stretches of CA 1. Rooms and cabins range from $95 to $165. Dinner or breakfast on the restaurant deck is sheer pleasure, (408) 667-2391.

BIG SUR

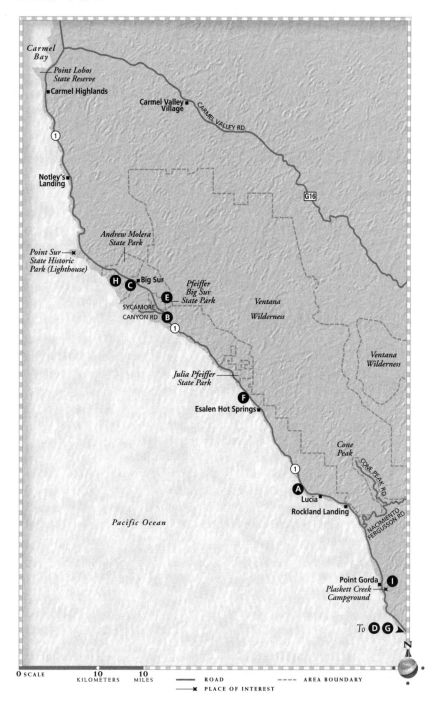

Carmel Bay

Point Lobos State Reserve

Carmel Highlands

Carmel Valley Village

CARMEL VALLEY RD.

G16

Notley's Landing

Andrew Molera State Park

Point Sur State Historic Park (Lighthouse)

H **C** ■ Big Sur

Pfeiffer Big Sur State Park

E

SYCAMORE CANYON RD. **B**

Ventana Wilderness

Ventana Wilderness

Julia Pfeiffer State Park

F

Esalen Hot Springs

Cone Peak

CONE PEAK RD.

A

Lucia

Rockland Landing

NACIMIENTO FERGUSSON RD.

Pacific Ocean

Point Gorda **I**

Plaskett Creek Campground

To **D** **G**

N

0 SCALE

10 KILOMETERS

10 MILES

—— ROAD

- - - - AREA BOUNDARY

✳ PLACE OF INTEREST

Food

(A) Lucia Lodge

(B) Nepenthe

(C) Ripplewood Café

(C) Village Pub

(D) Whalewatcher Café

Lodging

(E) Big Sur Lodge

(B) Deetjen's Big Sur Inn

(F) Esalen Institute

(A) Lucia Lodge

(G) Ragged Point Inn

(B) Ventana Big Sur Country Inn Resort

Camping

(H) Andrew Molera State Park Campground

(C) Big Sur Campground and Cabins

(E) Pfeiffer Big Sur State Park Campground

(I) Plaskett Creek Campground

(B) Ventana Big Sur Campground

Note: Items with the same letter are located in the same town or area.

Near Hearst Castle and San Simeon, the **Ragged Point Inn** is on a bluff above the sea. A nature trail leads to a seasonal, 300-foot waterfall. Rooms range from $90 to $115—ask for a cliff-side room, (805) 927-4502.

CAMPING

Walk-in sites at the **Andrew Molera State Park Campground** are only $3, and the walk is easy! Call (408) 667-2315 for information.

To reach the happy jumble of **Big Sur Campground and Cabins**, you have to cross the Big Sur River on a narrow bridge just off the highway. There are tent sites for $24 and RV sites for $27, several of both are right on the river, Big Sur, (408) 667-2322. Down the road, the **Pfeiffer Big Sur State Park Campground** has good sites for $14 to $18, (408) 667-2315 for information, (800) 444-7275 for reservations.

The **Ventana Big Sur Campground** is the nice but poor cousin to the resort in the hills above. The 60 good and fair sites are strung through a narrow valley, $24, near Nepenthe, (408) 667-2688.

In the south, **Plaskett Creek Campground** is in the National Forest. It features 43 nice sites spread above the road, $9.

Scenic Route: Nacimiento Road

Five miles south of the tiny town of Lucia, on the Big Sur coast, the Nacimiento Fergusson Road climbs in great, winding switchbacks up to the crest of the Santa Lucia Mountains, 3,000 feet above the ocean. At the ridgeline, the road continues inland to Fort Hunter Leggett, but you can turn right or left to wind along the crest, enjoying occasional views. By turning left, winding Cone Peak Road will bring you to the parking area at the base of Cone Peak. Hike up to the lookout to stand on the highest coastal peak in the Santa Lucias, 5,155 feet in elevation.

Free camping is available at any of several pullouts along the ridgecrest. Two official campgrounds can be reached by continuing 6 or 8 miles past the ridgecrest on the Nacimiento Road. Another is located a few miles from the ridge junction on the Coast Ridge Road.

A loop up from Lucia and back with a hike to Cone Peak will take at least four hours. A simple driving loop with a short stint south along the ridgecrest can be done in 1½ hours. The closest services are in Lucia.

NACIMIENTO ROAD

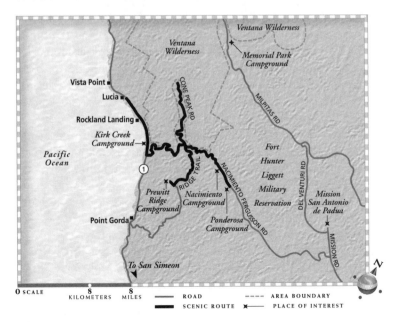

7

WINE COUNTRY

The nation's finest wines are produced in the several valleys north of San Francisco, known collectively as the "Wine Country." It's delightful to explore the region, visiting vineyards for a taste or a tour, enjoying fine dining as the sun sets, and soaking in hot mineral waters in the evenings. Budget lodging and camping are available in several areas, as are historic sites, recreation options, and family activities.

The greatest concentration of vineyards is in the northern half of the famous and heavily visited Napa Valley. Take CA 29, north of the town of Napa, to pass wineries like Robert Mondavi, Sutter Home, Beringer, and Christian Brothers. Across the river, the less traveled Silverado Trail provides access to wineries on the valley's east side. The town of Calistoga sits at the head of the valley, home to several resorts that channel the area's hot springs into pools, tubs, and mud baths.

West of Napa, the Sonoma Valley features wineries, resorts, and the wonderful, historic town of Sonoma, the birthplace of the short-lived Bear Flag Republic. The pace here is slower, and the wineries less crowded. Other northern wine growing areas are found in or near the Russian River Valley and scattered through the Coast Range south of San Francisco, the Central Valley, and the Sierra foothills.

A nice alternative to the Napa-Sonoma region is the peaceful Anderson Valley. North of Cloverdale, CA 128 leaves the Russian River basin, climbs over a divide, and drops into the Anderson Valley on its way to the Mendocino Coast. Several charming wineries line the way between Boonville and Navarro. ◼

A PERFECT DAY IN WINE COUNTRY

Start in Sonoma with breakfast on the square. Visit the mission, M. G. Vallejo's mansion, and Buena Vista Winery and Vineyards—the first in California. Take CA 12 to the cutoff for Glen Ellen. Visit the tiny center of this historic town before heading to Jack London State Historic Park. Take winding Trinity Road over the ridge and down into the Napa Valley. Visit a winery or two and the waterwheel-powered Bale Grist Mill. After registering at your spa resort in Calistoga, soak in a hot tub as you muster the courage for a soaring trip in the morning.

SIGHTSEEING HIGHLIGHTS

★★ **Sonoma and the Sonoma Valley**—Nowhere else in Wine Country can you enjoy such a perfect blend of regional history, charming surroundings, good food, pleasant strolling, and, of course, fine wine. The **Sonoma Plaza** is the heart of town. Here you'll find the interesting **City Hall**, with its four identical facades, and the **Bear Flag Monument**, honoring Sonoma's brief stint as the capital of an independent California. Stop in at the **Vasquez House** just off the square for tea, cookies, and a look at the historic library collection. Details: Located on El Paseo Plaza, 1st Street East; (707) 938-0150; open Wednesday through Sunday from 1:30 p.m. to 4:30 p.m. Admission is free. (½ hour)

The Sonoma Valley Historical Society's **Depot Park Museum** features regional heritage exhibits, one block north of the plaza. Details: 1st Street West one block north of the plaza; (707) 938-1762; open Wednesday through Sunday from 1 p.m. to 4:30 p.m. Admission is free. (½ hour)

Sonoma is a great place to put together a picnic. Stop at the **Artisan's Bakery** at Seventh and Napa Street for some bread, visit the **Vella Cheese Company** at 315 Second Street East for cheese, team them up with that bottle you bought while wine tasting, and find a pleasant place to dine.

Like the Napa Valley, two main roads pass through the Sonoma Valley. **CA 12** is the busy route that connects the town of Sonoma with Santa Rosa to the north and the Bay Area to the south. On the western side of the valley, **Arnold Drive** is the equivalent of the Silverado Trail, offering a quieter route from Sonoma to Glen Ellen.

WINE COUNTRY

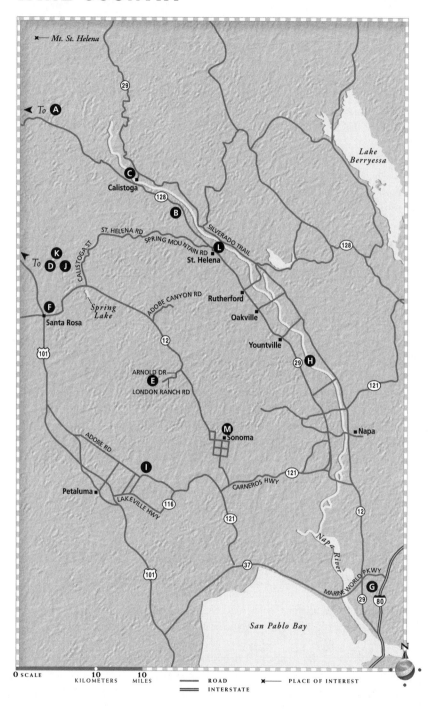

×— Mt. St. Helena

Lake Berryessa

29

To Ⓐ

Ⓒ
Calistoga

128

Ⓑ

SILVERADO TRAIL

ST. HELENA RD
SPRING MOUNTAIN RD

Ⓛ
St. Helena

128

CALISTOGA ST

Ⓚ
Ⓓ Ⓙ
To

ADOBE CANYON RD

Rutherford

Oakville

Ⓕ
Santa Rosa

Spring Lake

12

Yountville

29 Ⓗ

121

ARNOLD DR

101

Ⓔ

LONDON RANCH RD

Ⓜ
Sonoma

Napa

121

ADOBE RD

Ⓘ

CARNEROS HWY

121

Petaluma

LAKEVILLE HWY

116

12

121

Napa River

101

37

MARINE WORLD PKWY

Ⓖ

29 80

San Pablo Bay

N

O SCALE
10 KILOMETERS
10 MILES
——— ROAD   ×— PLACE OF INTEREST
═══ INTERSTATE

Sightseeing Highlights

Ⓐ Anderson Valley

Ⓑ Bale Grist Mill State Historic Park

Ⓒ Calistoga

Ⓓ Healdsburg

Ⓔ Jack London State Historic Park

Ⓕ Luther Burbank Home and Gardens

Ⓖ Marine World and Africa U.S.A.

Ⓗ Napa Valley

Ⓘ Petaluma Adobe State Historic Park

Ⓙ Real Goods Solar Living Center

Ⓚ Russian River

Ⓛ St. Helena

Ⓛ Silverado Museum

Ⓜ Sonoma and the Sonoma Valley

Ⓜ Sonoma State Historic Park

Ⓜ Sonoma Traintown Railroad

Note: Items with the same letter are located in the same town or area.

★★ **Wine Tasting**—It would simply be unfair to recommend any particular wineries for visiting. The joy of wine tasting is in the sense of exploration, spontaneity, and discovery that accompanies your search for the one that's just right. Perhaps it's a name remembered from a good bottle you enjoyed on a special occasion. Maybe you spot some inviting buildings on a sunny hillside. It could be the artfulness of a roadside sign or the colorful landscaping around a gate that leads you to turn up a drive. Whatever it is, your Wine Country tour will be more enjoyable because you responded to inspiration rather than targeting a famous name.

Pick up a map, brochure, or winery guide so you can choose your driving route wisely. Bookshops, convenience stores, tourist offices, and the wineries themselves offer such resources. Pay special attention to tasting hours and to whether or not tours are offered. Ask the opinions of local folks, using words like "charming," "small," and "friendly" in your inquiries. Take a chance—leave Robert Mondavi to the masses.

Roads where you will pass by several good wineries include **CA 29** and the **Silverado Trail** between Napa and Calistoga, the **Westside Road** from Guerneville to Healdsburg, **CA 128** from Geyserville south to the higher hills, **Dry Creek Road** from Healdsburg to Lake Sonoma, **U.S. 101** from Hopland to Redwood Valley, and **CA 128** between Yorkville and Navarro. Sonoma Valley wineries are more dispersed, as are those for other areas.

A number of wineries host concerts or festivals throughout the summer. Free visitor guides and newspapers that list these events are available throughout the area.

Note: The police throughout Wine Country know full well that wine tasting is the same thing as wine drinking. DUI laws in California are no picnic. Decide wisely.

Despite the preceding words, you might still want a suggestion or two. The following are attractive choices:

In Napa Valley:
Beringer Brothers—This large winery, the oldest continuously operated in the valley, is worth a visit for a look at the splendid Rhine House, built in 1883. Details: 2000 Main Street, St. Helena (on CA 29); (707) 963-4812; open daily with tours every half hour. There is a free tasting, but for a premium wines tasting it is $2 or $3. (1 hour)

The Hess Collection—In the hills between Sonoma and Napa, this fine winery has a museum-quality art gallery. Details: 4411 Redwood Road (from CA 29 north of Napa); (707) 255-1144; open daily from 10 a.m. to 4 p.m. Admission to the gallery is free; the tasting is $2.50. (1 hour)

Nichelini Winery—Head into the quiet hills for a relaxing visit to the oldest continuously family run winery in the county. Details: Hwy. 128 (10 miles east of CA 29); (707) 963-3312; open weekends from 10 a.m. to 6 p.m. or by appointment. (1 hour)

Robert Mondavi Winery—This extensive winery features excellent tours of a large wine-making operation. Details: 7801 St. Helena Highway (CA 29), Oakville; (707) 226-1395; open 10 a.m. to 4:30 p.m. A free tour is available with a free tasting; other tastings are $2 to $4. (1½ hours)

In Sonoma Valley:
Buena Vista Winery—This is California's oldest winery, dating back to 1857. Enjoy the lovely, wooded grounds and tasting in the original press room. Details: 18000 Old Winery Road, from East Napa Street, Sonoma; (707) 938-1266 or (800) 926-1266; open daily from 10 a.m. to 5 p.m. Self-guided tours are offered. (1 hour)

Gundlach-Bundschu Winery—Founded in 1858 and reconstructed in the 1970s, this easy-going winery has a quiet hills setting, small lake, and nice picnic spots. Details: 2000 Denmark Road, from Eighth Street East, Sonoma; (707) 938-5277; open daily from 11 a.m. to 4:30 p.m. (1 hour)

In Russian River:
Hop Kiln Winery—This backroad winery is housed in a restored barn with three large chimneys that were once used in the drying of hops. Details: 6050 Westside Road, from Healdsburg; (707) 433-6491; open daily from 10 a.m. to 5 p.m. A self-guided tour is offered, along with a free tasting. (1 hour)

Johnson's of Alexander Valley—In the Alexander Valley along the Russian River, this small winery features a 1925 pipe organ in the tasting room. Details: 8329 Hwy. 128, Healdsburg, north of Calistoga; (707) 433-2319; open daily from 10 a.m. to 5 p.m. Free tasting. (1 hour)

Korbel Champagne Cellars—This stately and popular winery, dating to the 1880s, sits among lovely gardens and redwood trees. Details: 13250 River Road, east of Guerneville; (707) 887-2294; open from 9 a.m. to 5 p.m.; tours are given from 10 a.m. to 3 p.m. (1 hour)

In Anderson Valley:
Husch Vineyards—Husch was the first winery in the Anderson Valley and is still a great place for a taste and a visit. Details: 4400 Hwy. 128,

between Philo and Navarro; (707) 895-3216; open from 10 a.m. to 6 p.m. (1 hour)

Lazy Creek Vineyards—You won't find a more easy going, family winery than this one. Call for an appointment and meet Hans and Theresia. Details: 4610 Hwy. 128 (up a long drive); (707) 895-3623; by appointment only. (1 hour)

Pepperwood Springs Vineyards—Great Pinot Noir and a fabulous view are found at this small winery 2 miles from the valley floor. Details: 1200 Holmes Road, just beyond Husch Vineyards; (707) 895-2920. Call for current hours. (1 hour)

✿ **Bale Grist Mill State Historic Park**—The **Old Bale Mill** was built in 1846 and has been restored to full operating condition. You can buy stone-ground flour made at the mill for $2 a bag and enjoy a pleasant minute watching the water tumble over the 36-foot, wooden waterwheel. Details: 5 miles north of St. Helena on CA 29; (707) 963-2236; open daily from 10 a.m. to 5 p.m. Admission is $2. (1 hour)

✿ **Calistoga**—Sam Brannan, newspaper mogul and big dreamer, founded this pleasant town in 1859. The name blends "California" with the New York spa town "Saratoga." Brannan spent a fortune building a glorious resort for weary and wealthy San Franciscans. Not enough of them showed up, however, and he lost everything. Today, Lincoln Avenue is a pleasant street for strolling and dining between rejuvenation sessions at one of the many spas. Check out the **Calistoga Depot**, the second oldest train depot in the state.

While here, you might also visit the **Old Faithful Geyser**—that's right, there's another one. At least, until recently it was faithful. Call ahead to see if conditions are right for a good showing. Details: 1299 Tubbs Lane (between CA 29 and CA 128), Calistoga; (707) 942-6463; open daily from 9 a.m. to 6 p.m. Admission is $5. (½ hour)

Just west of town at the **Petrified Forest**, a quarter-mile trail leads past ten varied examples of petrified trees. Details: 4100 Petrified Forest Road, Calistoga, (707) 942-6667; open daily from 10 a.m. to 5:30 p.m. Admission is $3. (½ hour)

In town, the **Sharpsteen Museum** features the historical dioramas of Ben Sharpsteen, one of Walt Disney Studio's original animators, as well as numerous other heritage exhibits. Next door is the restored and relocated **Brannan Cottage**, a remnant of Sam Brannan's ill-fated Calistoga Resort. Details: The museum is at 1311 Washington Street,

Calistoga; (707) 942-5911; open daily from 10 a.m. to 4 p.m. (noon to 4 p.m., November through March). Admission is free. (1 hour)

✻ **Jack London State Historic Park**—In the hills above Glen Ellen, Jack London lived the last years of his life in a small cottage with his wife, Charmian. He had commissioned the construction of the magnificent **Wolf House** nearby, but it mysteriously burned a month before completion in 1913. He intended to rebuild it, but he died in 1916 at age 40. An easy, 1¼-mile loop hike through woodsy parkland takes you to the Wolf House ruins and the Londons' graves. A museum of his memorabilia and park headquarters are in **Happy Walls**, the home built by Charmian after London's death. Details: Take London Ranch Road from Arnold Drive in Glen Ellen; (707) 938-5216; open from 10 a.m. to 5 p.m. Fee is $5 for day use. (2 hours)

✻ **Petaluma Adobe State Historic Park**—This living history park features a large, balconied, adobe structure that served as the central building for General M. G. Vallejo's 66,000-acre ranch. The *hacienda* sits on a hill, overlooking the Petaluma River Valley. On weekends, costumed park volunteers reenact farm routines from the 1850s. Details: 3325 Adobe Road, 5 miles north of CA 116; (707) 762-4871; open daily from 10 a.m. to 5 p.m. Admission is $2. (1 hour)

✻ **Sonoma State Historic Park**—Remnants and reconstructions of several historic structures are preserved on the north side of Sonoma's central plaza. Little is left of the original **Mission San Francisco Solano de Sonoma**, except one wing, the 1840 mission chapel, and the courtyard which can be visited. Other adobe and historic structures include soldiers' barracks, nineteenth-century hotels and residences, and **La Casa Grande**, General M. G. Vallejo's first home.

A half mile west of the square on West Spain Street is the entrance to **Lachryma Montis**, the Vallejo Home, built 1851–1852. General Vallejo and his wife lived here for more than 35 years. Many of the current furnishings belonged to the Vallejos, and the gardens have been restored to their original beauty. Details: Sonoma Plaza, Sonoma; (707) 938-1519; open daily from 10 a.m. to 5 p.m. Admission to the home and park is $2. (2 hours)

✻ **Sonoma Traintown Railroad**—A mile south of the town square in Sonoma, Traintown features 10 acres of miniature settings, accessed by a scaled-down train that carries passengers. Built in the 1950s by rail buff, Stanley Franks, the facility is lovingly maintained. There's a petting zoo for the kids, but you won't be alone if you come kidless. Details: 1 mile south of downtown Sonoma on CA 12, Sonoma; open daily June through September from 10:30 a.m. to 5 p.m. (October through May, open only Friday through Sunday). The $3 ride takes about twenty minutes. (1 hour)

☆ **Marine World and Africa U.S.A.**—This popular family attraction features killer whales, dolphins, tigers, elephants, birds, and more in shows and exhibitions. In the **Shark Experience**, you walk through a large shark aquarium in an acrylic tunnel. Enter **Butterfly World** to interact with hundreds of free-flying butterflies. There are elephant rides, robotic dinosaurs, a playground, and more. Details: Take Marine World Parkway from Interstate 80, Vallejo; (707) 643-6722; open daily from 9:30 a.m. to 6:30 p.m. in the summer (until 5 p.m. the rest of the year). Admission is $26. (half day)

Healdsburg—This is a pleasant village for strolling, dining, and relaxing. The shady town square is surrounded by well-kept shops and cafés. Healdsburg Avenue, the town's main street, parallels the freeway to the east. The **Healdsburg Museum** features regional heritage items. Details: 221 Matheson Street, Healdsburg; open Tuesday through Sunday from 11 a.m. to 4 p.m. Admission is free. (45 minutes)

Luther Burbank Home and Gardens—A renowned horticulturist, Luther Burbank introduced over 800 new varieties of plants, including 200 varieties of fruit. The home where he lived from 1884 to 1906 and the gardens where he did much of his work are open to the public. Details: The gardens are on Santa Rosa Avenue across from Julliard Park in Santa Rosa. The main entrance is on Tupper Street. Call (707) 524-5445 for information; open daily. House tours are offered April through October, Wednesday through Sunday, every half hour from 10 a.m. to 3:30 p.m. Admission and tours are free. (1 hour)

St. Helena—This town is certainly worth a stop and a stroll, with the disadvantage being that CA 29 and the town's Main Street are one in the same. North of town, you'll easily spot the old Christian Brothers Winery that is now the **Culinary Institute of America**. Details: 2555

Main Street, St. Helena; (707) 967-1100. Stop in for a "kitchen view-ing" weekdays at 11:30 a.m., 1:30 p.m., or 3:30 p.m. (½ hour)

For some valley heritage, visit the **Napa Valley Museum**. Details: 473 Main Street, St. Helena; (707) 963-7411; open weekdays from 9 a.m. to 4 p.m.; weekends from 11 a.m. to 3 p.m. (45 minutes)

Real Goods Solar Living Center—Just south of Ukiah, Real Goods is both a store and an ongoing experiment featuring the latest goods and technologies for environmentally friendly design and construction. Explore the crafted grounds, examine the architecture, and browse the shelves to orient your thinking toward a sustainable future. Details: 555 Leslie Street, on U.S. 101, Ukiah; (707) 744-2100; open daily from 10 a.m. to 7 p.m. (½ hour)

Silverado Museum—Located next to the public library in St. Helena, the Silverado Museum is devoted to the life and works of Robert Louis Stevenson. Some 8,000 items are in the collection, including original letters and manuscripts, first editions, artwork, and the last words he ever penned. Details: 1490 Library Lane, St. Helena; (707) 963-3757; open Tuesday through Sunday from noon to 4 p.m. Donations accepted. (½ hour)

FITNESS AND RECREATION

From the trailhead in **Robert Louis Stevenson State Park**, you can hike to the top of 4,344-foot Mount St. Helena, the tallest in the region. The 10-mile roundtrip hike takes the better part of a day and is best in the spring or fall when temperatures are moderate. The views from the summit are spectacular—be sure to carry plenty of water. The park is 6 miles north of Calistoga on CA 29.

Several outfits offer hot air balloon rides. **Napa Valley Balloons, Inc.** has daily flights from the **Domaine Chandon Winery** in Yountville. One-hour trips are $165 and leave at sunrise. Plan on a 3-to-5-hour morning due to preparation and shuttling time, (707) 944-0228 or (800) 253-2224.

Cycling is great on area backroads. **Saint Helena Cyclery** rents OK bikes for $7 an hour or $25 a day, 1156 Main Street, St. Helena, (707) 963-7736. The **Good Time Bicycle Company**, located 1.5 miles north of Sonoma Plaza at 18503 Hwy. 12, has rentals for $5 per hour or $25 per day. Guided trips are also offered, (707) 938-0453.

Scenic biplane and glider flights from the Sonoma Valley Airport are offered by **Aeroschellville**. They have several, vintage military planes in their fleet. The 15-to-40-minute flights range from $70 to $195. Try the "Kamikaze" flight for some aerial acrobatics, 23982 Arnold Drive (CA 121), (707) 938-2444. **Calistoga Gliders** offers glider and biplane rides from the **Calistoga Gliderport**, right in town. Flights of 20 to 30 minutes range from $80 to $160, (707) 942-5000.

The **Sonoma Cattle Company** offers rides through **Jack London State Historic Park**, **Sugarloaf Ridge State Park**, or **Bothe-Napa Valley State Park**. Scheduled rides range from $30 to $45, private rides are $40 per hour. Call (707) 996-8566.

Canoeing and tubing on the Russian River are popular activities. Several places rent the needed equipment.

South of the Healdsburg town center, at 20 Healdsburg Avenue, **W.C. "Bob" Trowbridge** offers canoe and kayak trip packages. Half-day trips are $25, overnight trips start at $50, (707) 433-7247 or (800) 640-1386.

FOOD

In the town of Napa, stroll down First Street and along the brick walks of the pedestrian mall for a good selection of eateries. **Downtown Joe's** is a popular brewpub and restaurant serving breakfast, lunch, and dinner. It's next to the Riverfront Park, at 902 Main Street, (707) 258-2337.

For an elegant and unusual meal, take a lunch or dinner trip on the **Napa Valley Wine Train**. The train makes two 3-hour roundtrips daily from Napa to St. Helena and back. The lunch train runs daily at 11:30 a.m. on weekdays and 12:30 p.m. on weekends, $63. The dinner train runs Wednesday through Friday at 5:30 p.m., and on weekends at 6:30 p.m., $70. Prices include a gourmet meal, but not wine, (707) 253-2111 or (800) 427-4124.

In Yountville, **Domaine Chandon**, at the winery of the same name, offers fine French-California cuisine in elegant surroundings. Sit on the patio if weather permits, 1 California Drive, (707) 944-2892. **The French Laundry** has pricey but wonderful California cuisine, 6640 Washington, (707) 944-2380.

In Rutherford, **Auberge du Soleil** is the place to rub elbows with the platinum card set while enjoying exquisite California-French entrées and stellar views from the patio, 1050 Charter Oak Avenue (from CA 29), (707) 963-4444. Right on the highway, the **Rutherford Grill** is deservedly popular. Stylish American fare anchors the menu—notice the chickens rotating deliciously on spits behind the glass, (707) 963-1792.

The raves for **Tra Vigne** in St. Helena keep coming. Choose between a full-scale Italian meal in the grand, high-ceilinged dining room or lighter fare in the wonderful, walled courtyard patio. Prices are in the ballpark for most average travelers; lunch and dinner, break-fast on weekends, 1050 Charter Oak (off CA 29), (707) 963-4444. Expectations are high at the **Greystone**, 2555 Main Street (north of St. Helena). It shares space in the magnificent old Christian Brothers Winery with the Culinary Institute of America, (707) 967-1010. There are also several good places right on Main Street in town.

The **Calistoga Inn** on the Napa River in Calistoga is a wonderful place to enjoy fine patio dining and a home-brewed beer, 1250 Lincoln Avenue, (707) 942-4101. For Cajun dishes prepared California style, **Catahoula** is an excellent, upscale choice. Dinner entrées range from $8 to $21, 1457 Lincoln Avenue, (707) 942-2275.

There are over 20 restaurants around the Sonoma Plaza and many more nearby. You won't do better than the **Feed Store** for breakfast or

Robert Holmes

WINE COUNTRY

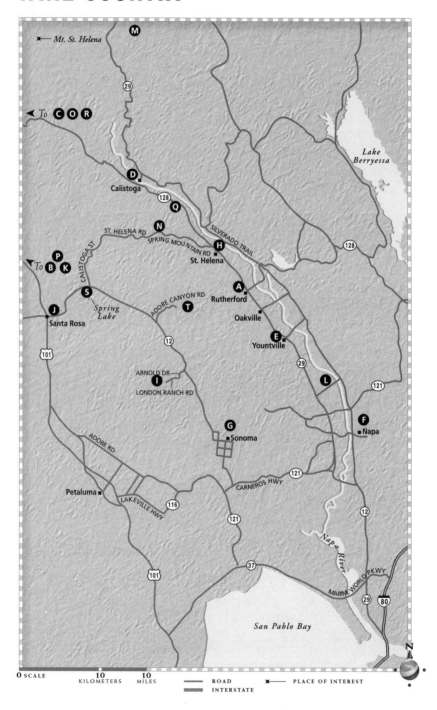

Mt. St. Helena

To Ⓒ Ⓞ Ⓡ

Lake Berryessa

Ⓜ

29

128

Ⓓ
Calistoga

128

Ⓠ

ST. HELENA RD

SILVERADO TRAIL

Ⓝ

SPRING MOUNTAIN RD

Ⓗ
St. Helena

CALISTOGA ST

Ⓟ
Ⓑ Ⓚ

To ◄

Ⓢ

Spring Lake

ADOBE CANYON RD

Ⓐ
Rutherford

Ⓙ
Santa Rosa

Ⓣ

Oakville

128

101

12

Ⓔ
Yountville

29

Ⓛ

121

ARNOLD DR

Ⓘ

LONDON RANCH RD

Ⓕ
Napa

Ⓖ
Sonoma

ADOBE RD

121

CARNEROS HWY

12

Petaluma

LAKEVILLE HWY

116

121

Napa River

101

37

MARINE WORLD PKWY

29 80

San Pablo Bay

N

O SCALE 10 KILOMETERS 10 MILES   ROAD   ✖ PLACE OF INTEREST
                                     INTERSTATE

Food

Ⓐ Auberge du Soleil

Ⓑ Bear Republic Brewing Co.

Ⓒ Boonville Hotel

Ⓓ Calistoga Inn

Ⓓ Catahoula

Ⓔ Domaine Chandon

Ⓕ Downtown Joe's

Ⓖ Feed Store

Ⓔ The French Laundry

Ⓗ Greystone

Ⓘ Jack London Café

Ⓙ La Gare

Ⓑ Mangia Bene

Ⓚ Mendocino Brewing Company

Ⓖ Murphy's Irish Pub

Ⓛ Napa Valley Wine Train

Ⓐ Rutherford Grill

Ⓗ Tra Vigne

Ⓙ Westside Espresso Café

Lodging

Ⓒ Boonville Hotel

Ⓔ Burgundy House

Ⓓ Calistoga Inn

Ⓗ El Bonita Motel

Ⓜ Harbin Hot Springs

Ⓝ Hilltop House

Ⓗ Hotel St. Helena

Ⓓ Nance's

Ⓞ Philo Pottery Inn

Ⓐ Rancho Caymus

Ⓓ Roman Spa

Ⓖ Sonoma Hotel

Ⓚ Thatcher Inn

Ⓟ Vichy Springs Resort

Camping

Ⓠ Bothe-Napa Valley State Park

Ⓡ Cloverdale Alexander Valley KOA

Ⓞ Hendy Woods State Park

Ⓞ Indian Creek County Park

Ⓓ Napa County Fair Campground

Ⓢ Spring Lake Regional Park

Ⓣ Sugarloaf Ridge State Park

Note: Items with the same letter are located in the same town or area.

lunch. Try the Jalisco Club Sandwich, 529 First Street West, (707) 938-2122. **Murphy's Irish Pub** offers fish and chips or Irish stew to go with a pint—traditional live music Thursday through Sunday, 464 First Street East, (707) 935-0660.

In the tiny historic end of Glen Ellen, enjoy a meal on the streamside deck at the **Jack London Café**. Sandwiches are around $8, entrées are $10 to $15.

West of U.S. 101 in Santa Rosa is Historic Railroad Square, featuring shops and restaurants in a couple of blocks of renovated buildings. At 10 Fourth Street, the **Westside Espresso Café** has tasty $6 breakfasts and sandwiches, (707) 541-7392. **La Gare**, at 208 Wilson Street, is a delightful and romantic French restaurant, (707) 528-4355.

The brand new **Bear Republic Brewing Co.** in Healdsburg has good site-brewed ales and fine pub grub. The brewpub is spacious and light, and it faces the small park across the street from the plaza, 345 Healdsburg Avenue, (707) 433-2337. **Mangia Bene** has good Italian entrées at very reasonable prices, 241 Healdsburg Avenue, (707) 433-2340. There are many other wonderful cafés on or near the plaza.

Lots of U.S. 101 travelers stop in Hopland for a bite and a pint at the **Mendocino Brewing Company**. The beer garden is a simple pleasure, 13351 U.S. 101, (707) 744-1361.

In Boonville, the **Boonville Hotel** has California cuisine that strays wonderfully in several directions. Entrées run from $12 to $20, CA 128 in Boonville, (707) 895-2210.

LODGING

The cities of Vallejo, Napa, Petaluma, Santa Rosa, and Ukiah all have budget and moderate chain motel outlets. Use the numbers on the "Resources" page to contact them. Elsewhere, accommodations tend to be more expensive.

In Yountville, the **Burgundy House** is a charming, French country-style B&B built in the 1890s. The six guest rooms start at $135, 6711 Washington Street, (707) 944-0889.

Next to the Rutherford Grill, **Rancho Caymus** offers spacious comfort. This hacienda-style inn has beamed ceilings, individually designed rooms and suites, stained glass, fireplaces, and all the amenities. Rooms are from $125 (a bargain) to $295, 1140 Rutherford Road, (707) 963-1777 or (800) 845-1777.

Dating back to 1881, the downtown **Hotel St. Helena** is a lovely choice with gracious hosts, complimentary breakfast, garden patio, wine bar, and an air of history. Rooms range from $130 to $250, 1309 Main Street, (707) 963-4388. At 195 Main Street, the **El Bonita Motel** has rooms from $50 to $110, (707) 963-3216.

Calistoga has several spa resorts featuring mud baths, massages, and mineral pools. None of them really stand out as accommodations, but each has its strengths. **Nance's** has the lowest spa and lodging rates, $50 to $75, 1614 Lincoln Avenue, (707) 942-6211. The **Roman Spa** is more intimate and decorated, and it has nice pools, $68 to $128 (includes in-room whirlpool spa), 1300 Washington Street, (707) 942-4441. For a non-spa stay, try the charming and historic **Calistoga Inn**, right on the Napa River at 1250 Lincoln Avenue. All rooms are shared-bath and are priced from $50 to $60. There's a wonderful restaurant with a riverside patio. A tiny brewery offers lagers and ales on the premises, (707) 942-4101.

A great, cheap spa option out of town is **Harbin Hot Springs**, about 23 miles north of Calistoga. You can stay in a dorm for $25 to $35. There's a vegetarian restaurant and a clothing-optional pool. Bring your own linens. Take CA 29 to Middletown and then to Harbin Springs Road, (707) 987-2477.

On the top of the ridge separating the Napa and Sonoma Valleys, you'll find **Hilltop House**. Sip wine on the deck as you enjoy the incredible views, or soak in the hot tub under the stars, 9550 St. Helena Road (take Spring Mountain Road north of St. Helena), (707) 944-0880.

Right on the square in Sonoma, the charming vintage **Sonoma Hotel** has private and shared-bath rooms from $75 to $120, 110 West Spain Street, (707) 996-2996 or (800) 468-6016.

Located on the highway in the center of Hopland, the **Thatcher Inn** was built in 1890. The splendid library is a great place to sit and read by the fire. Rooms are from $100 to $150, (707) 744-1890 or (800) 266-1891.

In the Anderson Valley, Boonville offers the **Boonville Hotel**, a tasteful and spacious B&B with gardens and a fine restaurant. Rooms run from $70 to $150, CA 128 and Lambert Lane in central Boonville, (707) 895-2210. At the south end of Philo, the **Philo Pottery Inn** is a wonderfully rustic B&B. The main building was built in 1888 and was once used as a stagecoach stop. Rooms range from $80 to $95, 8550 CA 128, (707) 895-3069.

In Ukiah, consider a night at the **Vichy Springs Resort**. The warm, bubbling mineral springs, named after the almost identical waters of Vichy in France, have been used for centuries. A stay at this B&B inn includes soaking and relaxing on the quiet, sprawling grounds. Rooms are $130 and cabins are $170, 2605 Vichy Springs Road, (707) 462-9515.

CAMPING

Just south of Calistoga on CA 29, **Bothe-Napa Valley State Park** has 50 very nice sites stretching up along Ritchey Creek. There's an interesting Native American Garden by the park headquarters. Reservations are advised, 3801 St. Helena Highway North, (707) 942-4575. In Calistoga, RVs might want to camp at the **Napa County Fair Campground**, sites are $18. The fairgrounds are on Oak Street, a few blocks north of downtown, (707) 942-5111.

In the upper Sonoma valley, **Sugarloaf Ridge State Park** has very nice sites surrounding a meadow for $12 to $16. Trail rides are available and hiking trails lead to the summits of Red Mountain and Mt. Hood. Take Adobe Canyon Road from CA 12 north of Kenwood, (707) 833-5712 for information or (800) 444-7275 for reservations.

Near Santa Rosa, **Spring Lake Regional Park** has sites on a small reservoir. Take Montgomery Drive from CA 12 to Summerfield Drive, $14, (707) 539-8082.

The **Cloverdale Alexander Valley KOA** is well off the highway on the east side of the Russian River, not far from Cloverdale. Take the Asti exit and follow the signs for a few miles. Tent sites are $21, RV sites $26, "Kamping Kabins" $36, (707) 894-3337 or (800) 368-4558.

Just east of Philo in the Anderson Valley, **Indian Creek County Park** has a few nice, but primitive tent sites, $10. West of Philo, **Hendy Woods State Park** has sites for $12 to $14, (707) 937-5804.

8

THE NORTH COAST: SONOMA AND MENDOCINO

The southern half of California's North Coast extends from Bodega Bay to the town of Rockport above Fort Bragg. Though the stretch is beaded with points of interest, the chief attraction is the magnificent coast itself. The Coast Highway, CA 1, snakes along at the brink of the continent, hugging treacherous bluffs one minute, and winding through gentle pastures the next. Always, it is the stunning junction of land and sea that draws the eye. It is perfectly legitimate to spend your entire time on the North Coast alternating between headland hikes, forest forays, cliff climbs, whale watches, and beach basks.

Several towns along the coast got their starts as mill and port towns, preparing lumber and then shipping it on sailing vessels to booming San Francisco. Today, the redwoods are all but gone, though the hills have a new beauty. Where once there were mills and saloons, you'll now find romantic inns, fine restaurants, and art galleries.

Visitors who cannot drive the entire Coast Highway can choose more limited explorations in two popular areas. Bodega Bay and the lower Russian River Valley are close to the Bay Area and are brimming with parks, attractions, and accommodations. Further north, the area around Mendocino and Fort Bragg is similarly blessed. Mendocino can be reached from San Francisco in as little as three hours via U.S. 101 and CA 128 through Anderson Valley. Traveling up CA 1 and back down U.S. 101 makes a good three-day loop. ◼

THE NORTH COAST

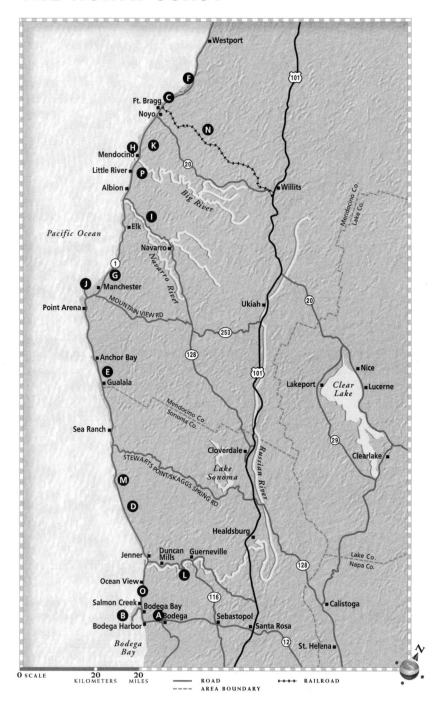

Westport

101

F

C Ft. Bragg
Noyo

N

H K
Mendocino

Little River P
Albion

20

Big River

Willits

Mendocino Co.
Lake Co.

I

Pacific Ocean

Elk

Navarro

Navarro River

1 G
J Manchester

MOUNTAIN VIEW RD

Ukiah

20

Point Arena

253

128

Anchor Bay

101

Nice

E
Gualala

Lakeport

Clear
Lake

Lucerne

Sea Ranch

Mendocino Co.
Sonoma Co.

Cloverdale

Russian River

29

Clearlake

STEWARTS POINT/SKAGGS SPRING RD

Lake
Sonoma

M

D

Healdsburg

Jenner Duncan
Mills

Guerneville

128

Lake Co.
Napa Co.

Ocean View

L

O

116

Salmon Creek Bodega Bay

B A Bodega

Calistoga

Bodega Harbor

Sebastopol

Santa Rosa

Bodega
Bay

12 St. Helena

0 SCALE   20   20
        KILOMETERS   MILES

——— ROAD
- - - - AREA BOUNDARY

╪╪╪╪ RAILROAD

Sightseeing Highlights

Ⓐ Bodega

Ⓑ Bodega Head

Ⓒ Fort Bragg

Ⓓ Fort Ross State Historical Park

Ⓔ Gualala

Ⓕ MacKerricher State Park

Ⓖ Manchester Beach

Ⓗ Mendocino

Ⓒ Mendocino Coast Botanical Gardens

Ⓘ Navarro River Redwoods

Ⓙ Point Arena Light Station

Ⓚ Russian Gulch State Park

Ⓛ Russian River Valley

Ⓜ Salt Point State Park

Ⓝ Skunk Train

Ⓞ Sonoma Coast State Beaches

Ⓟ Van Damme State Park

Note: Items with the same letter are located in the same town or area.

A PERFECT DAY AROUND THE NORTH COAST

In the cool of the morning, enjoy a recreational pursuit of your choice: hiking in Van Damme State Park, cycling in Jackson State Forest, or canoeing up Big River, for example. Drive to Fort Bragg and have lunch down at the wharf on the Noyo River. In the afternoon stroll along the sculpted paths of the Botanical Gardens to the ocean. Return to Mendocino for late afternoon shopping, gallery browsing, and aimless strolling. After a tasty dinner, walk out onto the headlands for sunset and evening views of the historic town.

SIGHTSEEING HIGHLIGHTS

✯✯✯ **Mendocino**—If you approach the town of Mendocino from the south, stop at the viewpoint below the mouth of Big River for a picture postcard view. Perched in historical splendor on protected bluffs, Mendocino began as a logging and milling town in the 1800s. When the wood was gone, it languished in obscurity until discovered first by artists, then by money and tourism. Despite the pressures, it has held its charm remarkably well and remains the top destination on the North Coast.

The town's finest feature is **Mendocino Headlands State Park**. On both sides of the mouth of Big River, the park protects open headlands with wonderful views of town and coast. The look of historic Mendocino perched on a grassy shelf high above the waves is classic. You can literally step off Main Street and onto the bluffs.

The **Ford House Visitor Center** features Mendocino heritage displays including a scale model of the historic town. Details: 735 Main Street, Mendocino; (707) 937-5397; open daily from 11 a.m. to 4 p.m. Admission is $1. (45 minutes)

At the **Kelly House Museum**, built in 1861, you'll discover more heritage items and a library with a history and genealogy collection. Details: 45007 Albion Street, Mendocino; (707) 937-5791; open Friday through Monday from 1 p.m. to 4 p.m. in July and August. Admission is $1. (1 hour)

The **Mendocino Art Center Showcase** on Main Street features works by local artists. The center also has galleries and offers classes that attract students from across the country. Enjoy a play put on by the Mendocino Theater Company at the **Mendocino Art Center**. Details: 45200 Little Lake Street, Mendocino; (707) 936-5818.

For great information on what's happening around town, check out the notices posted on the fence next to the **Corners of the Mouth Natural Foods Grocery** after you stock up on healthy stuff.

✯✯✯ **Mendocino Coast Botanical Gardens**—Established by retired nursery man Ernest Schoefer in 1961, the gardens lie at the south end of Fort Bragg on 47 acres, stretching from CA 1 to the Pacific. While visually stunning during blooming cycles from April to October, the garden is a wonderful place for easy walks and relaxation year-round. Whale watching is best in December and March. Details: 18220 North CA 1, Mendocino; (707) 964-4352; open daily from 9 a.m. to 5 p.m. Admission is $5. (1–3 hours)

★★ **Bodega Head**—For fine views of bay, coast, and open ocean, Bodega Head can't be beat. Whale watching is an option during the gray whale migration (best in and around December and March), and harbor seals can be seen and heard. Trails lead up and down the coast from the day use parking areas. To the north, the **Bodega Marine Reserve** and **Bodega Marine Laboratory**, extensions of the University of California at Davis, are off-limits to hiking. The lab can only be visited on docent-led tours. Details: The entrance is along Bay Flats Road, Bodega Head; (707) 875-2211; tours are given Fridays from 2 p.m. to 4 p.m. Call for times and admission prices.

★★ **Point Arena Lighthouse**—Built in 1908 to replace a predecessor damaged in the 1906 earthquake, the Point Arena Lighthouse is one of California's tallest at 115 feet. A good museum, great coastal views, and the chance to climb to the top make the lighthouse an excellent stop on a North Coast tour. Details: Just north of Point Arena, turn left onto Lighthouse Road for the five-minute drive to the point. Details: (707) 882-2777; open daily from 11 a.m. to 2:30 p.m. Admission is only $2.50. (1½ hours)

★★ **Salt Point State Park**—With over 6,000 acres to explore, Salt Point is a great recreational resource. Miles of trails are available to hikers and horseback riders, providing access to headlands, sandy coves, and forested slopes. The associated **Gerstle Cove Reserve** preserves tide pools and shallows rich in marine life.

At the north end of the park, narrow Kruse Ranch Road winds up into the **Kruse Rhododendron State Preserve**. Here, the steep, forested hills feature a lush undergrowth of rhododendron that produces a magnificent display of pink blossoms in April and May. There are trailheads and turnouts along the road. Details: 20 miles north of Jenner on CA 1; (707) 847-3221.

★★ **Whale Watching**—Every year, gray whales swim close by the coast of California on their annual migrations, passing southward in

December and January, then northward from February through April.
During peak season, watchers enjoy a high rate of success in sighting
the passing behemoths from headland vantage points. Special whale
watching boat excursions leave from the larger coastal towns. Proper
timing, binoculars, and a little patience are all that's required.

✯ **Fort Ross State Historic Park**—In 1812, Russian traders seeking otter pelts established Fort Ross as a base of operations. Thirty
years later, the region's otter population was decimated and the site
was abandoned. Today, you can visit an accurate reconstruction of
the settlement and enjoy the library and historical exhibits in the visitor center. There are also several good hiking trails on the coast and
in the hills above the highway. Details: 12 miles north of Jenner on
CA 1; (707) 847-3286; open daily from 10 a.m. to 4:30 p.m.
Admission is $5. (1 hour)

✯ **Manchester Beach**—CA 1 cuts away from the coast to get around
this sprawling beach. The San Andreas Fault, which runs along the
North Coast above Bolinas, exits the continent here once and for all. If
you want miles of sand, wind, waves, driftwood, and shore birds, you'll
love it here. Details: Access is via Kinney Road, ½ mile north of
Manchester.

✯ **MacKerricher State Park**—Located north of Fort Bragg, the 8
miles of wide beach backed by dunes make this park one of the sandiest
stretches on the North Coast. Near the campground is a small lake
with a perimeter trail. An old logging haul road runs the length of the
park behind the beach, providing a great route for cycling, walking, or
jogging. Harbor seals are common visitors and migrating whales can be
seen from November through March. Details: 3 miles north of Fort
Bragg on CA 1; (707) 937-5804.

✯ **Navarro River Redwoods**—Turn up CA 128 south of Mendocino
to pass through a narrow corridor of old-growth redwoods, saved
from the chainsaw because of their proximity to the fragile riverine
environment—and their proximity to the eyes of drivers who prefer
forest to clear cuts. There are several spots to stop along the way to
enjoy both river and trees. If you are zooming to or from the
Anderson Valley, this is a great place to slow down. Details: CA 128,
south of Mendocino.

✹ **Russian Gulch State Park**—Just north of Mendocino, a mile of protected coast features the **Punch Bowl**, a churning inlet in a collapsed sea cave that has a "boiling cauldron" look. A lovely waterfall is one possible hiking destination on the miles of trails through the inland portion of the park. Details: Located 2 miles north of Mendocino on CA 1; (707) 937-5804.

✹ **Russian River Valley**—Hwy. 116 follows the final miles of the Russian River from the town of **Guerneville** to the coast at **Jenner**. The entire region, including the towns of **Forestville**, **Occidental**, **Monte Rio**, and **Cazadero**, is a resort area that is replete with vacation homes, riverside inns, fishing lodges, and other attractions.

Duncans Mills is a tiny, "historic" town, with shops largely owned by one family. It's a bit too cute to be believable, though the museum and rail cars may be worth a look. **Monte Rio** offers a public beach, mini-golf, and a small amusement park. Cross the river on the Bohemian Highway to reach the town center. **Bohemian Grove**, retreat of the rich and powerful, sits in the hills east of Monte Rio, but it is closed to the public.

Located just north of Guerneville, on the Armstrong Woods Road, is **Armstrong Redwoods State Reserve**. The park preserves the largest grove of old-growth redwoods in Sonoma county and offers several short hikes. Adjacent to the park on the north is **Austin Creek State Recreation Area**, offering 20 miles of hiking in a rugged terrain of open forest and rolling hills. Details: Armstrong Woods Road, Guerneville; (707) 869-2015; open daily from 8 a.m. to sunset. Day use parking for both areas is $5. (1½ hours)

✹ **Skunk Train**—Named after the foul fuel smells of yesteryear, the historic Skunk Trains run through redwood country along the Noyo River between Fort Bragg and Willits. Details: The station is east of CA 1 at 100 Laurel Street, Fort Bragg; (707) 964-6371; roundtrip train trips leave Fort Bragg at 9:20 a.m. or 10 a.m., and at 2 p.m. or 2:20 p.m. The schedule is a bit complex so call ahead. Half-day trips are $21 and full-day trips are $26.

✹ **Sonoma Coast State Beaches**—From Bodega Bay north to Stewart's Point, much of the Sonoma County coastline is preserved in the **Sonoma Coast State Beaches**, **Fort Ross State Historic Park**, and **Salt Point**

State Park. Choose any of the coastal access points for picnicking and beachcombing. Details: (707) 875-3483.

✯ **Van Damme State Park**—This park is a favorite of joggers and cyclists who enjoy the 3-mile paved road along Little River. An easily accessible beach attracts abalone divers, and there's a golf course . An unusual pygmy forest is easily reached by a wheelchair accessible trail. Details: 3 miles south of Mendocino; (707) 937-5804.

Bodega—One mile east of the Coast Highway, the small town of Bodega offers a few art and antique shops, along with a chance for a meal and supplies. Historic **Santa Teresa's Catholic Church**, a National Historical Landmark, sits on the south slope above the road. Of greatest interest, perhaps, is **The Potter School**, now a private residence. Behind Santa Teresa's, on a side road across from **The Little Duck Antique Shop**, the Potter School catches the eye with its mildly odd appearance and interesting architectural highlights. No wonder Alfred Hitchcock used it in his film *The Birds*.

Fort Bragg—Easy to overlook because of its obvious status as Mendocino's ugly relative, Fort Bragg has two areas worth exploring. The somewhat scruffy Wharf area along the mouth of the Noyo River is often only glimpsed by people as they zoom over the bridge, but it offers great eating, boat trips, and loads of character. Drop down from the east side of CA 1 at the north end of the Noyo River Bridge. In the historic downtown area around North Main (CA 1) and Redwood, there are pleasant shops and cafés, several of which are located in restored historic buildings.

Gualala—This pleasant town lies north of Sea Ranch at the mouth of the Gualala River. A hundred years ago, the town was one of several up and down the coast that milled redwood and hauled it offshore to waiting schooners. Today, it's a charming, fast-growing hamlet of 500 or so that serves tourists and Sea Ranch residents.

FITNESS AND RECREATION

Tame and easy fun for the kids can be had at **Hagemann Ranch Trout Farm** just east of CA 1 between Bodega and Bodega Bay— watch for the sign. For $2 and up, you can catch lunch while the young ones hunt forfrogs. Pole rental is available, and picnicking is permitted. Open 9 a.m. to 6 p.m., Thursday through Monday, June through September, (707) 876-3217.

In Bodega Bay, **Wil's Fishing Adventures** on East Shore Road offers daily ocean fishing excursions for around $50, (707) 875-2323. The **Bodega Harbour Golf Links** offers beautiful ocean views on a "Scottish-style" course. Green fees are $35 to $45. Take Heron Drive, just south of Bodega Bay, (707) 875-3538. Beach and headlands hiking is possible from many access points along the Sonoma Coast.

Located in the Armstrong Redwoods State Reserve, **Armstrong Woods Pack Station** offers private and scheduled trail rides through the reserve and Austin Creek State Recreation Area that range from two hours to three days in length. Rides start at $40, (707) 887-2939.

With outlets in Fort Bragg and Van Damme State Park, **Lost Coast Adventures** offers sea kayaking and diving tours, as well as gear rental, 19275 South Harbor Drive, Fort Bragg, (707) 961-1143 or (800) 961-1143.

Catch-a-Canoe is a great place to rent canoes or kayaks for a paddle on Big River. They also rent mountain bikes and recommend routes on the thousand miles of bikeable roads in **Jackson State Forest**. Turn south on Comptche-Ukiah Road just south of the Big River Bridge below Mendocino, then left down the hill, (707) 937-0273 or (800) 320-2453.

From the wharf, along the north shore of the Noyo River in Fort Bragg, several companies offer charter and scheduled ocean fishing and whale watching trips. Try the **Noyo Bell**, (707) 964-3104, the **Tally Ho II**, (707) 964-2079, or **Trek II/Cavalier**, (707) 964-4550. Turn east at the north end of the Noyo River Bridge.

FOOD

Bodega Bay has the **Lucas Wharf Restaurant and Bar**, offering good seafood at tourist prices, 595 CA 1, (707) 875-3522. The **Sandpiper Dockside Café and Restaurant** is where you might go for $6 to $7 breakfasts if you lived here, as well as for salad and sandwich lunches and a wide dinner menu, 1410 Bay Flat Road, (707) 875-2278. The **Breakers Café** is darn good and more reasonable than the rest. How about Belgian waffles with hot spiced peaches and whipped cream for $6? They serve lunch and dinner too, 1400 CA 1, (707) 875-2513.

There are numerous dining options in the Russian River region. The **Blue Heron** in Duncans Mills has delicious entrées from $8 to

THE NORTH COAST

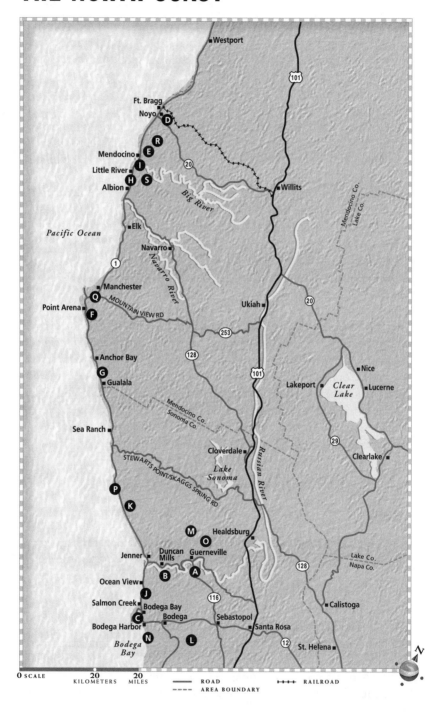

Westport

101

Ft. Bragg
Noyo ■ **D**

■ **R**
Mendocino ■ **E**
Little River ■ **I**
H **S**
Albion ■

20

Big River

Willits

Mendocino Co.
Lake Co.

Pacific Ocean

■ Elk

Navarro ■

1

Manchester ■ **Q**

Point Arena ■ **F**

MOUNTAIN VIEW RD

Ukiah ■

20

Navarro River

253

128

101

■ Anchor Bay

G
Gualala ■

Sea Ranch ■

Mendocino Co.
Sonoma Co.

Lakeport ■

Clear Lake

Nice ■

Lucerne ■

29

Cloverdale ■

Lake Sonoma

Clearlake ■

STEWARTS POINT/SKAGGS SPRING RD

Russian River

P

K

M
O
Duncan Mills
Jenner ■ ■ Guerneville
B
A

Healdsburg ■

128

Lake Co.
Napa Co.

Ocean View ■

Salmon Creek ■
J
Bodega Bay
Bodega

116

Sebastopol ■

Calistoga ■

Bodega Harbor ■ **C**
N

Bodega Bay

L

Santa Rosa ■

12

St. Helena ■

N

0 SCALE 20 20
KILOMETERS MILES

ROAD
AREA BOUNDARY

+++ RAILROAD

Food

- **A** Applewood Restaurant
- **B** Blue Heron
- **C** Breakers Café
- **D** Carine's Fish Grotto
- **D** Gardens Grill
- **A** The Hiding Place
- **C** Lucas Wharf Restaurant and Bar
- **E** McCallum House
- **E** Mendocino Bakery and Café
- **D** North Coast Brewing Company Tap Room and Grill
- **F** Pangaea Café
- **C** Sandpiper Dockside Café and Restaurant
- **G** St. Orres Restaurant

Lodging

- **H** Andiron Lodge
- **A** The Applewood Inn
- **C** Bodega Harbor Inn
- **I** Brewery Gulch Inn
- **J** Chanslor Guest Ranch
- **F** Coast Guard House
- **D** Coast Motel
- **G** Gualala Hotel
- **C** The Inn at the Tides
- **E** McCallum House
- **E** Mendocino Hotel
- **K** Salt Point Lodge
- **G** St. Orres
- **K** Stillwater Cove Ranch
- **K** Timber Cove Inn
- **L** Valley Ford Hotel

Camping

- **M** Austin Creek State Recreation Area
- **J** Bodega Dunes
- **B** Casini Family Campground
- **N** Doran Regional Park
- **O** Faerie Ring Campground
- **P** Gerstle Cove
- **G** Gualala Point Regional Park Campground
- **D** MacKerricher State Park
- **Q** Manchester State Park
- **P** Ocean Cove Camping
- **R** Russian Gulch State Park
- **S** Van Damme State Park
- **P** Woodside

Note: Items with the same letter are located in the same town or area.

$20, including the house special of "Heronhouse Steamed Clam Feast," featuring a white wine and shallots broth. Go three-fourths of a mile east of downtown Guerneville on Main Street to reach **The Hiding Place** for a tasty meal on the deck overlooking the water. Good sandwich plates run from $6 to $9. Open for breakfast, lunch, and dinner. A must for fine dining is the **Applewood Restaurant** in the inn with the same name, on Hwy. 116 across the bridge from downtown Guerneville. Prix fixe dinners served Tuesday through Saturday, (707) 869-9093 for reservations.

The **St. Orres Restaurant** at the St. Orres Inn is one of the finest places to dine on the north coast—doubly nice if you have a room at the inn to walk back to after dinner. The North Coast-style, French country cuisine features amazing wild game recipes. Reserve in advance (even if you're an inn guest!), 36601 CA 1 (2 miles north of Gualala), (707) 884-3303.

In Point Arena, try the **Pangaea Café** for a tasty meal, entrées $13 to $18, (707) 882-3001.

Mendocino has enough options to keep you busy for a few days. A stop at the **Mendocino Bakery and Café**, 10485 Lansing Street, seems like the right thing to do. It's friendly, reasonable, and just plain pleasant, (707) 937-0836. For fancy fare, the historic **McCallum House** blends traditional and California cuisines with great success. Entrées run from $15 to $20, 45020 Albion Street, (707) 937-5763.

The **Gardens Grill** overlooks the beautiful Mendocino Coast Botanical Gardens at the south end of Fort Bragg on CA 1. Dinner entrées range from $10 to $18, 18220 CA 1, (707) 964-7474. From the north end of the bridge over the Noyo River in Fort Bragg, head east and down to the wharf for a huge and tasty seafood dinner at **Carine's Fish Grotto**. Grace Carine herself may guide you through the feast, (707) 964-2429. The **North Coast Brewing Company Tap Room and Grill**, 444 Main Street, has great microbrews and better-than-pub-grub food, (707) 964-3400.

LODGING

The North Coast has lots of romantic getaway inns and B&Bs, most hoping that you leave the kids at home. If you're particularly interested in this type of lodging, consult a B&B or country inn guide like those noted in "Recommended Reading." Options that have particular charm, character, or historic interest are listed below, as are budget and family friendly choices. One thing that *all* North

Coast lodging and camping options have in common is that they are booked solid on summer weekends! Make reservations if your schedule calls for it.

In Valley Ford, the **Valley Ford Hotel**, built in 1864, offers charming rooms for $70 to $90 in a ranch country setting. At dinner, served Friday through Sunday, a locally renowned Basque White Bean Soup is featured, 14415 CA 1, (707) 876-3600 or (800) 696-6679.

A good budget option in Bodega Bay is the **Bodega Harbor Inn** with motel rooms from $50 to $70, 1345 Bodega Avenue (one block above CA 1), (707) 875-3594. **The Inn at the Tides** offers several buildings that climb the hills above the harbor, separated by landscaped walks and lawns. Plenty of luxury at $125 to $230 per room, 800 CA 1, (707) 875-2751 or (800) 541-7788.

North of Bodega Bay on CA 1 is the family-oriented **Chanslor Guest Ranch**, offering lodging, guided horseback rides, hiking, fishing, and more on a 700-acre spread. There's even a petting zoo for the kids. Rooms start at $60, 2660 CA 1, (707) 875-2721.

The lower Russian River Valley has many lodging options. Elegant but friendly, **The Applewood Inn** is one of the area's finest. Built in 1922 as a private home, the inn has nine rooms with woodsy or vineyard views. A full breakfast is served to inn guests only. Pricey but worth it, 13555 Highway 116 (1 mile south of Guerneville), (707) 869-9093.

Once a school for boys, **Stillwater Cove Ranch** is a unique and inexpensive option located just south of Salt Point State Park. Peacocks strut through the rustic grounds of this working farm, shrieking whenever the mood takes them (including, sometimes, at night). There are cottages and a small bunkhouse for groups up to eight, $30 to $70, 22555 CA 1, (707) 847-3227.

Just 17 miles north of Jenner, the **Salt Point Lodge** offers reasonable North Coast rates and family friendly accommodations. Set above the highway, just south of Salt Point Park, there are gardens and a small playground, $50 to $107, 23255 CA 1, (800) 956-3437. The **Timber Cove Inn** is worth a stay for its lofty lobby, Japanese pond, and knoll-top obelisk. What makes it truly outstanding is its location on a ragged coastal headland with exclusive trails. Rooms start at $78, but climb quickly toward $350, 21780 CA 1 (north of Fort Ross State Historical Park), (707) 847-3231 or (800) 987-8319.

For a taste of history, try the **Gualala Hotel** in central Gualala. Built in 1903, it features shared-bath rooms for only $44. Private bath, ocean view rooms are $55 to $65. The "logging bar" retains all the charm that made Jack London a frequent visitor, (707) 884-3441. One of the best known inns on the coast, **St. Orres** is uniquely styled like a Russian dacha with onion-shaped domes. Rooms are reasonable at $90 to $180, and breakfast is included, 36601 CA 1 (two miles north of Gualala), (707) 884-3303.

Just south of central Point Arena, Port Road follows Point Arena Creek to the ocean. There you'll find the **Coast Guard House**. Long used by the Coast Guard as a base for life-saving operations, it is now a friendly and historic B&B. Scooter the dog greets you when you arrive, 695 Arena Cove, Point Arena, (707) 882-2442.

The **Andiron Lodge** in Albion has no-frills, family friendly cottages above the road with rooms from $45 to $60, and cabins (sleep four) from $100 to $125, (707) 937-1543.

In the fields east of the highway, Ann and her dog Ben keep the wonderful **Brewery Gulch Inn**, a small B&B in an 1860s farmhouse. The charming gardens and grounds will make you sigh, 9350 CA 1, south of Mendocino, (707) 937-4752.

The **Mendocino Hotel**, built in 1878 sits right on Main Street overlooking the headlands and Mendocino Bay. Shared-bath rooms start at $55 and private bath at $75—a bargain, 45080 Main Street, (707) 937-0511 or (800) 548-0513. The classy, Victorian **McCallum House** has a variety of rooms and a couple for as low as $75, 45020 Albion Street, (707) 937-0289.

Fort Bragg has a real "motel row" at the south end of town. You *might* even find a vacancy sign still out on a Saturday afternoon in July. The **Coast Motel** is okay and one of the cheapest in the region with rooms from about $40, 18661 CA 1, a mile south of the river, (707) 964-2852 or (800) 280-2852.

CAMPING

The top camping choices on the North Coast are the beautiful California State Park campgrounds. Always in prime locations, state park sites are usually well designed and maintained, in addition to being spacious and relatively private. Most have coin showers. About half the parks can accommodate trailers or motor homes over 30 feet, though only a handful have hookups. All the campgrounds have clearly marked entrances along the Coast Highway. Call (800) 444-7275 to make reservations or to get a brochure describing all park facilities. The parks with developed campgrounds are listed below, from south to north.

- **Bodega Dunes** at Sonoma Coast State Beaches, just north of Bodega Bay—$12 to $16, (707) 875-3483.
- **Gerstle Cove** at Salt Point State Park—$12 to $16, (707) 847-3221.
- **Woodside** at Salt Point State Park—$12 to $16 (walk-ins $10 to $14), (707) 847-3221.
- **Manchester State Park**, 5 miles north of Point Arena—$7 to $9 (hike-ins $2), primitive sites, no reservations, (707) 937-5804.
- **Van Damme State Park**, 3 miles south of Mendocino—$12 to $16 (some sites for self-contained vehicles on the water, regular camping above the highway), (707) 937-5804.
- **Russian Gulch State Park**, just north of Mendocino—$12 to $16, (707) 937-5804.
- **MacKerricher State Park**, north of Fort Bragg—$12 to $16, (707) 937-5804.

In Bodega Bay, **Doran Regional Park** has pretty good sites on the open, sandy spit that separates Bodega Bay from Bodega Harbor. There's a good beach and hiking trails. Take Doran Beach Road where CA 1 meets the coast south of town.

A few miles from the coast on Hwy. 116, **Casini Family Campground** has 225 sites on a 120-acre spread with a long river frontage. Sites range from spacious, private tent sites to RV pull-throughs with hookups. There are a store and recreation hall, canoe rental, fishing, a duck pond, playgrounds, river beaches, and Saturday night hayrides. It's a great family choice, $17 to $24, (800) 451-8400.

There are 24 sites at Bull Frog Pond in **Austin Creek State Recreation Area** at the end of the Armstrong Woods Road north of Guerneville, $10, (707) 869-2015. **Faerie Ring Campground** has 44 sites in a lovely setting, 1½ miles north of Guerneville on the Armstrong Woods Road. The campground features several "faerie rings," that is, circles of redwood trees that sometimes sprout up around the site of the dead "mother" tree. Tents can actually be placed within the rings at a couple of sites, $20 to $25, (707) 869-2746.

At $12 per vehicle with no charges for extra people, **Ocean Cove Camping** is a good budget option. Over 100 sites are scattered across low hills, including several at bluff's edge on the ocean. The campground is active with families, fisher folk, and abalone divers (in season), 23125 CA 1, (707) 847-3422.

Gualala Point Regional Park Campground has very nice sites in the redwoods along the Gualala River. Access to the river mouth is across the road. The entrance is south of the river, $14, (707) 785-2377.

9

THE REDWOOD PARKS

North of Mendocino, CA 1 ends and U.S. 101 becomes the sole coastal route. A freeway most of the way, it follows the course of the Eel River to Eureka, then continues up the coast to Oregon. U.S. 101 passes through a region known to as the "Redwood Empire." As you look out at the thick carpet of green that drapes the hills, you're seeing American decks and fences and resources for export.

The largest remaining groves of old-growth redwoods in the world are protected in park lands along U.S. 101. Humboldt Redwoods State Park lies south of Eureka, while the jointly administered Redwood National and State Parks are to the north. If your travels will take you as far north as Mendocino, driving an extra 110 miles to see the largest of all old-growth groves in Humboldt Redwoods is worth it. For the loveliest groves, you'll have to make your way to the northern parks where a healthy remnant of past splendor still grows almost to the ocean's edge.

California's fabled "Lost Coast" is the only significant stretch of the state without a shoreline highway. It lies west of U.S. 101, between Rockport to the south and Ferndale to the north. Access to the coastline here is time-consuming, but the rewards are many. The Lost Coast may no longer be lost, but it's still reluctant to be found.

Other attractions exist on the upper North Coast, and almost all are a stone's throw from U.S. 101. You'll notice a shift from the "California lifestyle" to one that is distinctly Pacific Northwestern. Everything from attitudes to art will reflect the difference. ◙

THE REDWOOD PARKS

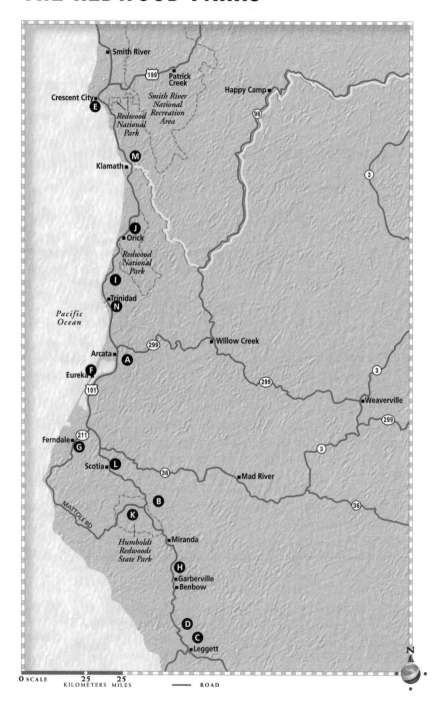

Smith River

199 Patrick Creek

Happy Camp

Crescent City
E

96

Redwood National Park

Smith River National Recreation Area

3

M

Klamath

J
Orick

Redwood National Park

I

Trinidad
N

Pacific Ocean

299 Willow Creek

Arcata
A

299

3

Eureka
F

101

299

Weaverville

Ferndale
211
G

3

Scotia
L

36

Mad River

36

MATTOLE RD

B

K

Humboldt Redwoods State Park

Miranda

H
Garberville
Benbow

D

C
Leggett

N

0 SCALE   25   25
KILOMETERS   MILES   ROAD

Sightseeing Highlights

Ⓐ Arcata

Ⓑ Avenue of the Giants

Ⓒ Chandelier Tree

Ⓓ Confusion Hill

Ⓔ Crescent City

Ⓕ Eureka

Ⓖ Ferndale

Ⓗ Garberville

Ⓘ Patrick's Point State Park

Ⓙ Redwood National and State Parks

Ⓚ Rockefeller Forest and Humboldt Redwoods State Park

Ⓛ Scotia

Ⓜ Trees of Mystery

Ⓝ Trinidad

A PERFECT DAY IN THE REDWOODS

Leave your campsite early at Gold Bluffs Beach to be the first one to
the Fern Canyon Trailhead. Relish a hike through the canyon and
onward to the mist-shrouded, primeval groves. Drive south to Patrick's
Point State Park for a short headlands walk, a picnic lunch, and some
beachcombing on aptly named Agate Beach. If you're in a people
mood, pick a sight or two from the list in Trinidad, Arcata, and Eureka.
Your hotel room awaits in Ferndale, or perhaps it's a campsite at the
mouth of the Mattole River near Petrolia. You'll fall asleep convinced
you need another day for the upper North Coast.

THE REDWOOD EMPIRE

Less than four percent of the old-growth trees from the western coastal forests still stand, and the redwoods have been as hard hit as any. Where are the remaining trees? Over 90 percent of those that are left are protected, most in parks, yet even park boundaries are deceiving. Most of the land in the North Coast's dedicated redwood parks was logged in this century. When you look at the parks on your map, less than a third of what you see has virgin forest. The rest of the old growth—and that of virtually all the sprawling private timberlands of the Redwood Empire—is gone.

The battle lines have been drawn, but there really is no compromise. Either you cut them, or you don't. Enjoy the splendor of the remaining groves. They are all the more amazing for their rarity.

SIGHTSEEING HIGHLIGHTS

★★★ **Humboldt Redwoods State Park and Rockefeller Forest**—About 50 miles south of Eureka, Humboldt Redwoods preserves over 17,000 acres of old growth, including the 10,000-acre **Rockefeller Forest**, which is the largest contiguous tract of virgin redwoods in the world.

Bull Creek runs through the heart of the forest, paralleling the Mattole road about a half mile to the south. The **Bull Creek Trail** is easily accessible from the road at **Bull Creek Flats**, where the creek meets the Eel River, and also 4 miles upstream at the sites of **Flat Iron Tree** and **Giant Tree**. Loop hikes of varying length can be designed using the trail map in the park brochure. Plan on more time than the mileage indicates. You will find yourself drawn to a quiet spot among the great sentinels for some moments of quiet reverence. To reach the forest from U.S. 101 or the Avenue of the Giants, take the Mattole Road west into the park interior.

In the southern end of the park, the Avenue of the Giants is particularly nice because it runs between the freeway and the river. Lovely riverside groves offer good short walks undisturbed by traffic noise. Details: Located on CA 101, north of Leggett; (707) 488-2041.

★★★ **Redwood National and State Parks**—Between Eureka and Crescent City, an almost continuous band of jointly managed federal and state land preserves the finest remaining examples of several old-growth redwood ecosystems: **Redwood National Park, Prairie Creek Redwoods State Park, Del Norte Redwoods State Park**, and **Jedediah Smith Redwoods State Park**. Together with the **Smith River National Recreation Area**, they offer the traveler numerous recreational opportunities.

In the main body of Redwood National Park, only about 20 percent of the trees are old growth, but two areas deserve special note. There is a pleasant, 1-mile loop trail through the impressive **Lady Bird Johnson Grove**. Take Bald Hills Road (no trailers or large RVs) 2½ miles to the parking area. For the trailhead of the 8½-mile path along Redwood Creek to the **Tall Trees Grove**, take a right to the picnic area just after you turn onto Bald Hills Road. The easier route to see the grove is via a shuttle bus and guided ranger tour, or by getting one of 35 free daily car permits to drive down the shuttle road. Permits and tours are arranged at the Redwood Information Center a mile south of Orick.

One of the nicest parks is Prarie Creek Redwoods, practically the only place where ancient redwoods grow down almost to the Pacific. Old Hwy. 101, now **Newton B. Drury Scenic Parkway**, provides a lightly traveled pathway through a very large stand of old growth along Prarie Creek. Several trails head deep into the groves and to the ocean. The short **Cal-Barrel Road** (no trailers or large RVs) offers a vehicular dip into solitude. Winding, 8-mile **Davison Road** (no trailers or large RVs) leads to the low dunes of **Gold Bluffs Beach**. Roosevelt elk browse between the base of the bluffs and the dunes. The road ends at the trailhead for mystical **Fern Canyon** where tiny waterfalls drip down the 70-foot, fern-covered canyon walls. Connecting trails lead to the old-growth stands, as well as up and down the coast.

Howland Hills Road in **Jedediah Smith State Park** is a great route through a fine old-growth forest. Take Elk Valley Road from the south end of Crescent City. It connects to U.S. 199. There is no fee to drive through the redwood parks, though a $5/day use fee is charged for Gold Bluffs Beach and Fern Canyon. Call (707) 822-7611 for information.

☆☆ **Avenue of the Giants**—Whether you're approaching Humboldt Redwoods State Park from the north or south, leave U.S. 101 and drive the 30-mile long Avenue of the Giants, a segment of the old Highway 101 that passes through several fine redwood groves. Stop at one of many turnouts for a dip in the pleasant waters of the Eel River. Watch for egrets wading in the shallows. Enjoy the groves as you go, but save your hiking time for the Rockefeller Forest.

The central segment of the Avenue of the Giants is the best, passing through a continuous corridor of public land between the freeway and the Eel River. Enjoy the tunnel of green and the river vistas on your way to the junction with Mattole Road and access to the park's interior. Watch for exit signs on U.S. 101 between Leggett and Scotia.

★★ **Patrick's Point State Park**—This small and wonderful coastal park features a 2-mile headlands hike with interesting rock formations, some fine tide pools, a replica of a Yurok Indian village to explore, and good whale watching in season. Ocean-polished agates can indeed be found along **Agate Beach**. Hike to **Wedding Rock** for that rugged, coast feel. There are three nice campgrounds. Details: Located 5 miles north of Trinidad on U.S. 101; (707) 677-3570; open daily from dawn to dusk. As with most California state parks, there is a day use fee of $5. (3 hours)

★ **Crescent City**—In the early morning of March 28, 1964, the most powerful earthquake ever recorded in North America struck in Alaska, devastating parts of Anchorage and several smaller communities. Several hours later, four tsunamis (or tidal waves), each progressively larger, struck Crescent City. Half of this town of 9000 was washed away. Fourteen people were killed or never found. It doesn't take too sharp an eye to find evidence of the disaster in the current layout and architectural variation of the town.

For photographic insights into this event, as well as good displays on many aspects of the region's heritage, visit the **Del Norte Historical Society Museum**. Details: 577 H Street; Crescent City; (707) 464-9533; open Monday through Saturday, May to September. Admission is $1.50. (45 minutes)

The **Battery Point Lighthouse** can be reached across a walkway at low tide. Now a museum, tours are available. Details: Located at the end of A Street on Battery Point Island; (707) 464-3089; tour given Wednesday through Sunday from 10 a.m. to 4 p.m., April through September. Admission is $2. (½ hour)

★ **Eureka**—As the state's largest port city north of San Francisco, Eureka is the site of commercial activity and the unattractive industrial sprawl that goes along with it. Look past the blight until U.S. 101 splits into Fourth Street and Fifth Street as it passes through downtown. Head down to Second and Third, between C Street and M Street, to reach the almost successful Victorian renaissance **Old Town**. While there, don't miss a look at the **Carson Mansion** at Second and M Street, one of the most ornate Victorian structures to be found anywhere. You can't go inside unless you manage to be invited as a guest of "Ingomar," the resident men's club.

If you visit the rich collection at the **Humboldt Bay Maritime Museum**, ask for Bill, the 80+-year-old who has all the answers. Details: 1410 Second Street, behind the new library, Eureka; (707) 444-9440; open daily from 11 a.m. to 4 p.m. Admission is free. (45 minutes)

Consider a visit to the **Clarke Memorial Museum** for a look at American Indian history and regional heritage artifacts. Details: 240 East Street, Eureka; (707) 443-1947; open Tuesday through Saturday from noon to 4 p.m. Admission is free. (45 minutes)

Try a guided, one-and-a-half-hour cruise on the *Madaket* to see the sights on Humboldt Bay. The *Madaket* is the oldest boat in continuous service on the Pacific Coast. Details: Located where C Street meets Humboldt Bay below 1st Street; (707) 445-1910 for schedule and reservations; tours are available from May through October. Admission is $9. (1½ hours)

Fort Humboldt State Historic Park preserves the site of Fort Humboldt, which served as a base to suppress Indian activity in the area. There is a good museum of logging and Native American history, as well as an excellent walk-through, outdoor logging history exhibit. Details: At the south end of Eureka, turn east on Highland Avenue, then left into the park, Eureka; (707) 445-6567; open daily from 9 a.m. to 5 p.m. Admission is free. (1 hour)

Several diversions offer themselves to travelers in the vicinity of Eureka and Arcata. Bird watching is good in the estuarine and sheltered inlet environments of the **Eel River Wildlife Area** and **Humboldt Bay National Wildlife Refuge** south of Eureka, or the **Mad River Slough and Dunes** north of Arcata. Enjoy the sands at **Samoa Dunes Recreation Area** as you watch the boat traffic flow in and out of Humboldt Bay. If you're here in the spring, walk the short loop path through the stunning blooms at the small **Azalea State Reserve**, 1 mile east of U.S. 101 on CA 200, the southernmost McKinleyville exit.

✯ **Arcata**—Take the CA 255, Samoa Boulevard exit west from U.S. 101 to reach the home of **Humboldt State University**. Arcata provides a somewhat liberal counterpoint to Eureka's conservative, resource-harvest economics. The **Arcata Plaza**, a large square at G Street and Ninth Street, is the heart of the town and worth a look. The Chamber of Commerce, two blocks from the plaza, provides information and

walking tour maps. Details: 1062 G Street, (707) 822-3619; open
Monday to Friday from 10 a.m. to 4 p.m.; Saturday, 9 a.m. to 3 p.m.
	The people of Arcata own 600 acres of second-growth redwood in
the **Arcata Community Forest**. Ten miles of roads and paths are open
for hiking and biking. The **Historic Logging Trail** features displays
on historic logging practices. A forest management plan allows for the
harvesting of trees while protecting watershed and habitat. Revenue
from timber sales supports park and recreation projects in the community. Access is through Redwood Park at the east end of 14th Street. At
the bottom of I Street, the **Arcata Marsh** is a good spot for bird
watching. Details: Located at 600 South G Street; (707) 826-2359;
open Monday to Friday from 1 p.m. to 5 p.m.; weekends, 11a.m. to 5 p.m.

✭ **Ferndale**—The town of Ferndale, 5 miles west of the Fernbridge
exit on U.S. 101, anchors a large dairy farming region. So many
Victorian buildings of historic importance clutter the town center that
all of Main Street was dedicated as an historic landmark. It's worth a
look, though the current commercial emphasis on tourism has made it
easier to find frozen yogurt than bulk beans and hardtack. Details:
Take the Fernbridge exit from U.S. 101 and follow CA 211 for 5 miles.

✭ **Garberville**—Much of California's "sinsemilla" marijuana is grown
in Humboldt County. As the area's main town, Garberville has become
renowned as the home of a hidden culture of pot growth and distribu-
tion. Two decades ago, the town was alive with the trappings of the
marijuana subculture. Today, growers have become very savvy indeed.
It's fun to guess who might be in the business, and who might work for
the D.E.A. Drive through town for a bite and a peek. Details: Located
on U.S. 101 between Leggett and Humboldt Redwoods State Park.

✭ **Scotia**—As a shock to the system and a study in contrasts, stop several miles north of the Humboldt Redwoods in the town of Scotia to
see the **Pacific Lumber Company Mill**—the largest sawmill in the
world. Scotia is the last of the once common "company towns," owned
in its entirety by Pacific Lumber. Every structure in town is built
entirely of redwood. Mill workers and their families rent the uniformly
designed and flawlessly maintained homes at low rates. The company
provides some of the best wages, benefits, and pensions in the industry.
	Details: The mill entrance is on Scotia's one main street so you
can't get lost. Call (707) 764-2222 for information. Free, self-guided

tours of the mill last about an hour. Get a permit at the museum across Main Street from the company headquarters (skip the museum unless you're into company history). Show up at the entrance gate to begin the tour between 7:30 a.m. and 10 a.m., or between 11:30 a.m. and 1:30 p.m. The mill shuts down completely from 11 a.m. to 11:30 a.m. and at 2:30 p.m. for the day. (1½ hours)

✴ **Trinidad**—This is one of the more pleasant and relaxing towns on the upper North Coast. A lovely beach curves away to the south along Trinidad Bay. Enjoy a bite at the wharf or a walk around **Trinidad Head**. The small headland is connected by a short, narrow neck of land to the broader shelf where the town is located. A loop trail goes around the head, though the trailhead is awkward at the beginning where a block of private land forces a detour. Trinidad Head Lighthouse is closed to visitors.

The Yurok Indian village of Tsurai existed for hundreds of years on the shores of Trinidad Harbor, below the present day location of the **Trinidad Memorial Lighthouse**—a scaled-down mockup of the real thing on Edwards Street at Trinity Street. Drive down to **Trinidad State Beach** for some beachcombing. Details: Located 12 miles north of Arcata from the Trinidad exit off U.S. 101.

Chandelier Tree—If you want to drive through a living redwood tree, here's your chance. Details: Follow the "Drive-Thru Tree" road signs near Leggett; (707) 925-6363. The cost is $3 per vehicle (6'8" limit on vehicle height).

Confusion Hill—Your kids will swear that gravity doesn't work here. You might have your doubts too. It's a hokey attraction, but . . . you never know! Details: It's 9 miles north of Leggett on U.S. 101; (707) 925-6456; open daily from 10 a.m. to 5 p.m. Admission is $3. (½ hour)

Trees of Mystery—Just north of Klamath and Requa on U.S. 101, you'll pass Trees of Mystery, an attraction more famous, perhaps, for its bumper stickers than for anything else. Featured are a gift shop, the **"End of the Trail" Indian Museum**, a nature walk with mildly interesting redwood sights, and giant statues of Paul Bunyan and Babe the Blue Ox. Kids will like the statues and the hype, and the museum is perhaps worth a stop. Details: Just north of Klamath and Requa on U.S. 101; (707) 482-2251; open daily from dawn to dusk. (1 hour)

FITNESS AND RECREATION

There are over a hundred miles of trails in **Humboldt Redwoods State Park**, many of which are open to cyclists (no single track). The 5-mile **Bull Creek Flats Trail** follows Bull Creek and accesses the larger trees. It's an easy walk, though the logical return loop runs close to the Mattole Road on the north side of the creek. Several loops and overnights that climb to the ridges are possible, including a good 12-mile bike loop to **Grasshopper Peak and Fire Lookout**. Trailheads are along the Mattole Road.

The 24-mile **Lost Coast Trail** is good for a three-day or a long two-day backpack. Hike south from the mouth of the Mattole River (Lighthouse Road from the Mattole Road, south of the bridge into Petrolia) so that the often strong wind is likely to be at your back. The trail ends in Shelter Cove. For a great seven-mile loop, hike as far as the abandoned **Punta Gorda Lighthouse**, then return via the bluffs by following the old lighthouse access road that climbs up near the tiny cluster of cabins north of the light. Watch out for poison oak!

In **Redwood National Park**, the moderately easy, 8½-mile **Redwood Creek Trail** runs from the **Tall Trees Grove** to a picnic area near the base of Bald Creek Road. Loops are awkward but possible. A park shuttle can get you to Tall Trees for a one-way, downhill walk. A half mile north of the Bald Creek Road junction, on U.S. 101, are a picnic area and trailhead for the **Coastal Trail**. A great two-day hike will take you through old growth and down to **Gold Bluffs Beach** in **Prairie Creek Redwoods State Park** for the night. In the morning, head up through **Fern Canyon** and back to the road for a hitch to your car. Great day hike loops are possible from Fern Canyon.

There's a bikeable segment of the **Coastal Trail** through old growth in **Del Norte Redwoods State Park**. Look for the trailhead on the west side of U.S. 101, about 2 miles north of the overlook, near the park's south end. A beautiful loop circles the **Mill Creek Campground** and access road to the north.

Jedediah Smith Redwoods State Park has great old growth walks from trailheads on U.S. 199 and the narrow Howland Hill Road.

Smith River National Recreation Area has good opportunities for fishing, canoeing, rafting, and kayaking.

FOOD

You'll shake your head and wonder what the marvelous **Benbow Inn** is doing in the middle of nowhere, but you'll be glad it's here. It's a fine dining oasis in the wilderness, 445 Lake Benbow Drive, take the Benbow exit from U.S. 101, (707) 923-2124.

The **Woodrose Café** in Garberville is *the* place to go for a fine breakfast or lunch. Sandwiches and pasta plates are in the $4 to $7 range, 911 Redwood Drive, (707) 923-3191.

Don't miss the **Samoa Cookhouse** in Eureka. Breakfast, lunch, and dinner are served up family-style, all-you-can-eat American fare at long tables—and it's good! It's on the way to Samoa Dunes across the CA 255 bridge, (707) 442-1659. **Tomaso's Tomato Pies** has fantastic pizzas, calzones, and other Italian standards, 2120 Fourth Street, (707) 444-3318. Splurge on the unbelievable breakfast buffet at the **Hotel Carter**, 301 L Street, (707) 444-8062.

In Arcata, fine dining with a fresh face is available at the excellent and always crowded **Folie Douce**, 1551 G Street, (707) 822-1042. The **Humboldt Brewing Company** is the pub grub brewpub in town. The beers are very tasty, 956 Tenth Street, (707) 826-2739. About the only bohemian oasis on the hard-working upper North Coast is the **Café Mokka Coffeehouse**, on J Street at Fifth. They have live folk music on the weekends, (707) 822-2228.

At the harbor in Trinidad, the **Seascape Restaurant** offers okay seafood in a great location, (707) 677-3862. Better fare is available at the **Larrupin' Café** at 1658 Patrick's Point Drive, north of town, (707) 677-0230.

LODGING

About 3 miles north of Leggett, on U.S. 101, the **Bell Glen B&B** and **Eel River Redwood Hostel** make a wonderful oasis in the woods. The various B&B cabins range from $95 to $130, while the friendly, Euro-style hostel has bunks for only $15 and a free, do-it-yourself breakfast! The ten-acre, redwood-dotted grounds feature lovely paths, an all-night sauna, and a jacuzzi. There's an English-style pub, a restaurant, free use of bikes, and even a heated swimming hole in the river (in season)! Gene and Sandra Bennett are the excellent keepers, 70400 U.S. 101, (707) 925-6425.

THE REDWOOD PARKS

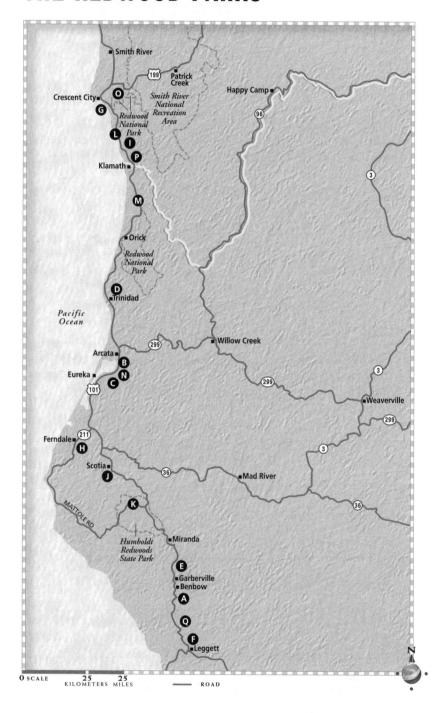

Food

- **A** Benbow Inn
- **B** Café Mokka Coffeehouse
- **B** Folie Douce
- **C** Hotel Carter
- **B** Humboldt Brewing Company
- **D** Larrupin' Café
- **C** Samoa Cookhouse
- **D** Seascape Restaurant
- **C** Tomaso's Tomato Pies
- **E** Woodrose Café

Lodging

- **F** Bell Glen B&B
- **A** Benbow Inn
- **G** Crescent Beach Motel
- **C** Downtowner Motel
- **F** Eel River Redwood Hostel
- **C** Eureka Inn
- **H** Francis Creek Inn
- **B** Hotel Arcata
- **I** Redwood National Park Hostel
- **J** Scotia Inn
- **H** Victorian Inn

Camping

- **K** Albee Creek Campground
- **A** Benbow Lake State Recreation Area
- **L** Del Norte Redwoods State Park
- **M** Elk Prairie Campground
- **N** Eureka KOA
- **M** Gold Bluffs Beach Campground
- **K** Humboldt Redwoods State Park
- **O** Jedediah Smith Redwoods State Park
- **P** Mystic Forest RV Park
- **D** Patrick's Point State Park
- **Q** Richardson Grove State Park
- **F** Standish-Hickey State Recreation Area

Note: Items with the same letter are located in the same town or area.

Take the Benbow exit from U.S. 101 to reach the **Benbow Inn**, a grand edifice that seems splendidly out of place. This historical landmark has rooms for $115 to $295. Visit this palace even if you can't stay, 445 Lake Benbow Drive, (707) 923-2124.

In the Pacific Lumber company town of Scotia, the **Scotia Inn** offers quite an illusion to the visitor. It appears to be quite large, but only ten of the many rooms are open. Other wings and floors are collecting dust. Still, the available rooms, lobby, and restaurant are excellent. Rooms run from $60 (a bargain) to $165, Main Street and Mill Street, (707) 764-5683.

Another fine old hotel is the **Victorian Inn** at 400 Main Street in Ferndale. The ornate Victorian exterior can't be missed as you walk through town. Rooms are $85 to $125, (707) 725-9686. More reasonable is the **Francis Creek Inn** with nice rooms and a morning danish for $55, 577 Main Street, (707) 786-9611.

Most of the chain motels are represented in Eureka, right along U.S. 101. Use the numbers on the Resources page to contact them. In the center of town, the **Eureka Inn** is a fine, English Tudor style, historic landmark hotel with a player grand piano gracing the elegant lobby. Rooms start at a surprisingly low $85 and range upward to $200. The inn is famous for its Christmas displays, 518 Seventh Street, (707) 442-6441 or (800) 862-4906. A nice budget choice is the **Downtowner Motel**, 424 Eighth Street. Rooms are $40 to $50, pool and sauna available, (707) 443-5061.

Several chain outlets are available on the outskirts of Arcata. In town, the **Hotel Arcata**, an historical landmark on the square, is dignified in a humble way. Rooms run from $60 to $100, 708 Ninth Street, (707) 826-0217 or (800) 344-1221.

Near the south end of Del Norte Redwoods, the **Redwood National Park Hostel** has beds for $10 to $12, and they're often booked in advance. There are curfews and checkout rules, 14480 U.S. 101 (entrance on Wilson Creek Road), (707) 482-8265.

Crescent City is also blessed with chain motels and wannabes. The **Crescent Beach Motel** is on the beach along U.S. 101 south of town. Rooms are $50 to $60, 1455 U.S. 101 South, (707) 464-5436.

CAMPING

Standish-Hickey State Recreation Area has nice sites for $12 to $16. The park features great Eel River access and hiking trails to small redwood groves, (707) 925-6482 for information, (800) 444-7275 for reservations.

Further north, **Richardson Grove State Park** has two campgrounds with $12 to $16 sites. This 1,300-acre park offers fishing and swimming in the Eel, as well as grove walks, (707) 247-3318 for information, (800) 444-7275 for reservations.

Benbow Lake State Recreation Area has waterside and other open sites for $12 to $16. Take the Benbow exit from U.S. 101, (707) 247-3318 for information, (800) 444-7275 for reservations. A nine-hole golf course is nearby.

There are four campgrounds in **Humboldt Redwoods State Park**, each with sites for $12 to $16. They're all good, but the **Albee Creek Campground** is the most remote, (707) 946-2409 for information, (800) 444-7275 for reservations.

Between Eureka and Arcata, the **Eureka KOA** has typical sites for $18 to $25, 4050 North U.S. 101, (707) 822-4243 or (800) 562-5754.

Several private campgrounds and RV parks are located on Patrick's Point Road between Trinidad and Patrick's Point. All are bearable except "Big D." **Patrick's Point State Park** has two campgrounds with great sites for $12 to $16, five miles north of Trinidad on U.S. 101, (707) 677-3570 for information, (800) 444-7275 for reservations.

There are many RV parks at the mouth of the Klamath River. One of the better ones is **Mystic Forest RV Park**, 15875 U.S. 101, (707) 482-4901. Several nice tent sites are isolated from the rest.

Only **Elk Prairie Campground** in Prarie Creek Redwoods State Park takes reservations. The wonderful **Gold Bluffs Beach Campground** has first-come, first-served primitive sites, but it is closed to trailers and large RVs, (707) 445-6547. **Del Norte Redwoods State Park** has sites for $12 to $16, (707) 464-9533, as does **Jedediah Smith State Park** on U.S. 199, (707) 464-9533. Call (800) 444-7275 for reservations at all three parks.

Scenic Route: The Mattole Road

A wonderful 80-mile detour from U.S. 101 connects the Humboldt Redwoods with the historic town of Ferndale, via the fabled Lost Coast. Follow the Mattole Road as it climbs through Rockefeller Forest. Enjoy the views of the Mattole Valley as you wind down to the riverside village of Honeydew.

Continue about 12 miles along the Mattole Valley. At the Lighthouse Road turnoff, just before the bridge into Petrolia, turn left to reach the mouth of the Mattole at the northern end of King Range National Conservation Area. Primitive camping is permitted. If time allows, hike the windy Lost Coast Trail for 3 miles south along the shore to the abandoned Punta Gorda Lighthouse. For spectacular views, return via the old road that climbs up onto the headlands just north of the lighthouse. Allow four hours for the hike—and watch out for poison oak!

Return to the Mattole Road and cross the river to Petrolia, named during the days when the valley produced oil. Continue to Cape Mendocino Lighthouse, enjoying the views before winding inland to the Eel River delta and Ferndale.

THE MATTOLE ROAD

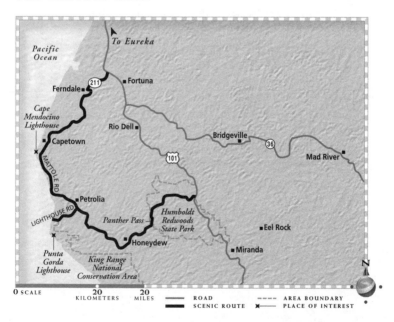

10
VOLCANOES

The Cascade Range extends from southern British Columbia, down through Washington and Oregon, and a hundred miles into Northern California. Throughout the range, volcanic peaks rise thousands of feet above what is otherwise a generally low range of mountains. California hosts two such volcanoes: Mount Shasta in the north and Mount Lassen at the range's southern tip.

Mount Shasta is a splendid, glacier-capped cone, visible for miles. At 14,162 feet, it is the second tallest volcano in the lower 48, only 250 feet shorter than Mount Rainier. A national forest wilderness protects its upper reaches, while some logging activity occurs on the lower slopes. The Mount Shasta Ski Park is high on a southern spur. Interstate 5 passes by to the west, crossing from the Upper Sacramento River Valley and over into the broad basin of Shasta Valley. The towns of Mount Shasta and Weed are on either side of the divide that separates the Central Valley from the Klamath River watershed.

Mount Lassen is very different from its perfect neighbor, 75 miles to the northwest. In 1915, the mountain blew its top, much as Mount St. Helens did in 1980. Now the broken peak reaches a mere 10, 457 feet in elevation. After the eruption, the area was made into a national park.

At the head of the Central Valley, the city of Redding hosts a superb recreational area. Whiskeytown, Shasta, and Trinity lakes offer boating, fishing, swimming, and camping. To the west, the peaks and valleys of Trinity Alps draw backpackers from throughout the region. Castle Crags south of Shasta is a favorite for rock climbers. ◣

VOLCANOES

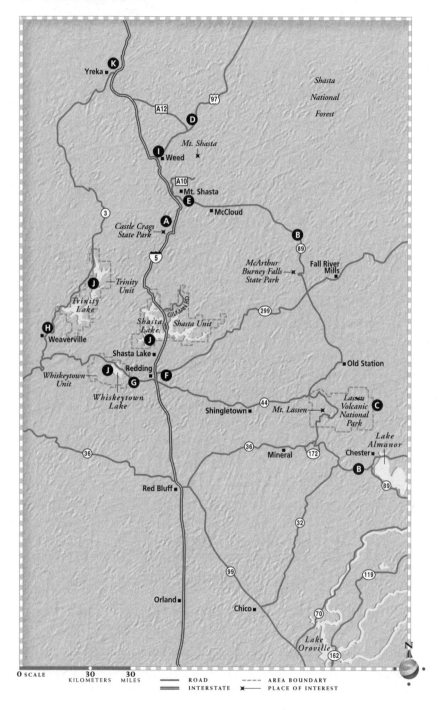

Sightseeing Highlights

Ⓐ Castle Crags State Park

Ⓑ Highway 89 South

Ⓒ Lassen Volcanic National Park

Ⓓ Living Memorial Sculpture Garden

Ⓔ Mount Shasta (town)

Ⓕ Redding

Ⓖ Shasta State Historic Park

Ⓗ Weaverville

Ⓘ Weed

Ⓙ Whiskeytown-Shasta-Trinity National Recreation Area

Ⓚ Yreka

A PERFECT DAY FROM SHASTA TO LASSEN

Enter Lassen Volcanic National Park from the south, stopping for a look and a sniff at the Sulfur Works. Near the pass, park at the trailhead and ascend 2,000 feet to Lassen's summit. Bask in the stunning panorama and explore the high ridge. After your descent, enjoy a picnic lunch at King's Creek or Lupine. Cruise north on CA 89, watching Mount Shasta loom ever larger in your view. From the town of Mount Shasta, take the Everitt Memorial Highway (A10) to Panther Meadows, high on Shasta's southern slopes. From here, prepare for your summit attempt, camp, or retreat to town for a hot shower and a cool drink.

SIGHTSEEING HIGHLIGHTS

★★★ **Lassen Volcanic National Park**—After several months of volcanic activity, Mount Lassen exploded in 1915, showering the region with ash and devastating several square miles of land in the blast zone.

Lassen's summit was shortened, and it's roughly conical shape was made much rougher. Today, Lassen is somewhat of a wonderland. Dwarfed trees grow in the recovering **Devastated Area**. Sulfurous mudpots and steaming springs bubble up in thermal areas. Pristine lakes share the forest with cinder cones. Relatively few visitors come here, both because it's off the beaten track and because CA 89, the main park road, can be closed by snow well into the summer.

Much of Lassen Volcanic National Park is designated as wilderness. Miles of trails criss-cross the forest, though access to the fragile soils and loose gravel around the peak is limited. A good trail climbs 2,000 vertical feet to the summit, affording a 360-degree panorama that can't be beat. Access is from the parking area close to the summit of the road. Another trail descends from near Lake Helen down to the thermal features of **Bumpus Hell**. If you can't do the hike, the **Sulfur Works** has many similar features. The **Summit Lake Campgrounds** are the nicest, though they're often closed until midsummer. Check out the early photos and other exhibits at the **Loomis Museum**. Details: Park information is available at (916) 595-4444. (all day)

★★ **Castle Crags State Park**—The park and adjacent **Castle Crags Wilderness** protect splendid granite cliffs and pinnacles. Climbers and hikers alike enjoy formations that resemble those of Yosemite. The **Pacific Crest Trail** passes through on its way from Mexico to Canada. Take the Castle Crags exit to reach a viewpoint and trailheads. Other views are had from the north. Try the Mount Bradley Lookout Road, the second exit north of the state park exit. Details: For park information, call (916) 235-2684. (1½ hours)

★★ **Living Memorial Sculpture Garden**—Next to U.S. 97, 13 miles east of Weed, is a remarkable collection of sculpture dedicated to " . . . all the veterans of all conflicts that the United States has been involved in." Created by Vietnam veteran Dennis Smith, sculptures such as *Coming Home, The Peaceful Warrior,* and *The Refugees* offer windows into core issues of war and peace. Spread across an acre or so of open land, the garden features open vistas of Mount Shasta. Careful placement of sculptures, paths, and viewing benches enhances the perspective of relationships between various themes. The Living Memorial Sculpture Garden is a "must see" for anyone driving U.S. 97 with a half hour to spare. Look for the large turnout and entrance about 1 mile east of the junction of U.S. 97 and A12.

✷ **Highway 89 South**—As you travel south between Mount Lassen and the Lake Tahoe region, the Sierra Nevada mountains grow ever taller. The road winds through forested valleys and over easy passes, running through small towns oriented toward logging, ranching, and vacationers.

Watch for debris from passing logging trucks as you drive past lovely **Lake Almanor** and over into the Indian Creek Valley. CA 70 from Paxton leads down through the sometimes spectacular **Feather River Canyon**. For a good loop after a day exploring Lassen Volcanic National Park, drop down CA 32 into **Chico** to spend the night, then return to the high country through the Feather River Canyon in the morning.

The town of **Quincy** is the county seat for Plumas County and the site for the **Plumas County Museum**. Buck's Lake Road (County 119) heads south from town, providing access to the lovely **Buck's Lake, Pacific Crest Trail**, and **Buck's Lake Wilderness**. The lake has two small resorts. Canoes can be rented allowing access to the north and east shore wilderness.

Further south, the area around **Graeagle** has vacation rentals, golf courses, and the **Plumas Eureka State Park**. The historic mining village of **Johnsville** and a ski basin are within the park. From Graeagle, the Gold Lake Forest Highway (N.F. 24) climbs into the beautiful **Lakes Basin**, then heads down to join CA 49. Staying south on CA 89 from Graeagle, the road drops into the wide **Sierra Valley** and the swampy headwaters of the Feather River.

✷ **Mount Shasta (the town)**—Nestled below its volcanic namesake, this pleasant town offers a respite from the freeway race. The exits funnel you right onto Mount Shasta Boulevard, the only street of consequence. You can visit the headwater springs of the Sacramento River in Mount Shasta's **City Park**, north of downtown on Nixon Road.

The **Everitt Memorial Highway** heads east from town and climbs to **Panther Meadows**, almost 8,000 feet up on Mount Shasta's southern flank. This drive is your best way to get close to the mountain by car. Take any Mount Shasta exit from Interstate 5.

✷ **Weaverville**—At the base of the Trinity Alps, on CA 299, little Weaverville owes its charm, as do so many other towns, to its Gold Rush history. Unlike many others, however, that charm has aged well, without the pressures of the tourist masses. All of Weaverville is listed on the National Register of Historic Places. Stop at **Joss House State Historic Park** to see the oldest Chinese temple in California. Details: 508 Main Street, Weaverville; (916) 623-5284; open Thursday through Monday from 10 a.m. to 5 p.m.; tours given hourly until 4 p.m. Admission is $2. (1 hour)

✳ **Weed**—Abner Weed moved his lumber mill onto the low slopes of Mount Shasta so that the highland winds would dry his lumber faster. Thus, Weed was born. It's not much today, but visit the **Weed Historic Lumbertown Museum** on Camino Avenue at Gilman Avenue. Sam and Elmer will give you the lowdown—and they know their stuff! It's amazing what you can dig up on the back streets of nowhere.

✳ **Whiskeytown-Shasta-Trinity National Recreation Area**— Boating, fishing, and lakeside fun are the primary activities along the miles of shoreline these three lakes offer. All of them were created to increase and control the flow of water for Central Valley irrigation.

In the U.S., only Hoover Dam is more massive than **Shasta Dam**. The impressive spillway of the Shasta Dam is the world's

Robert Holmes

highest at 487 feet. Details: Take Shasta Dam Boulevard (CA 151) from Interstate 5 (stop at the viewpoint on the way); (916) 275-4463; free tours are available at the visitor center. Visitor center open daily from 7:30 a.m. to 5 p.m.; one-hour tours depart hourly from 9 a.m. to 4 p.m. Call for off-season hours.

Typical lake recreation opportunities abound around **Shasta Lake**. The lake also features the **Shasta Caverns**. Details: Take the O'Brien exit from Interstate 5 to Shasta Cavern Road. A boat and bus take you to the caverns, (916) 238-2341. Tours are given daily, leaving every half hour from 9 a.m. to 5 p.m. in summer, from 9 a.m. to 3 p.m. in winter. Admission is $14. (2½ hours)

Whiskeytown Lake is easily accessed from Redding on CA 299. You can enjoy recreational gold panning in this unit of the park, but not the others. Details: Located 10 miles west of Redding on CA 299; (916) 246-1225; visitor center open daily from 9 a.m. to 5 p.m.; get a $1 permit at the visitor center at the southeast end of the lake.

Trinity Lake is a thousand feet higher in elevation than the other two, and it's also more remote. Lake recreation of all sorts can be enjoyed here. Details: Take Dam Boulevard from Lewiston or CA 3 north from Weaverville.

✯ **Yreka**—If you can, enter (or exit) Yreka via CA 283 to the north of town. You'll enjoy the climb from the Klamath River through the steep canyon of Yreka Creek. It gives some added perspective to the perky, busy town. Check out the fake gold nuggets in the lobby of the 1857 **Siskyou County Courthouse**, 311 Fourth Street. Visit the collected historic buildings of the **Siskyou County Museum**, as well as the heritage exhibits inside. Details: 910 S. Main Street, Yreka; (916) 842-3836; open Tuesday through Saturday from 9 a.m. to 5 p.m. Admission is $2. (1 hour)

The "Blue Goose" steam train of the **Yreka Western Railroad** takes passengers on three-hour, roundtrip excursions from Yreka to the historic cattle and railroad town of Montague. The train passes wood processing plants and a large sawmill. Views of Mount Shasta and a crossing of the Shasta River are featured. Check out the amazing model train in the depot.

Details: Yreka Depot, east of Interstate 5 in central Yreka; (916) 842-4146; trains depart at 10:00 a.m., Wednesday through Saturday in the summer; weekend trips continue through Halloween. Admission is $9. (3½ hours)

Redding—Poor Redding is one of those towns where they decided to build a center city mall to revitalize the area and the idea failed. Now downtown is ugly and without character, while the suburbs offer what suburbs always do: strip malls, real malls, and houses.

Redding's one redeeming zone is **Caldwell Park**, which has two good museums. The **Redding Museum of Art and History** has Indian art, local historical art and artifacts, and changing exhibits. Details: Quartz Hill Road, in the park, across the river north of downtown, Redding; (916) 225-4155; open Tuesday through Sunday from 10 a.m. to 5 p.m. in the summer (noon to 5 p.m. in the off season). Admission is free. (1 hour)

Northern California natural history is on display at the **Carter House Natural Science Museum**. Details: Quartz Hill Road, in the park, across the river north of downtown, Redding; open Tuesday through Sunday from 10 a.m. to 5 p.m. Admission is $1. (1 hour)

Shasta State Historic Park—If you travel CA 299, you can't miss the historic buildings of this park along either side of the road, 6 miles west of Redding. The sites, ruins, and restorations are interesting to examine as you get a feel for the layout of this once bustling mining town. Details: Located 6 miles west of Redding on CA 299; (916) 243-8194; open Thursday through Monday from 10 a.m. to 5 p.m. Most of the park is free to see, except the museum, where admission costs $2. (45 minutes)

FOOD

In Chester, stop at the **Chester Saloon and Italian Restaurant**, 159 Main Street, for a plate of culinary goodness from the old country, (916) 258-2887.

For steaks in Redding, hit **Jack's Grill**, south of the hideous downtown mall at 1743 California Street, (916) 241-9705. At 1344 Market Street, **Maxwell's** has good mixed grill lunches and dinners in a nice setting, (916) 246-4373.

In Weaverville, the **Pacific Brewery** has good beer and good grub at 107 Main Street. Read as you eat at the **Gooseberry Café** where shelves of used books go well with the light meals and desserts, Center Street, (916) 623-4666.

The town of Mount Shasta has several good places, most on or near Mount Shasta Boulevard. **Café Bellissimo** takes top honors for fine cuisine, including some unusual vegetable dishes, 204A West Lake Street, (916) 926-4461. Enjoy the beer garden and German menu at **Willy's Bavarian Kitchen**, 107 Chestnut Street.

Grandma's House in Yreka has just what you'd expect on the menu. It's next to the freeway at 123 East Center Street.

LODGING

The **Chester Manor Motel** is a comfortable place with lots of space and rooms from $40 to $70, 306 Main Street, Chester, (916) 258-2441. At the east end of Chester on CA 36 is the **Bidwell House**, a lovely bed and breakfast with a fascinating history. It overlooks the lake at 1 Main Street, (916) 258-3338.

Twelve miles west of CA 89 on CA 299 is the town of Fall River and the **Fall River Hotel**. Built in 1936, the hotel combines well-kept history with rural charm. Shared-bath rooms are $40, private-bath rooms from $45 to $50, 24860 Main Street, (916) 336-5550.

Redding has many chain motels, including **Best Western**, **Comfort Inn**, **Red Lion**, **Super 8**, **Motel 6**, and others. Use the numbers on the "Resources" page to contact them. For something more charming, try the **Tiffany House**, a Victorian B&B with a pool and a great view. The three rooms range from $75 to $125, 1510 Barbara Road (from Benton Drive), (916) 244-3225.

The **Weaverville Hotel** is historic, well-kept, and cheap, with rooms from $35. It's at 201 Main Street (CA 299), (916) 623-3121.

The town of Mount Shasta has the **Mount Shasta Ranch Bed and Breakfast**, west of Interstate 5 at 1008 Barr Road. It's an easy and comfortable place, and there's a great fireplace in the main lodge, (916) 926-3870. There are several budget and moderate choices along Mount Shasta Boulevard.

In Dunsmuir, you can stay in a caboose at the **Railroad Park Resort**, 100 Railroad Park Road (from Interstate 5). Cabins and cabooses are $65, (916) 235-4440 or (800) 974-7245.

The **Grand Manor** in Weed is a nice motel with rooms from $60 to $80, 1844 Shastina Drive, (916) 938-1982. A bit cheaper, the **Sis-Q-Inn Motel** has good basic rooms from $40 to $45, 1825 Shastina Drive, (916) 938-4194.

Yreka has several chain motels. Use the phone numbers on the "Resources" page to contact them. There are budget options at the north and south end of town, paralleling the freeway, including the

VOLCANOES

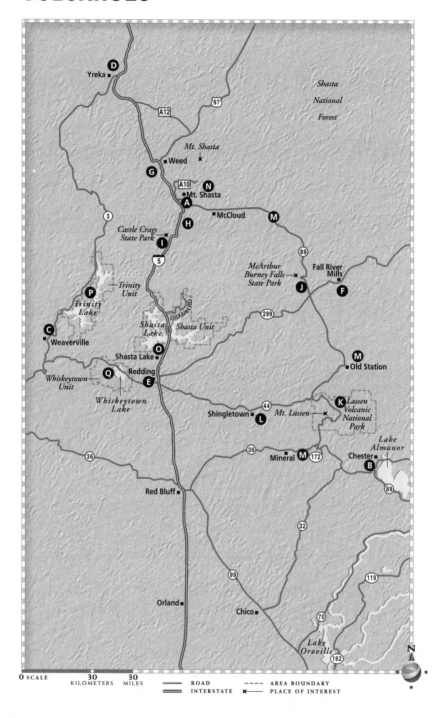

Food

A Café Bellissimo

B Chester Saloon and Italian Restaurant

C Gooseberry Café

D Grandma's House

E Jack's Grill

E Maxwell's

C Pacific Brewery

A Willy's Bavarian Kitchen

Lodging

B Bidwell House

B Chester Manor Motel

F Fall River Hotel

G Grand Manor

D Klamath Motor Lodge

A Mount Shasta Ranch Bed and Breakfast

H Railroad Park Resort

G Sis-Q-Inn Motel

E Tiffany House

D Wayside Inn

C Weaverville Hotel

Camping

I Castle Crags State Park

J McArthur-Burney Falls Memorial State Park

K Mount Lassen National Park

L Mount Lassen—Shingletown KOA

M National Forest Campgrounds

N Panther Meadows

O Shasta Lake

P Trinity Lake

Q Whiskeytown Lake

Note: Items with the same letter are located in the same town or area.

Klamath Motor Lodge, 1111 South Main Street, (916) 842-2751, and the **Wayside Inn**, 1235 South Main Street, (916) 842-4412.

CAMPING

Many National Forest and National Recreation Area campgrounds are found in the region. South of Mount Lassen, three campgrounds are located near **Mineral**, on CA 89 and CA 172. North of Mount Lassen, six campgrounds are along CA 89 near **Old Station**. Three campgrounds are along CA 89 within 18 miles, east of **McCloud**. There are two National Forest campgrounds on Everitt Memorial Highway above the town of Mount Shasta, including **Panther Meadows** at the end of the road.

Just off of CA 3 along the west shore of **Trinity Lake** are several National Recreation Area and National Forest campgrounds. **Whiskeytown Lake** has a campground at the end of Kennedy Memorial Drive and one at the lake's west end on CA 299. The campgrounds for **Shasta Lake** are accessible from Interstate 5.

Castle Crags State Park has sites for $12 to $16 during the summer. Take the Castle Crags/Castella exit from Interstate 5, (916) 235-2684 for information, (800) 444-7275 for reservations.

The campground at the lovely **McArthur-Burney Falls Memorial State Park** has $12 to $16 sites. The park is on CA 89, five miles north of the CA 299 junction, (916) 335-2777 for information, (800) 444-7275 for reservations.

The **Mt. Lassen—Shingletown KOA** has RV and tent sites from $16 to $22, 7749 KOA Road (off CA 44), Shingletown, (916) 474-3133 or (800) KOA-3403.

Scenic Route: The Lava Loop

Few travelers ever venture onto the Modoc Plateau, which spreads across the sparsely populated northeastern corner of California. East of Mount Shasta, this is a land of broad forested uplands, low buttes and hills, tight canyons, and lonely roads. As you drive from Shasta to Lassen, you will see both subtle and vivid signs of the volcanic activity that shaped the area. Open the car windows, set the cruise control, sit back, and just say, "Aaahhh."

From Weed, take U.S. 97 northeast. Stop at the Living Memorial Sculpture Garden (see preceding chapter), then drive over Mount Hebron Summit and down through Butte Valley, enjoying the sudden flatness of the irrigated plain as you continue to the state line. Turning east on Stateline Road (CA 161), enter the Lower Klamath National Wildlife Refuge. Turn south onto CA 139, then right 8 miles later onto Great Northern Road, and then south along the edge of Tule Lake National Wildlife Refuge.

These two refuges are vital stopovers for millions of migrating water birds. Viewing is possible from the main roads through the refuges and via several perimeter roads. Migrating populations peak March through April and September through October. Many species come and go well into the summer, some remaining to nest and raise young. From December through February, up to a thousand bald eagles winter in the region.

The road soon enters Lava Beds National Monument. Most of the monument is covered with smooth pahoehoe (pa-hoy-hoy) lava, overlain by thicker flows of aa (ah-ah) lava. Volcanic cones and craters dot the area. Stop and hike in to Captain Jack's Stronghold. In this lava maze in 1872, Modoc Indian "Captain Jack" and 160 members of his tribe held off the U.S. Army for over six months. Visit Schonchin Butte, taking the short hike to the top for a marvelous view of the monument. Borrow a helmet and flashlight from the visitor center and explore one of the lava tube caves along Cave Loop Road. To see where much of the pahoehoe originated, drive to Mammoth Crater, 3 miles south of the visitor center. If it's time to camp, continue 12 miles to Medicine Lake, a water-filled volcanic crater.

Head southeast out of the Lava Beds National Monument and back to CA 139. Stop at the store in Tionesta, and ask about its history as a saloon and brothel catering to lumberjacks.

Continue to CA 299 in Canby, or save a dozen miles by turning south on Lookout Hackamore Road.

Take CA 299 west, more or less following the Pit River Valley. If it's late, stop in Fall River at the old Fall River Lodge. You'll find a homemade quilt on every bed, rooms as low as $40, and a fine restaurant, (916) 336-5550. Two miles past town, stop at the viewpoint for a look into the Pit River Canyon.

At the junction of CA 89 and CA 299, you can opt to return north to Mount Shasta, or continue west to Redding. Otherwise turn south towards Lassen Volcanic National Park and the scenic route through the Sierras. Remember, CA 89 through the park may not open until late May or June.

THE LAVA LOOP

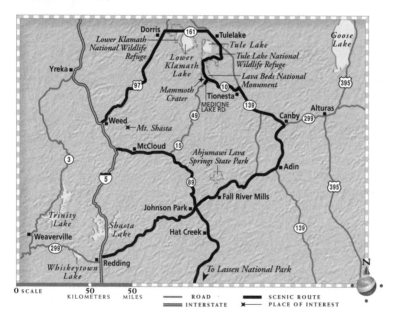

11

SACRAMENTO AND THE CENTRAL VALLEY

In 1839, German-born John Augustus Sutter arrived in California. The Mexican government granted him 76 square miles of land at the confluence of the American and Sacramento rivers, the site of present day Sacramento. He called it "New Helvetia" and built Sutter's Fort to secure his ownership. When the gold rush came along, entrepreneur Sam Brannan and others constructed buildings and started businesses. Sutter's son named the town, and, in 1850, it became the capital of the brand new state of California.

Today, Sacramento has a population of 390,000, with sprawling exurban communities spreading along the major arteries into the Sierra foothills. The region is one of the fastest growing in the state, and the resulting "Los Angelization" is an unfortunate byproduct. Unless you have loads of time or a compelling interest in the attractions, I don't recommend putting it on your itinerary.

If you decide to spend some hours in "Sacto," head for the heart of downtown. U.S. 50 and Interstate 5 intersect just south of the central district. If you're on Interstate 80 West, take Interstate 5 (CA 99) South into town. The main sights are within a 1-square-mile area from Capitol Park to the Sacramento River. A good walking loop takes in the capitol, Governor's Mansion State Historic Park, Old Sacramento, the Wells Fargo History Museum, Crocker Art Museum, and the Leland Stanford Mansion. ◼

SACRAMENTO

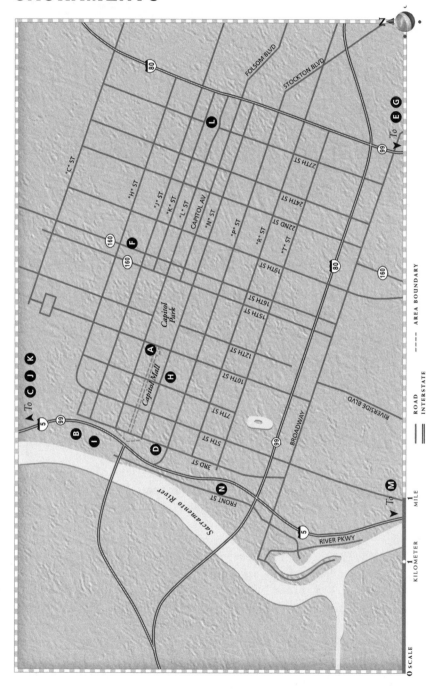

Sightseeing Highlights

A California State Capitol

B California State Railroad Museum

C Chico

D Crocker Art Museum

E Fresno

F Governor's Mansion State Historic Park

G Hershey Chocolate Factory

H Leland Stanford Mansion

I Old Sacramento and Old Sacramento State Historic Park

J Red Bluff

K Sacramento National Wildlife Refuge

L State Indian Museum

M Stockton

O Sutter's Fort State Historic Park

N Towe Ford Museum

Note: Items with the same letter are located in the same place.

A PERFECT DAY IN SACRAMENTO

Do your walkabout before the heat sets in. Start with a 10 a.m. visit to
Sutter's Fort State Historic Park for a taste of local roots. Park near
the capitol, then take a look at the workplace of those who govern 30
million Californians. Walk the K Street pedestrian mall toward the
river, then cross the freeway to Old Sacramento via J Street or Capitol
Mall. Spend the afternoon moving slowly, exploring museums. Loop
over to the Crocker Museum for an hour of browsing before closing.
Now smile and head for your reserved room or campsite in the Sierras
or on the coast.

THE CENTRAL VALLEY

A 400-mile swath of pancake-flat basin and barely-rolling lowlands
covers close to 20,000 square miles in the heart of California. Once an
inland sea, this great "Central Valley" now hosts mile upon mile of irrigated farmland, surrounded by pastures that blend into the foothills.
The rivers of the Sierras and northern mountains are plugged with
scores of dams, enabling the waters to be fed through thousands of
miles of aqueducts and canals. Little is left of the natural environment—the sea of grass that once hosted huge populations of elk and
antelope, predators, and birds has given way to enormous farms and
sprawling subdivisions.

   The Central Valley is devoted to agricultural production and has
relatively little of interest to the tourist. The smaller cities of the valley
each have something to offer, but they tend to show up near the bottom of most prioritized sightseeing checklists. The land is flat and
largely devoid of natural features. Human habitation is characterized
by working farms, sprawling new developments, tacky old ones, and
relatively artless urban centers. The Central Valley can be unbearably
hot in the summer months. Air conditioning and a fast freeway may
seem like your best friends.

   I say all this, not because the valley isn't a fine place to live and
work, but because the mountain and coastal destinations of Northern
California are so compelling. With only two or three weeks to see the
state, visiting old homes and historic museums in Modesto or Yuba
City won't make sense for most of you. Think of the Central Valley
sites as places to drop in if you're passing through. A few noteworthy
towns are mentioned in the following section.

SIGHTSEEING HIGHLIGHTS: SACRAMENTO AND THE CENTRAL VALLEY

✯✯ **California State Capitol**—Built from 1860–1874 and recently restored to glory, the Capitol building is a classic structure with a dome that reaches 210 feet above the base. There's a nice rotunda, historic exhibits, statues, and murals. Details: The Capitol sits at the west end of **Capitol Park** facing the mall and river. The park is bounded by L, N, Tenth, and 15th Streets, (916) 324-0333; free guided tours are given daily, on the hour, from 9 a.m. to 4 p.m. (1 hour)

✯✯ **Old Sacramento and Old Sacramento State Historic Park**— The restored, riverside district of Old Sacramento includes the four blocks of Front Street and Second Street north of the Capitol Mall. Among the buildings that hold the tourist shops and restaurants are several dating back to gold rush days.

At the north end of the district, the Old Sacramento State Historic Park has two fine museums. The **California State Railroad Museum** has a marvelous collection of 21 historic cars and locomotives, as well as exhibits, films, and dioramas related to rail history. It's a must for rail buffs and the nostalgic. Details: Second and I Streets, Sacramento; (916) 445-4209; open daily from 10 a.m. to 5 p.m. Admission is $5. The reconstructed **Central Pacific Passenger Station** across the street can be visited on the same ticket. (1½ hours)

Next to the Railroad Museum is the hands-on **Discovery Museum**. Interactive science and technology exhibits feature a million-dollar gold display from the mother lode (this one's not hands-on). Kids will like it here. Details: 101 I Street, Sacramento; (916) 264-7057; open summers Tuesday through Sunday from 10 a.m. to 5 p.m.; open the rest of the year Wednesday through Sunday from noon to 5 p.m. and Saturday and Sunday from 10 a.m. to 5 p.m. Admission is $3.50 for adults, $2 for kids. (1½ hours)

✯ **Chico**—This pleasant college town is worth a stop on your way to or from Mount Lassen. CA 99 splits into Main Street and Broadway, opposing one-ways that pass through the heart of town. The **Chico Museum** has regional heritage displays, including Ishi Indian and Chinese Temple exhibits. Details: Second Street and Salem Street, Chico; (916) 891-4336; open Wednesday through Sunday from noon to 4 p.m. (½ hour)

CA 99 unites again into the Esplanade to cross north over Big Chico Creek. The **Bidwell Mansion State Historic Park** preserves the home of town founder, General John Bidwell, on wide grounds at the edge of the California State University campus. Details: 525 Esplanade; (916) 895-6144. Tours start from the visitor center, weekdays from noon to 4 p.m.; Saturday and Sunday from 10 a.m. to 4 p.m. Admission is $2. (1 hour)

The **Sierra Nevada Brewery** offers tours of its building. Details: 1075 East 20th Street, Chico; (916) 893-3520; tours Tuesday through Friday at 2:30 p.m., and Saturday between noon and 3 p.m. Admission is free. (1 hour)

☆ **Crocker Art Museum**—A good collection of modern California artists is featured in the one-time home of Edwin and Margaret Crocker. The house itself is one of Sacramento's most elaborate Victorians and is worth seeing on its own. You can count on there being a high caliber touring exhibit on hand. Details: 216 O Street, Sacramento; (916) 323-3047; open Wednesday through Sunday from 10 a.m. to 5 p.m. (until 9 p.m. on Thursday). Admission is $2. (1½ hours)

☆ **Fresno**—This sprawling city on Hwy. 99 never seems to end. If you find downtown (take the downtown exits at Fresno Street or Stanislaus Street), you can visit the very nice **Fresno Art Museum**, which hosts good rotating exhibits and a fair permanent collection with interesting highlights. Details: 2233 North First Street, Fresno; (209) 485-4810; open Tuesday through Friday, 10 a.m. to 5 p.m., weekends from noon to 5 p.m. Admission is $2. (1 hour)

The kids will like the hands-on exhibits and lasers at the **Fresno Metropolitan Museum**. Details: 1515 Van Ness Avenue, Fresno; (209) 441-1444; open daily from 11 a.m. to 5 p.m. Admission is $4.

☆ **Governor's Mansion State Historic Park**—Sacramento's first governor's mansion was built in 1877. Memorabilia and furnishings from past governors are displayed along with historic period pieces. Details: 16th and H Streets, Sacramento; (916) 323-3047; tours are given daily, on the hour, from 10 a.m. to 4 p.m. Admission is $2. (1 hour)

☆ **Red Bluff**—Where the flat Central Valley breaks upward into the hills, the pleasant town of Red Bluff sits on the Sacramento River. It's an easy on and off from Interstate 5. Drive or walk the **Victorian Homes Tour** to see lovely homes, dated by historical plaques, in the blocks near Main Street. Details: The Chamber of Commerce has tour information at 100 Main Street, Red Bluff; (916) 527-6220.

The **Kelly-Griggs House Museum** offers the chance for an inside look at a lovely Victorian. Details: 311 Washington Street, Red Bluff; (916) 527-1129; open Thursday through Sunday from 1 p.m. to 4 p.m. Donations accepted. (½ hour)

The **William B. Ide Adobe State Historic Park**, a small living history park on the Sacramento River, features the 1850 adobe home of Mr. Ide and family. Ide was the first and only president of the short-lived California Republic, established after the Bear Flag Revolt of 1846. Details: 2 miles north of Red Bluff on Adobe Road, right on the Sacramento River; (916) 529-8599; open daily 8 a.m. to dusk. Admission is free, but parking is $3. (½ hour)

☆ **Sacramento National Wildlife Refuge**—No state boasts a greater concentration of waterfowl than California. Snow geese, sandhill cranes, ducks, egrets, herons, and swans can all be seen at this large refuge 80 miles north of Sacramento on Interstate 5. A self-guided auto tour through the refuge is a good one-and-a-half-hour detour from the speeding freeway. Details: Take the Norman Road exit from Interstate 5; (916) 934-2801; open daily from dawn to dusk. Admission is free. (1–3 hours)

☆ **Sutter's Fort State Historic Park**—Originally built in 1839, Sutter's adobe fort has been restored to its original appearance. Furnishings and exhibits are true to the period. Visitors may take a self-guided, walkman tour. Details: L Street at 27th, Sacramento; (916) 324-0539; open daily from 10 a.m. to 5 p.m. Admission is $5. (1 hour)

Next to the fort on the large commons is the **State Indian Museum** with native history exhibits. Details: 2618 K Street, Sacramento; (916) 324-0539; open daily from 10 a.m. to 5 p.m. Admission is $2. (1 hour)

☆ **Towe Ford Museum**—This is a must-see attraction for car buffs. Over 150 vintage Fords in pristine condition are on display. Every model from 1903 to 1952 is represented. Don't be surprised if you see people drooling. Details: It's located between Interstate 5 and the Sacramento River on Front Street at V Street. Take Front Street south from Capitol Mall, Sacramento; (916) 442-6802; open daily from 10 a.m. to 6 p.m. Admission is $4.50. (1 hour)

Hershey Chocolate Factory—Located off CA 120 in Oakdale (conveniently on the way to Yosemite), this west coast chocolate factory still offers genuine plant tours, unlike its Pennsylvania counterpart. After the tour, you get a free chocolate bar and the chance to buy lots more. Details: 120 South Sierra Avenue, Oakdale; (209) 848-8126; open Monday through Friday from 8:30 a.m. to 3 p.m. Admission is free. (1 hour)

Leland Stanford Mansion—Stanford was one of the "big four" railroad magnates who dominated state politics in the mid- and late-1800s. The mansion, built in 1859, can be toured Tuesday, Thursday, and Saturday. Details: Located on the corner of Eighth and N Streets; (916) 324-0575. Admission is $2. (1 hour)

Stockton—The **Haggin Museum** has a wonderful collection of Native American artifacts, regional history items, and paintings. It is the best of the very few reasons to visit Stockton. Details: 1201 North Pershing Avenue, Stockton; (209) 462-4116; open Tuesday through Sunday from 1:30 p.m. to 5 p.m. Admission is $2. (1 hour)

FITNESS AND RECREATION

The 22½-mile **Jedediah Smith National Recreation Trail** follows the course of the American River through the sinuous American River Parkway park. The parkway stretches eastward from the point where the American flows into the Sacramento. It's a good path for jogging and cycling.

At 1600 Exposition Boulevard, just east of Business Interstate 80 and north of the American River, **WaterWorld USA** features water slides, a wading pool, and a play area, open daily, 10:30 a.m. to 6 p.m., (until 4 p.m. from Labor Day through Memorial Day); (916) 924-9556. Admission is $15.

FOOD

You'll probably find something you like as you browse the K Street Pedestrian Mall, Downtown Plaza, and Old Sacramento. The **River City Brewing Company** has a good mixed grill and selection of microbrew beer in the mall. Also in the mall is **Morton's of Chicago**, serving steaks and more for a price, 521 L Street, (916) 442-5091. In

Old Sacramento, **California Fats** has terrific seafood, pizzas, and more, 1015 Front Street, (916) 441-7966. Dine on the *Delta King* paddlewheeler for a taste of river history. The **Delta King Pilothouse Restaurant** offers fine continental cuisine. Bring your gold card, 1000 Front Street, (916) 441-4440.

Frank Fats is the place to throw a pricey eggroll at a state senator, 806 L Street, (916) 442-7092. For top quality traditional Italian fare, **Biba** is the clear, but not cheap choice. It's located on Capitol Street at 28th Street, a block from Sutter's Fort, (916) 455-2422. The beers are from the British Isles at **The Fox and Goose**, but the menu strays pleasantly into California cuisine. Play some darts, dine, and then enjoy live music into the night, 1001 R Street, (916) 443-8825.

LODGING

Several major highways and commercial avenues of Sacramento have concentrations of budget and chain lodging options. Many are found just north of the American River to the west of Business Interstate 80 on or near Arden Way (**Marriott, Hilton,** and **Red Lion**). Another cluster is found in Rancho Cordova (**Holiday Inn, Sheraton, Best Western, Motel 6,** and **Comfort Inn**), 12 miles west of downtown along U.S. 50. Use the numbers on the "Resources" page to locate the one you prefer.

For a unique experience, stay on the ***Delta King***, an old paddlewheel riverboat permanently moored in the Sacramento River, 1000 Front Street (at the end of L Street) in Old Sacramento. The smallish staterooms range from $100 to $140, (916) 444-5464 or (800) 825-5464. The **Hyatt Regency** is Sacto's big hotel. Across from the Capitol, it offers all the amenities, 1209 L Street, rooms from $80, (916) 443-1234 or (800) 233-1234. The best B&B choice is the **Amber House** at 1315 22nd Street (near Capitol Avenue). The lovely guest rooms are aptly named after classic artists, (916) 444-8085 or (800) 755-6526.

There are some inexpensive to moderately priced options downtown as well. The **Americana Lodge**, 818 15th Street, has nice rooms for $40, (916) 444 3980. The **Holiday Inn Capitol Plaza** is just two blocks from Old Sacramento. Rooms range from $86 to $120, 300 J Street, (916) 446-0100. Four blocks north of the capitol is the **Best Western Ponderosa Motor Inn**, 1100 H Street, $70 to $90, (916) 441-1314.

SACRAMENTO

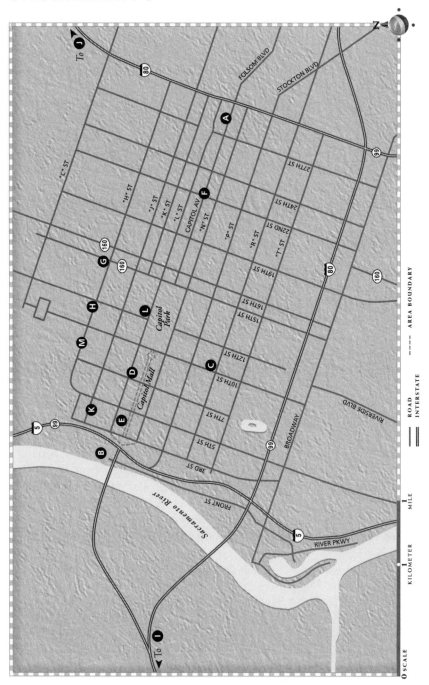

Food

A Biba

B California Fats

B Delta King Pilothouse Restaurant

C The Fox and Goose

D Frank Fats

E Morton's of Chicago

E River City Brewing Company

Lodging

F Amber

G Americana Lodge

I Best Western

H Best Western Ponderosa Motor

I Comfort Inn

B *Delta King*

J Hilton

I Holiday Inn

K Holiday Inn Capitol Plaza

L Hyatt Regency

J Marriott

I Motel 6

J Red Lion

M Sacramento Hostel

I Sheraton

Camping

J Cal Expo RV Park

I Sacramento Metropolitan KOA

Note: Items with the same letter are located in the same place or area.

The **Sacramento Hostel** has a great location at 900 H Street. Beds are $10 to $12, (916) 443-1691.

CAMPING

Three miles west of downtown, just off Interstate 80, is the **Sacramento Metropolitan KOA**. Take the West Capitol Avenue exit from Interstate 80. It's south of the freeway on Lake Road. Sites are $24 to $28, "Kamping Kabins", $35, 3951 Lake Road, (916) 371-6771 or (800) KOA-2747. The **Cal Expo RV Park** is adjacent to the California Exposition Grounds, American River Parkway, and Waterworld. There are tent sites available. Take Arden Way east from Business Interstate 80, then head south on Ethan Way, (916) 263-3187.

NIGHTLIFE

Near California State University Sacramento, the **Cattle Club** has live rock bands and a youthful crowd, 7042 Folsom Boulevard, (916) 386-0390. In the Downtown Plaza Mall, **America Live!** has five bars under one roof. You can dance, chat, laugh, drown your sorrows, or try out a pick-up line. Stop in at **Java City**, 1800 Capitol Avenue, for espresso, drinks, and tasty snacks. It's open until 11 p.m. (midnight on week-ends), (916) 444-5282. Genuine character is lacking, but people aren't, at K Street and Seventh Street. For a nighttime view of the impressive Capitol and bland cityscape, visit **Busby Berkeley's** at the top of the Hyatt Regency, 1209 L Street, (916) 443-1234.

12

GOLD COUNTRY

James Marshall's discovery of gold in 1848 revolutionized California. Within two years, thousands of "forty-niners" were at work in the western Sierra foothills. They sluiced every cubic foot of likely river gravel and tunneled through the hard rock to reach every vein. When the easy gold was gone, most of the treasure seekers left, abandoning towns right and left. Poor James Marshall's initial luck was never followed up. He died penniless. The treasure trove in the area today is tourism.

The aptly numbered CA 49 links the key sights of the Gold Country in a ribbon of touristic interest. The region features scores of abandoned, preserved, restored, and exploited historic sites. Whether it's a charming village, weathered ghost town, or strip-malled exurb, the towns along the way all have centers with nineteenth-century buildings and some degree of charm. Old mines, tailings, aqueducts, sluice boxes, and rusted hardware litter the land. Everything you see that appears mining-related probably is.

CA 49 will slow you down at every turn with the chance to see some attraction or another. Spend extra time at a single, great spot instead of spreading yourself too thin. There is a certain sameness to the history of Gold Country—each little town has a different variation on the same story. True buffs could spend a week or two exploring. Most travelers will want to choose a segment that coincides with a larger travel plan. The sights described below are the cream of a very large crop. They are grouped according to the prime attraction in an area. ◾

GOLD COUNTRY

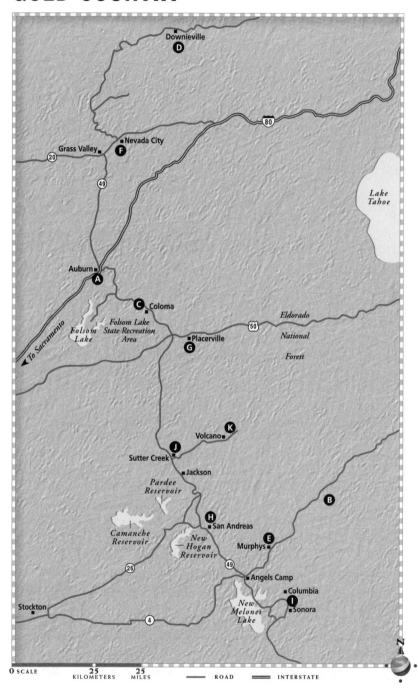

Downieville D

80

Nevada City
Grass Valley F

20

49

Lake
Tahoe

Auburn
A

Coloma
C

Folsom
Lake
State Recreation
Area

Folsom
Lake

Eldorado

50

Placerville
G

National

To Sacramento

Forest

K

Volcano

Sutter Creek J

Jackson

Pardee
Reservoir

B

Camanche
Reservoir

H
San Andreas

New
Hogan
Reservoir

E
Murphys

26

49

Angels Camp

Stockton

4

New
Melones
Lake

Columbia
I
Sonora

N

0 SCALE   25   25   ROAD   INTERSTATE
         KILOMETERS MILES

Sightseeing Highlights

Ⓐ Auburn

Ⓑ Calaveras Big Trees State Park

Ⓒ Coloma / Marshall Gold Discovery State Historic Park

Ⓓ Downieville

Ⓔ Murphy's

Ⓕ Nevada City Region

Ⓖ Placerville

Ⓗ San Andreas

Ⓘ Sonora Region

Ⓙ Sutter Creek Region

Ⓚ Volcano

A PERFECT DAY IN GOLD COUNTRY

My favorite segment of Gold Country is the Yuba River Valley between Grass Valley and Downieville. In the morning, visit Empire Mine State Historic Park. Travel on to Nevada City, one of the loveliest historic towns in the state. If you're not driving a huge RV or fifth wheel, visit Malakoff Diggins State Historic Park and the site of North Bloomfield. Drive up CA 49 as it winds up into the cool, forested country of the Yuba River Canyon. Finish your sightseeing with a walk around the interesting town of Downieville. Spend the night in town, or head to the high country.

MINING FOR GOLD

Gold occurs with the mineral quartz in *lodes*, or deposits, near the edges of large, granite masses. As the mountains erode, gold is mixed into the sediments in *placer* deposits. Most of the individual miners and low-budget outfits of the past engaged in placer mining; that is, extracting the gold from deposited sediments—usually the silt, sand, and gravels in and around stream beds. *Hardrock mining*, or deep mining, was much more expensive, requiring large investments of capital.

Gold's high density causes it to sink in moving water before lighter materials. Gold panners swirled grit and water in the bottom of shallow pans to sort out the good stuff. On a larger scale, streams were diverted to run through *sluice boxes*. Grit and gravel would be shoveled in at the upper end. Then, everything would be washed out at the other end except the gold, which caught in the *riffles* along the bottom of the box. The largest operations used dredges to remove deposits from river bottoms or hydraulic jets to scrub sediments (and everything else) from the underlying bedrock, then all was sluiced.

The original hardrock mines utilized blasted, drilled, and hand-dug shafts to find lodes and to follow veins deep into the earth. Ore was removed and then crushed in *stamp mills* so it, too, could be sluiced.

SIGHTSEEING HIGHLIGHTS

★★★ **Nevada City Region**—Mining history receives a classic veneer in this charming, historic town. The blocks around Broad Street are loaded with interesting shops and restaurants. You can still see a show up the hill on Broad Street at the **Nevada Theater**, opened in 1865, which makes it the oldest in the state. The **Firehouse Museum No. 1** has heritage items, including relics from the Donner party. Details: 214 Main Street, Nevada City; (916) 265-5468; open daily, April through October, from 11 a.m. to 4 p.m. Donations are accepted.

Four miles south on CA 49 is the very different town of **Grass Valley,** which reveals its history reluctantly. Exit the freeway and head to Main Street to see what there is. From Main, take Auburn Street under the freeway, then turn left on Empire Street to reach the **Empire Mine State Historic Park**. The deep rock Empire Mine was in operation until 1956, producing nearly 190 tons of gold, which were extracted via 370 miles of tunnel. Stop at the visitor center for an overview and to sign on for a free, one-hour guided tour. Details: 10791 East Empire Street, Grass Valley; (916) 273-8522; open daily from 9 a.m. to 5 p.m. Admission is $5. (2 hours)

From CA 49, twelve miles north of Nevada City, go east 17 miles on Tyler-Foote Road to reach **Malakoff Diggins State Historic Park** and the townsite of **North Bloomfield**. The park preserves an area of devastation that resulted from hydraulic mining. With this approach, water pressurized by pumps or gravity is shot through nozzles, washing everything, including gold-bearing placer deposits, from the surface to be sluiced. In North Bloomfield, a few restored buildings sit along the road, kept company by the marked sites of many more. Details: (916) 265-2740; open daily from 10 a.m. to 5 p.m. in summer (until 4 p.m. the rest of the year). Admission is $5. (1½ hours)

★★★ **Sonora Region**—The area around Sonora is ideal for exploring if you're on your way to or from Yosemite. CA 49 runs through the busy center of Sonora, but its historic charms are still intact. The **Tuolumne County Museum**, housed in the 1857 county jail, has the usual heritage displays. Details: The museum is located at 158 West Bradford Avenue, Sonora; (209) 532-1317; open Tuesday through Sunday from 10 a.m. to 4 p.m. (until 3:30 p.m. on Sunday). Admission is free. (1 hour)

Two miles north on CA 49 and another mile up Parrots Ferry Road is the wonderfully restored town of Columbia in the **Columbia State Historic Park**. The streets of Columbia are closed to cars, and historic businesses still sell old-time goods. Horse-drawn wagons roll through the streets. Two old hotels house guests, and a small theater offers period productions. Columbia is a great combination of living history museum and historic theme attraction. Details: Parrots Ferry Road, Columbia; (209) 532-4301; park open daily from 10 a.m. to 5 p.m. (though you can stroll through at any time). While individual attractions range in price, a walking tour is free. (2 hours)

Two miles south of Sonora is the town of **Jamestown**. Visit the **Railtown 1897 Historic Park** to see the historic **Sierra Railway Depot**, used as a set in such movie and TV productions as *High Noon* and "Petticoat Junction." Explore the 25-acre collection of rail history and take a one-hour ride behind the **Mother Lode Cannon Ball**. Details: Fifth Avenue, Jamestown; (209) 984-3953; tours run daily from 9:30 a.m. to 4:30 p.m. Cost is $3. The train runs weekends at 10:30 a.m., noon, 1:30 p.m., and 3 p.m. Cost is $9. (2 hours)

South of Jamestown, at the junction of CA 49 and CA 120, is the virtual ghost town of **Chinese Camp**. Stop at the visitors bureau where Main Street meets CA 49 or look around on your own. Details: 10 miles south of Sonora on CA 49; (209) 984-4636 (visitors bureau). Open anytime.

★★ Calaveras Big Trees State Park—Two marvelous groves of giant sequoia trees are preserved in this lovely state park. Hiking, fishing, camping, and swimming are enjoyed in the summer, while snow-shoeing and cross-country skiing through the upper grove are popular with a few knowing souls throughout the winter. If you can't visit Sequoia National Park, this is one of the best places to enjoy these amazing trees. Details: CA 4 east of Arnold; (209) 795-2334. All-day parking is $5. (2 hours)

★★ Coloma / Marshall Gold Discovery State Historic Park—This is where it all began. The park lies on either side of CA 49, on the banks of the American River. The centerpiece is a reconstruction of the sawmill where James Marshall spotted those first glitters in 1848. Up on the hill are Marshall's cabin and monument. Details: (916) 622-3470 for the park, (916) 622-1116 for the museum. The excellent visitor center and museum are open daily from 10 a.m. to 5 p.m. (until 4:30 p.m. in the winter). The park closes at dusk. Pay your $5 day use fee at the first site you visit and make sure the receipt is visible in your windshield.

Coloma is also the center of white-water rafting in the region. Several outfitters rent equipment and lead trips (see "Fitness and Recreation" below).

★★ Downieville—This humble and historic town is particularly attractive for its setting, nestled on the Yuba River well up the canyon from the hot foothills. It's a great place to pan for gold and have a picnic. The 1852 **Downieville Museum** on Main Street has a miniature working stamp mill model among other interesting items. Details: Main Street, Downieville; (916) 289-3423; open daily from Memorial Day through mid-October. Donations are accepted. (½ hour)

Further up CA 49 is the **Kentucky Mine Park and Museum**, notable for its impressive, working tin stamp mill. Details: 1 mile north of Sierra City on CA 49; (916) 862-1310; open Wednesday through Sunday in summer (weekends in October) from 10 a.m. to 5 p.m. The tour is $4. (1 hour)

★★ Sutter Creek Region—With its blend of history, charm, and hip romance, Sutter Creek is a popular destination for both tourists and weekenders. The lovely town with its sheltered walks and historic storefronts is great for browsing. Explore the **Historic Knight Foundry** where iron is still cast using waterwheel-powered machines. Details: 81 Eureka Street, Sutter Creek; (209) 267-5543; a self-guided tour is available Monday through Friday from 9 a.m. to 4 p.m. Admission is $2.50. (1½ hours)

Two miles north of Sutter Creek on CA 49, the town of **Amador City** has a short, charming stretch of shops, many selling antiques. As the smallest incorporated town in the state, Amador City has trouble competing with the thick highway traffic that rolls through downtown.

The large town of **Jackson** is 5 miles south of Sutter Creek on CA 49. As county seat, it's home to the **Amador County Museum**. The museum features a 1/12-scale, working model of the huge Kennedy mine which, along with the Eureka mine, dominated the scene until 1920. Details: 225 Church Street, Jackson; open Wednesday through Sunday from 10 a.m. to 4 p.m. Tours of the model are Saturday and Sunday only, on the hour, from 11 a.m. to 3 p.m. Tours are $1. (1 hour)

Visit **Kennedy Wheel Park** north of town to see huge mining wheels and other remnants of the Kennedy Mine. You can see the wheels from an overlook along CA 49.

★★ **Volcano**—This picturesque town gives a great feel for the way it once was. On Main Street, the St. George Hotel commands the scene. Shops and historic buildings, some unrestored, surround the town center. Nearby, **Daffodil Hill** is a magnificent sight in the springtime. Take Sutter Creek Road 14 miles east from Sutter Creek. It's worth it to wander off the beaten path to see this town.

Three miles to the south on Pine Grove-Volcano Road is **Indian Grinding Rock State Historic Park**. A rocky outcrop features numerous holes once used as bowls for the grinding of acorn meal. In addition, the rock face shows scores of historic petroglyphs. The **Chaw'Se Regional Indian Museum** has Miwok Indian heritage exhibits and a Miwok village. Details: Pine Grove-Volcano Road; (209) 296-7488; the park is open dawn to dusk; the museum is open from 11 a.m. to 3 p.m. Monday through Friday, and from 10 a.m. to 4 p.m. weekends. Fee is $5 for day use. (1½ hours)

★ **Auburn**—It will be obvious to the eye that Auburn has been captured by the exurban expansion of Sacramento. Deep within the sprawl, you will find the heavily touristed historic district, with its wooden sidewalks, shops, restaurants, and restored nineteenth-century buildings. Take Lincoln Street from CA 49. Visit the **Placer County**

Museum in the courthouse for excellent heritage exhibits. Details: Auburn; (916) 889-6500; open Tuesday through Sunday from 10 a.m. to 4 p.m. Admission is $1. (1 hour)

The fairgrounds host the **Gold Country Museum**, featuring historic mining and transportation exhibits. Details: 1273 High Street, Auburn; (916) 889-4134; open Tuesday through Sunday from 10 a.m. to 3:30 p.m. (11 a.m. to 4 p.m. weekends). Admission is $1. (1 hour)

A bit further south is the **Bernhard Museum**, a restored Victorian house, winery, carriage house, and grounds that exhibit the life of the times. Details: High Street, Auburn; (916) 889-6500; open Tuesday through Sunday from 11 a.m. to 3 p.m. (noon to 4 p.m. weekends). Admission is $1. (1 hour)

✯ **Murphys**—With lovely Victorian homes, Murphys has that classic, picturesque look that visitors love. Head 9 miles east on CA 4 from Angel's Camp, then left on Sheep Ranch Road. Stroll Main Street with your camera.

Another mile down on Sheep Ranch Road is **Mercer Caverns**. The one-hour tour reveals many interesting formations. Details: (209) 728-2101; open daily in the summer, weekends the rest of the year, 11 a.m. to 4 p.m. Admission is $5. (1 hour)

To the south of CA 4, beyond the town of Vallecito, is **Moaning Cavern** which features a huge, vertical chamber accessed by a 100-foot spiral staircase. Details: 2 miles south of Vallecito on Parrots Ferry Road; (209) 736-2708; open daily from 9 a.m. to 6 p.m. in the summer (10 a.m. to 5 p.m. the rest of the year). Admission is $6.75. Tours are 3 hours. (1–3 hours)

Continue south on Parrots Ferry Road for a view of **New Melones Lake** and to reach Columbia. At the junction of CA 49 and CA 4 is the town of **Angels Camp**. If you're here during the third weekend in May, you will endure the traffic and crowds assembled for the annual "Jumping Frog Jubilee," part of the celebrations of the Calaveras County Fair. Mark Twain was inspired to write his famous short story "The Celebrated Jumping Frog of Calaveras County" while here. His legacy lives on in all its hokey glory. Details: Call the Calaveras County Visitor Center for fair information; (209) 736-0049 or (800) 225-3764.

✯ **Placerville**—As a gas and burger stop on the heavily traveled U.S. 50 to Tahoe, Placerville suffers a bit from growth and wear. Fortunately, the highway bypasses Main Street, so browsing the historic center is relaxing.

Placerville was once called "Hangtown" for a spate of frontier justice that occurred during the gold rush. Notice the hanging figure in front of the building that now sits over the stump of the hanging tree. The free **Placerville Historical Museum**, open Friday through Sunday from noon to 4 p.m., and the historic **City Hall** are at the east end of Main Street.

The **El Dorado County Museum** is located 2 miles west of town at the fairgrounds. It features historic buildings, farm implements, logging and mining equipment, and more. Details: 100 Placerville Drive, Placerville; (916) 621-5865; open Wednesday through Sunday from 10 a.m. to 4 p.m. (from noon on Sunday). Admission is free. (1 hour)

Turn north on Bedford Avenue by the county courthouse and drive 1 mile to **Hangtown's Gold Bug Park and Mine**. You can take a self-guided, walkman tour deep into an almost horizontal mine shaft. Details: Bedford Avenue, Placerville; (916) 642-5232; open daily in the summer, weekends in shoulder seasons, 10 a.m. to 4 p.m., closed in the winter. Admission is $1. (45 minutes)

San Andreas—Check out the local heritage exhibits and California native plant garden of the **Calaveras County Historical Museum**.

Robert Holmes

Details: 30 North Main Street; (209) 754-6579; museum open daily
from 10 a.m. to 4 p.m. Admission is 50 cents. (½ hour)

The infamous Black Bart once graced the San Andreas jailhouse,
which has now been restored. The jail and other historic buildings
can be found on North Main Street.

Ten miles east of town, on Mountain Ranch Road, are the beautiful **California Caverns** at Cave City. Details: Take Mountain
Ranch Road 8 miles east from San Andreas. Follow the signs for 2
more miles on Michel and Cave City Roads to Cave City and the
caverns; (209) 736-2708. Cave tours last about 1½ hours, departing
hourly from 10 a.m. to 5 p.m. in summer, and from 10 a.m. to 4 p.m.
in fall. Cost is $6.25. Guided spelunking tours are also available.
(1½ hours)

FITNESS AND RECREATION

One of the best hikes around is the 9-mile trail that leads through the
South Grove of sequoias in **Calaveras Big Trees State Park**. The
trailhead of the **South Grove Trail** is at the Beaver Creek Picnic
Area, (209) 795-2334.

The **Downieville Downhill,** a popular mountain biking route,
follows Butcher Ranch and Third Divide trails in the hills near CA
49. Information, rentals, and trail shuttles are available from Coyote
Adventure Co.,123 Nevada St., Nevada City, (916) 265-6909

Coloma is a center for rafting, but other outfitters can be found
across the Sierra foothills. Earth Trek Expeditions is located in Lotus,
a stones throw from Coloma on Lotus Rd. (from CA-49). They offer
raft trips from 1/2 to 2 days, $70 to $250, on several oustanding river
runs, (916) 642-1900 or 800-229-8735. Whitewater Connections has
half-day to two day trips, from $70 to $220, (800) 336-7238.
American River rafting trips are offered by Whitewater Excitement
in Auburn. Call (800) 750-2386 for information.

FOOD

Downieville offers **Cirino's at the Forks**, featuring great Italian
food in a historic gold rush building, (916) 289-3479. The gourmet
pies at Nevada City's **Cowboy Pizza** are out of this world. Try the
"Popeye" with spinach, onions, garlic, feta cheese, and pine nuts, 315
Spring Street, (916) 265-2334. For fine dining, **Potager at Selayas**

offers a worldly menu at bearable prices, 320 Broad Street, (916) 265-0558.

In Auburn's historic heart, two fine options are **Bootlegger's**, 210 Washington Street, (916) 885-0249, and **Butterworth's**, 1522 Lincoln Way, (916) 889-2229.

At **Café Sarah's** in Placerville, Cathy will serve you monumentally huge pancakes or other large and tasty breakfast and lunch fare. It's next door to the hanging man on lower Main Street. **Lil' Mama D. Carlo's** is a classic and tasty little Italian place, 482 Main Street, (916) 626-1612.

In Sutter Creek, **Ruby's Café** is set back into a small courtyard at 15 Eureka Street. There's occasional live music to go with your burger, pasta, meat, or vegetable entrée, (209) 267-0556.

For fine dining in Jackson, try **Michael's Restaurant** in the National Hotel, 2 Water Street, (209) 223-3448.

Visit **Grounds** in Murphys for a great breakfast or lunch at a reasonable price, 402 Main Street, (209) 728-8663.

In Columbia, step back in time to dine on French cuisine at the **City Hotel Dining Room**, located in Columbia State Historic Park, (209) 532-1479.

Sonora has a number of good spots, including the **Coyote Creek Café and Grill**, with reasonably priced southwestern-style dishes, 177 South Washington Street, (209) 532-9225. **Good Heavens** has wonderful soups, sandwiches, and burgers at 49 North Washington Street, (209) 532-3663.

LODGING

Budget and chain motel lodging are available on CA 49 in Grass Valley (**Best Western**), Auburn (**Best Western, Holiday Inn, Super 8**), Placerville (**Best Western, Days Inn**), Jackson (**Best Western**), Sonora (**Best Western**), Mariposa (**Best Western, Comfort Inn, Holiday Inn**), and Oakhurst (**Best Western**).

In the Lakes Basin on Gold Lake Road (N.F. 24), between Graeagle and CA 49 at Bassetts, the **Graeagle Lodge** is a beautiful place to get away from it all. The best feature is a wonderful swimming hole at the base of a small waterfall; $160 for two people, (916)-836-2511.

Downieville offers **Saundra Dyer's Resort**, a down-home inn offering a good breakfast for $5. Rooms are $60, kitchen units $70 to $145, (916) 289-3308 or (800) 696-3308. North up CA 89 is Sierra

GOLD COUNTRY

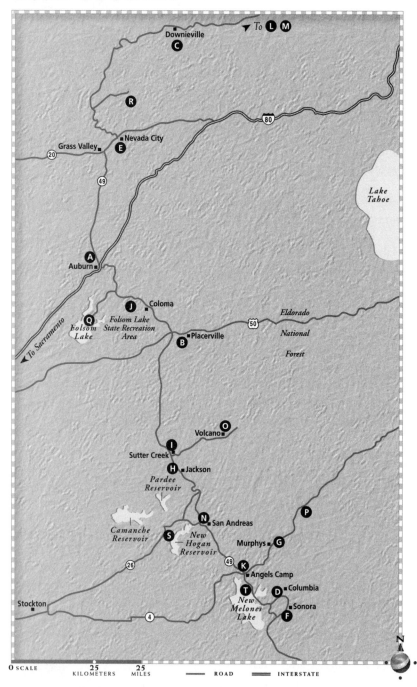

Downieville

To **L** **M**

C

R

Nevada City
Grass Valley ■ **E**

80

Lake Tahoe

49

20

A
Auburn ■

J ■ Coloma

Q
Folsom Lake

Folsom Lake State Recreation Area

B ■ Placerville

50

Eldorado

National

Forest

To Sacramento

O
Volcano ■

I
Sutter Creek

H ■ Jackson

Pardee Reservoir

Camanche Reservoir

N ■ San Andreas

S
New Hogan Reservoir

Murphys ■ **G**

P

26

49

K
■ Angels Camp

T
New Melones Lake

D ■ Columbia

F ■ Sonora

Stockton ■

4

N

0 SCALE   25
KILOMETERS   25
MILES   ROAD   INTERSTATE

Food

- **A** Bootlegger's
- **A** Butterworth's
- **B** Café Sarah's
- **C** Cirino's at the Forks
- **D** City Hotel Dining Room
- **E** Cowboy Pizza
- **F** Coyote Creek Café and Grill
- **F** Good Heavens
- **G** Grounds
- **B** Lil' Mama D. Carlo's
- **H** Michael's Restaurant
- **E** Potager at Selayas
- **I** Ruby's Café
- **B** Tortilla Flats

Lodging

- **B** Cary Hotel
- **D** City Hotel
- **J** Coloma Country Inn
- **K** Cooper House Bed and Breakfast Inn
- **L** Graeagle Lodge
- **M** Herrington's Sierra Pines Resort
- **K** Jumping Frog Motel
- **F** Llamahall Guest Ranch
- **G** Murphy's Historic Hotel and Lodge
- **H** National Hotel (Jackson)
- **E** National Hotel (Nevada City)
- **E** Red Castle Inn
- **N** Robin's Nest

- **O** St. George Hotel
- **C** Saundra Dyer's Resort
- **F** Sonora Inn
- **I** Sutter Creek Inn

Camping

- **P** Calaveras Big Trees State Park
- **J** Camp Lotus
- **J** Coloma Resort
- **Q** Folsom Lake State Recreation Area
- **D** 49er RV Ranch
- **R** Malakoff Diggins State Historic Park
- **S** New Hogan Lake Recreation Area

Note: Items with the same letter are located in the same town or area.

City and **Herrington's Sierra Pines Resort**, a rustic lodge with a great Yuba River location. Rooms start at $50, (916) 862-1151.

One of the nicest of the many B&B choices in Nevada City is the historic **Red Castle Inn**, built in 1860 and overlooking Nevada City from the hills across the river. Rooms range from $100 to $140, 109 Prospect Street, (916) 265-5135 or (800) 761-4766. The grand old **National Hotel** at 211 Broad Street in downtown Nevada City is steeped in history. Rooms with private baths start at $68, (916) 265-4551.

Near the heart of the Marshall Gold Discovery State Historic Park, the 1852 **Coloma Country Inn** is a fine, historic option. The innkeepers offer rafting and hot air ballooning trips, as well as use of their canoe on the nice pond, 345 High Street, (916) 622-6919.

The **Cary Hotel** in downtown Placerville offers history on a budget. Rooms at this landmark hotel range from $45 to $80 (suite), 300 Main Street, (916) 622-4271.

Sutter Creek has several nice places, including the **Sutter Creek Inn**, right in town at 75 Main Street. A few of the rooms have swinging beds (hanging from ceiling chains). Rooms start at $60, (209) 267-5606.

The old **St. George Hotel** in Volcano has shared baths, no air conditioning or heat, and 130 long years under its belt. If that's okay with you, don't miss the chance to spend a quiet night in this town of yesteryear. Dinner and breakfast are included, call for rates, (209) 296-4458.

In Jackson, the **National Hotel** has been in operation continuously since 1862. Many of the furnishings are original—as the plumbing seems to be. Rooms are very reasonable, 2 Water Street, (209) 223-0500.

Angels Camp has a good budget choice in the **Jumping Frog Motel**, with basic rooms from $45, (209) 736-2191.

Murphys has several B&Bs, in addition to **Murphys Historic Hotel and Lodge**, a local landmark and gathering place. There are nine rooms in the original building, 20 in a motel addition, $70 to $80, 457 Main Street, (209) 728-3444.

Spend a night in another era at the **Columbia City Hotel**, right on the main street of the closed-to-vehicles town. Rooms are from $75 to $95, (209) 532-1479.

In Sonora, the historic **Sonora Inn**, 160 South Washington Street, has rooms from $55 to $110, (209) 532-3400. For something different, stay at the **Llamahall Guest Ranch**, a great B&B and a working llama ranch. You can even meet the llamas, 18170 Wards Ferry Road, (209) 532-7264.

CAMPING

There are several National Forest campgrounds along CA 49 and Gold Lake Road (N.F. 24), both north and south of Downieville.

Three reservoirs near CA 49 have one or more campgrounds. For **Folsom Lake State Recreation Area**, take Rattlesnake Bar Road from Pilot Hill south of Auburn. Roads from CA 49, CA 26, and CA 12 provide access to **New Hogan Lake Recreation Area** near Valley Springs. CA 49 crosses New Melones Lake south of **Angels Camp**. Campground access is from the highway on either side of the lake.

Near Nevada City, **Malakoff Diggins State Historic Park** (see Sightseeing listing for directions) has a campground with $10 sites, (916) 265-2740 for information, (800) 444-7275 for reservations.

Calaveras Big Trees State Park on CA 4 above Arnold has a nice campground next to a sequoia grove. Sites are $12 to $16, (209) 795-2334 for information, (800) 444-7275 for reservations.

The **Coloma Resort** has RV and a few tent sites right on the American River, close to the sites of the state historic park. Sites run from $25 to $29, 6921 Mt. Murphy Road (from CA 49), (800) 238-2298. Nearby, down Lotus Road, **Camp Lotus** has tent sites from $15 to $22, (916) 622-8672.

Half a mile from Columbia State Historic Park on Italian Bar Road (from Pacific Street) is the **49er RV Ranch**, with nice shady sites for $23, (209) 532-4978.

Scenic Route: High Sierra Pass Roads

Four highways cross the Sierras between Yosemite and Lake Tahoe: U.S. 50, CA 88, CA 4, and CA 108. Each climbs from the foothills of Gold Country, through the vacation cabins and pine forests, up into high ski and lake basins, and over the Sierra crest. Only U.S. 50, a main route to Tahoe, experiences truly heavy traffic.

CA 88, a designated National Scenic Byway, is perhaps the nicest of the four, with CA 4 and CA 108 close behind. CA 88 features beautiful Caples Lake and Silver Lake, as well as access to Indian Grinding Rock Historic State Park and Volcano, a virtual ghost town. CA 4 rides the high ridge above the Mokelumne and Stanislaus valleys and features wonderful sequoia groves in Calaveras Big Trees State Park. CA 108, the highest of the three roads at 9,624 feet, crosses Sonora Pass.

For those desiring a three-to-six-day, 450-mile "Sierra sampler," take CA 120 through Yosemite with a tour of Yosemite Valley; U.S. 395 with stops at Mono Lake and a side trip to Bodie; CA 89 up to Emerald Bay on Lake Tahoe; back to CA 88 and across Carson Pass; then down to Gold Country and CA 49.

HIGH SIERRA PASS ROADS

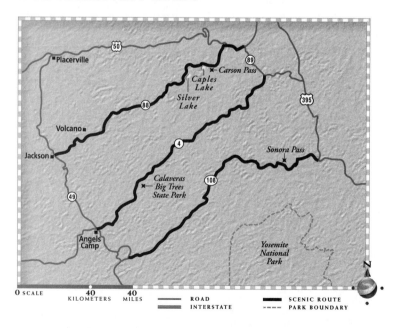

13
LAKE TAHOE

Straddling the California-Nevada border at 6,229 feet above sea level, beautiful Lake Tahoe attracts outdoor enthusiasts from all over the world. A dozen ski resorts surround the basin, including Squaw Valley U.S.A., which hosted events in the 1960 Olympics. Tahoe is a top weekend getaway spot, both in winter and summer. Don't get stuck on Interstate 80 and U.S. 50 at peak traffic times; that is, eastbound on Friday evenings and westbound on Sundays. Spring, fall, and midweek are the best times to be in the area.

Tahoe City on the northwest shore is the relaxed center for active outdoor sports enthusiasts. Some of the most serious skiing is done at Alpine Meadows and Squaw Valley just to the north on CA 89. The southwest shore features beautiful state parks and wilderness access. South Lake Tahoe hosts the largest concentration of accommodations and vacation homes. Cross into Nevada on either the north or south shores, and you shift immediately into the resort gambling scene.

Unless you're interested in gambling or specific Nevada sites, don't bother circling the lake. CA 89 passes through the most scenic areas. Your time is best spent in the hills, on the water, or at a café table on a deck where the two meet.

North of Tahoe, the area around Truckee offers attractions relating to the history of gold and silver mining, the transcontinental railroad, and cannibalism in America—that's right, cannibalism! It was around Donner Lake in the winter of 1846–1847 that some members of the ill-fated Donner Party survived by eating their loved ones. ◼

LAKE TAHOE

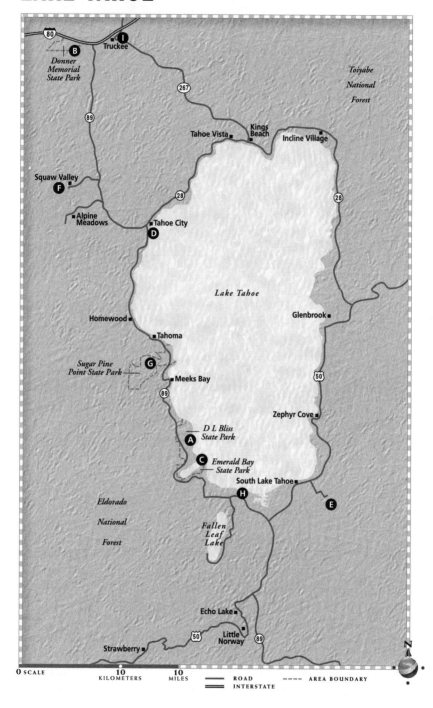

Truckee

80

Donner
Memorial
State Park

B

89

267

Toiyabe

National

Forest

Tahoe Vista

Kings
Beach

Incline Village

Squaw Valley

F

28

28

Alpine
Meadows

Tahoe City

D

Lake Tahoe

Homewood

Glenbrook

Tahoma

Sugar Pine
Point State Park

G

Meeks Bay

89

50

Zephyr Cove

D L Bliss
State Park

A

C

Emerald Bay
State Park

South Lake Tahoe

H

E

Eldorado

National

Forest

Fallen
Leaf
Lake

Echo Lake

50

Little
Norway

89

Strawberry

N

O SCALE   10
KILOMETERS   10
MILES   ——— ROAD   - - - - AREA BOUNDARY
═══ INTERSTATE

Sightseeing Highlights

Ⓐ D. L. Bliss State Park

Ⓑ Donner Memorial State Park

Ⓒ Emerald Bay State Park

Ⓓ Gatekeepers Museum

Ⓔ Heavenly Valley Tram

Ⓕ Squaw Valley Gondola

Ⓖ Sugar Pine Point State Park

Ⓗ Tallac Historic Site

Ⓘ Truckee

A PERFECT DAY AROUND LAKE TAHOE

What's your pleasure? If you arrive in winter or spring, a day of down-hill skiing at Alpine Meadows might be right. In summer or fall, a hike from Echo Lake into the edge of the Desolation Wilderness might fit the bill. If your just passing through, follow CA 89. Stop in Truckee and Donner Memorial State Park for some history. Spend half a day hiking and enjoying in D. L. Bliss and Emerald Bay State Parks. Pick a lakeside eatery to soak in the Tahoe scene. There's no place to go, you're already there.

SIGHTSEEING HIGHLIGHTS

☆☆☆ **D.L. Bliss State Park**—With the peaks of **Desolation Wilderness** looming above and the longest stretch of protected lakeshore below, this park should be at the top of your list. Walk the **Rubicon Trail** along the shore to find the patch of sand or granite boulder just right for basking. There are good spots to swim or to dive from the rocks. A 4-mile walk will take you to Vikingsholm in Emerald Bay State Park.

The parking lot at the end of the road is very small. At high times and during high season, you may have to walk an extra mile and a half from the upper lot to reach the main beach. Try to arrive early, especially if your schedule puts you in Tahoe on the weekend. Details: CA 89 runs through the park, south of Meeks Bay; (916) 525-7277; open 8 a.m. to dusk. Fee is $5 for day use.

★★★ **Emerald Bay State Parks**—Emerald Bay is one of the loveliest spots on this or any lake. Fed by a pristine stream draining from the Desolation Wilderness, a steady outflow assures that the water here will keep its crystal clarity, no matter how the larger lake fares in the long run. The bay's color is a feast for the eyes, the rich blue of the deeps blending into a turquoise that almost glows. CA 89 loops high above the bay, affording wonderful views. Details: On CA 89 south of Meeks Bay and D. L. Bliss State Park. For park information, call (916) 525-7277.

At the head of the bay is **Vikingsholm**, an imitation of a medieval Norse fortress built in 1929 by wealthy heiress Lora Josephine Knight. A steep, 1-mile path descends to the castle from the marked parking lot on the highway. Better yet, take the longer hike (about 4 miles) from the adjacent D. L. Bliss State Park to enjoy relative solitude and the best of the lakeside. Details: (916) 541-5155; open daily in summer from 10 a.m. to 4 p.m. Admission is $2. (3 hours)

★★ **Donner Memorial State Park**—In the spring of 1846, the Donners left Illinois with two other families, to be joined in Missouri by several others. The party was slowed in crossing the continent and became stranded by the shores of Donner Lake in one of the bitterest winters on record. Of the 87 who were snowbound, over half died, some resorting to cannibalism to survive.

In the forested flats around Donner Lake's eastern end, there's little to see besides sites, plaques, and a monument. However, don't miss the excellent **Emigrant Trail Museum** to gain a rich perspective of this compelling story. Details: (916) 582-7892; open daily from 10 a.m. to 5 p.m. Admission is $2; free with $5 park day use fee. The state park features trails and lake access. It's open until dusk, $5 day use. (1 hour)

★ **Gatekeepers Museum**—You'll probably see a small crowd of visitors at this three-way attraction in Tahoe City. Features include the museum, the **Lake Tahoe Dam**, and the small **William B. Layton**

State Park. It's hypnotic to watch the waters tumble over the small spillway that controls the lake level and serves as the headwaters of the Truckee River. The museum is a reconstruction of the original gate-keepers' log cabin in which dam attendants lived. There are good local heritage displays inside. Details: On CA 89 just south of the CA 89–CA 28 junction in Tahoe City; (916) 583-1762; open daily through the summer, Wednesday through Sunday in shoulder seasons, 11 a.m. to 5 p.m. Donations are accepted. (45 minutes)

✯ **Sugar Pine Point State Park**—More developed and accessible than D. L. Bliss State Park, Sugar Pine has a popular beach, swimming dock, and tennis courts. There's an informative **Nature Center** near the water. Trails visit **Sugar Pine Point**, while a longer route climbs toward the high peaks through the large portion of the park that's above the road. Details: On CA 89, 1 mile south of Tahoma; (916) 525-7982; open from 8 a.m. to dusk. Fee is $5 for day use.

The star attraction is the **Ehrman Mansion**, a beautiful Queen Anne-style structure built in 1902. Details: 1 mile south of Tahoma; (916) 525-7982. Mansion tours depart daily, on the hour, from 11 a.m. to 4 p.m., July 1 through Labor Day. Admission is free. (1 hour)

✯ **Heavenly Valley Tram**—For a spectacular, panoramic view of the lake basin without the challenge of a tough hike, take a tram ride. At the top, you'll be 2,000 feet above the lake surface. Hiking trails can take you even higher. Details: Take Ski Run Boulevard south from U.S. 50 between South Lake Tahoe and the Nevada border; (916) 586-7000; a tram departs every 15 minutes, daily in the summer, from 10 a.m. to 9 p.m. (from 9 a.m. on Sundays, closed Sundays in shoulder season). Cost is $6. (1 hour)

✯ **Squaw Valley Gondola**—At the top of this lift, there's a swimming pool and an ice skating rink as well as a fabulous view. Enjoy a cool drink as you soak in the alpine splendor. Details: 1960 Squaw Valley Road; (916) 583-6985 or (800) 545-4350; the gondola runs from July through March—call ahead to make sure scheduled maintenance isn't underway. Admission is $13. (1½ hours)

✯ **Tallac Historic Site**—Located on CA 89, three miles north of its junction with U.S. 50, the Tallac site features three historic estates on the shores of the lake. The **Pope Estate**, built in 1894, serves as visitor center and art gallery. The **Tallac Museum**, featuring heritage and

Indian displays, is housed in the **Baldwin Estate**, built in 1924. Details: North of Camp Richardson and South Lake Tahoe on CA 89; (916) 541-4975; the site is open from dawn to dusk in the summer only. **Pope Estate Visitor Center** hours are 8 a.m. to 5 p.m. daily, summer only, (916) 573-2674. (1½ hours)

☆ **Truckee**—The tracks for Northern California's main east-west rail route dominate this fine, historic town. Mining put Truckee on the map, and the completion of the transcontinental railroad through Donner Pass kept it there. Enjoy the shops, restaurants, and historic buildings while avoiding the outdoor chic of the lake and ski areas.

FITNESS AND RECREATION

There are many excellent skiing areas in the region. See the chart following for a breakdown:

Royal Gorge is the largest cross country ski area in the nation, featuring 200 miles of trails. Take the Soda Springs exit from I-80, turn right at the flashing light and follow the signs, (916) 426-3871. Northeast of Tahoe City at the **Lakeview Cross Country Ski Area**, the extensive network of trails starts on a never-finished golf course, then heads up into Burton Creek State Park. Take CA 28, turning onto Fabian at the Shell Station, take the first right onto Village, then left on Country Club. Trail fees range from $5 to $15, rentals $12 to $15, (916) 583-9353. **Squaw Valley**, **Kirkwood**, **Northstar-at-Tahoe**, and other ski areas have cross country trails as well.

A very nice bike path follows the north and west shores of the lake between Dollar Point and Sugar Pine Point State Park, with an extension down the Truckee River to Squaw Valley. Another designated path runs from South Lake Tahoe almost to Emerald Bay. For a major mountain bike ride, ask about the **Flume Trail** along the ridge in Lake Tahoe–Nevada State Park. The rental shops all have good information on rides. **Mountain Cyclery** in Kings Beach rents and repairs mountain bikes in the summer, 8299 North Lake Boulevard, (916) 546-3535. A couple miles south of Tahoe City on CA 89 is Sunnyside, where you'll find **Cycle Paths**, a good place to rent a bike. Guided day rides range from $30 to $50. 1785 West Lake Boulevard, (916) 581-1171.

Just north of the posh homes of Tahoe Pines is the trailhead for **Eagle Rock**. A short, steep hike earns you marvelous views. It's a great way to spend an hour or so. The **Tahoe Rim Trail** circles the lake on the ridges, covering 150 miles in the process. There is access at several points. **Desolation, Granite Chief**, and **Mt. Rose Wilderness** areas have good trail systems.

FOOD

In and around Tahoe, there's plenty of good food for the discerning and big food for the hungry.

In the Truckee Hotel, **The Passage** has great food with live music on weekends, 10007 Bridge Street (just off Commercial), (916) 587-7619. The place is tiny, but the omelettes and sandwiches are giant and tasty at the **Squeeze In**, 10060 Donner Pass Road.

In Kings Beach, the **Log Cabin Caffé** advertises the fact that they've been voted as having the best breakfast in Tahoe. I'll call it one of the best three which, in this restaurant happy region, is close enough. **Lanza's** pasta, pizza, and meat dishes are the real thing.

There are two good fine dining options in Tahoe Vista. **Captain John's** features dinner entrees in the $16 to $20 range. Deck and pier seating is more casual. Next door, **Le Petit Pier** is even more upscale, featuring Americanized French cuisine with a view. Entrees are in the $16 to $25

LAKE TAHOE AREA SKIING

Name	Closest Tahoe Town	Phone	Vertical Drop	Lifts	Weekend $ Day/Half
Alpine Meadows	Tahoe City	(800) 441-4423	1802'	12	45/30
Boreal	Truckee	(916) 426-3666	600'	9	34/26
Diamond Peak	Incline Village	(800) 468-2463	1840'	7	35/27
Donner Ski Ranch	Truckee	(916) 426-3635	750'	6	20/16
Granilibakken	Tahoe City	(916) 583-9896	300'	2	15/10
Heavenly	S. Lake Tahoe	(916) 541-1330	3500'	26	44/30
Kirkwood	S. Lake Tahoe	(209) 258-6000	2000'	11	41/31
Mt. Rose	Incline Village	(800) 754-7673	1440'	5	38/26
Northstar	Kings Beach	(916) 562-1010	2280'	12	43/29
Sierra-at-Tahoe	S. Lake Tahoe	(916) 659-7453	2212'	10	39/27
Ski Homewood	Homewood	(916) 525-2992	1658'	8	34/25
Soda Springs	Truckee	(916) 426-1010	650'	2	15/15
Squaw Valley	Tahoe City	(800) 545-4350	2850'	40	45/31
Sugar Bowl	Truckee	(916) 426-3651	1500'	10	40/26
Tahoe Donner	Truckee	(916) 587-9444	600'	3	26/15

range, 7238 North Lake Boulevard (CA 28), (916) 546-4464. The **Seedling Café and Coffeehouse** is an excellent, inexpensive vegetarian option for a bite to eat or some espresso. Check the schedule for readings and music upstairs, 7081 North Lake Boulevard (CA 28), (916) 546-3936.

The best known place in Tahoe City is **Rosie's Café**. You can't go wrong, breakfast, lunch or dinner, 571 North Lake Boulevard (CA 28), (916) 583-8504. **Za's Pizza** hits the spot for lunch or dinner, 395 North Lake Boulevard (CA 28), (916) 583-1812.

Two miles south of Tahoe City is the **Fire Sign Café** in Sunnyside, another of the top three breakfast places around, 1785 West Lake Boulevard (CA 89), (916) 583-0871 (good lunches too).

Across the highway from the Homewood Ski Area is the **West Shore Café**, featuring mixed cuisine lunches from $10, dinner from $15, with great outdoor seating on the lake, 5180 West Lake Boulevard (CA 89), (916) 525-5200.

Third of the top three for breakfast is the **Stony Ridge Café** in Tahoma, located with the Tahoma Meadows B&B, (916) 525-0905.

Sit outside at the **Beacon** on the beach at Camp Richardson, just west of South Lake Tahoe. Enjoy a salad, sandwich, or seafood as you bask. There's live music, too, 1900 Jamisonn Beach Road, (916) 541-0630. Drop in at the **Red Hut** for breakfast or a burger. It's no-nonsense American fare done right, 2723 Hwy. 50, South Lake Tahoe, (916) 541-9024.

LODGING

Lodging at Lake Tahoe is often booked weeks in advance. Prices are generally highest in the summer, a bit lower in the winter, and much lower in the spring and fall shoulder seasons.

The **Truckee Hotel** offers a fine dose of history with all the comforts of a recent restoration, 10007 Bridge Street (just off Commercial). Shared-bath rooms range from $70 to $115, private bath rooms from $90 to $115, (916) 587-4444 or (800) 659-6921.

The biggest concentration of North Shore lodging options is in Tahoe Vista. Right on the water, **Lakeside Chalets** has nice cabins with fireplaces and kitchens. In the summer, Alvina the friendly innkeeper offers windsurfing lessons. Cabins run from $95 to $135, 7276 North Lake Boulevard (CA 28), (916) 546-5857. **Beesley's Cottages** is clean, cute, on the beach, and family friendly. Rooms and

Robert Holmes

LAKE TAHOE

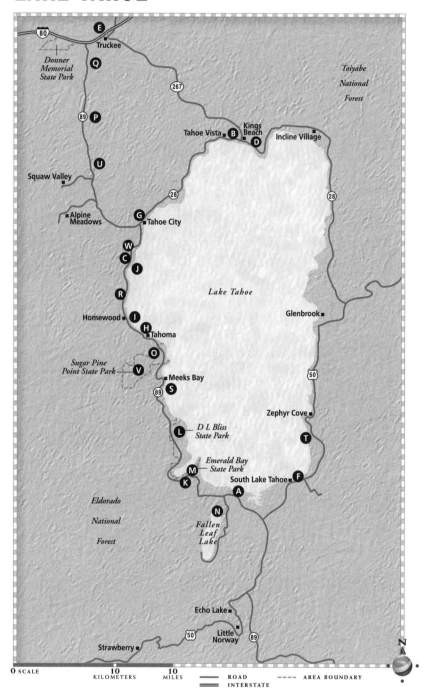

Truckee
Donner Memorial State Park
Toiyabe National Forest
Tahoe Vista
Kings Beach
Incline Village
Squaw Valley
Alpine Meadows
Tahoe City
Lake Tahoe
Homewood
Tahoma
Glenbrook
Sugar Pine Point State Park
Meeks Bay
Zephyr Cove
D L Bliss State Park
Emerald Bay State Park
South Lake Tahoe
Eldorado National Forest
Fallen Leaf Lake
Echo Lake
Little Norway
Strawberry

O SCALE
10 KILOMETERS
10 MILES
ROAD
INTERSTATE
AREA BOUNDARY

N

Food

- (A) Beacon
- (B) Captain John's
- (C) Fire Sign Café
- (D) Lanza's
- (B) Le Petit Pier
- (D) Log Cabin Caffé
- (E) The Passage
- (F) Red Hut
- (G) Rosie's Café
- (B) Seedling Café and Coffeehouse
- (E) Squeeze In
- (H) Stony Ridge Café
- (I) West Shore Café
- (B) Za's Pizza

Lodging

- (B) Beesley's Cottages
- (A) Camp Richardson Resort
- (F) Christiania Inn
- (F) Inn by the Lake
- (B) Lakeside Chalets
- (J) Sunnyside Lodge
- (G) Tahoe City Travelodge
- (G) Tahoe Marina Lodge
- (H) Tahoma Meadows Bed and Breakfast
- (E) Truckee Hotel

Camping

- (K) Bayview Campground
- (A) Camp Richardson
- (L) D. L. Bliss State Park
- (M) Emerald Bay State Park
- (N) Fallen Leaf Campground
- (O) General Creek Campground
- (P) Goose Creek
- (Q) Granite Flat
- (R) Kaspian Camping
- (S) Meeks Bay Campground
- (T) Nevada Beach
- (U) Silver Creek
- (V) Sugar Pine Point State Park
- (W) William Kent Campground

Note: Items with the same letter are located in the same town or area.

cottages range from $80 to $120, 6647 North Lake Boulevard (CA 28), (916) 546-2448.

Tahoe City has several good places to stay. The **Tahoe Marina Lodge** is a nice motel with tennis courts, a pool, and beachfront. Rooms start at $83 midweek in the shoulder season, $160 in August, (916) 583-2365 or (800) 748-5650. **Tahoe City Travelodge,** next to the golf course, is more reasonable with rooms from $50 to $115, 455 North Lake Boulevard (CA 28), (916) 583-3766 or (800) 578-7878.

The moderately luxurious **Sunnyside Lodge** at the Sunnyside Marina has rooms from $80 to $185—cheapest in spring and fall, priciest in the summer, 1850 West Lake Boulevard (CA 89), (916) 583-7200 or (800) 822-2754.

The cozy cabins of **Tahoma Meadows Bed and Breakfast** have that Tahoe "feel"—a fine place with a great breakfast. Cabins run from $95 to $125, 6821 West Lake Boulevard, Tahoma, (916) 525-1553 or (800) 355-1596.

West of South Lake Tahoe, the **Camp Richardson Resort** has nightly rentals in a lodge, condos, or rustic cabins ranging from $64 to $125. The resort is next to the Tallac Historic Site and features a marina, the Beacon Bar & Grill, and a private beach, (916) 541-1801 or (800) 544-1801.

South Lake Tahoe is motel central. A number of budget and chain motels are found along U.S. 50. Others are clustered near the state line and casino action. Use the numbers on the "Resources" page to contact the chains. For general reservation assistance, call the South Lake Tahoe Visitors Authority at (800) 288-2463. The **Inn by the Lake** at 3300 Lake Tahoe Boulevard (U.S. 50) has nice rooms from $85. Near the base of the Heavenly Valley ski lifts is the **Christiania Inn** with a range of rooms and romantic suites, 3819 Saddle Road, (916) 544-7337.

CAMPING

Each of the three main state parks have very nice campgrounds. **Sugar Pine Point State Park**, located above the highway, has access to mountain trails and is open year-round, $12 to $16, (916) 525-7982. **D. L. Bliss State Park** has easy access to the lakeshore and Rubicon Trail, $12 to $20, (916) 525-7277. **Emerald Bay State Park** has great sites on Eagle Point, the south side of Emerald Bay, $12 to $16, (916) 541-3030. Call (800) 444-7275 for reservations.

Several National Forest campgrounds are located around Lake Tahoe and along the Truckee River. Many more are nearby, especially along CA 89, both north and south of the lake, and along CA 88 between Nevada and Silver Lake. Between Truckee and Tahoe City on CA 89 are: **Granite Flat** (fairly large and close to Truckee), **Goose Creek** (the nicest of the three because it's set back from the highway), and **Silver Creek** (closest to Squaw Valley and the lake).

Around the lake, you'll find: **William Kent** (above CA 89 just south of Tahoe City), **Kaspian** (close to Eagle Rock, above Tahoe Pines, with shore access across the road), **Meeks Bay** (in the trees next to Meeks Bay resort with beach access), **Bayview** (undeveloped sites above Emerald Bay with access to great views and rocky climbs), **Fallen Leaf** (at the end of lovely Fallen Leaf Lake, take Fallen Leaf Lake Road from Camp Richardson), **Camp Richardson** (beach access, near South Lake Tahoe), and **Nevada Beach** (just over the Nevada border with great beach access). Prices range from $11 to $17. Some sites are reservable, call (800) 280-2267 ($7.85 per reservation).

NIGHTLIFE

Two popular spots are located down by the lake, behind the Safeway, at the east end of Tahoe City. The **Bluewater Brewing Company** has tasty site-brewed beer and excellent pub grub, pool tables, and Todd, the happy bartender. Next door, the **Pierce Street Annex** has a full line of drinks with a broil-your-own grill deal, 950 North Lake Tahoe Boulevard (CA 28), (916) 583-5800. Across the road is **Humpty's**, a bar, grill, and rock and roll club with good bands and a bad attitude, 877 North Lake Boulevard (CA 28), (916) 583-4867. **Pete and Peter's** is a good sports bar in the heart of town.

14
OWENS VALLEY AND MONO LAKE

E ast of Yosemite, the land drops steeply into the shallow, undrained
Mono Lake Basin. The surrounding land is dry and desolate, a
sagebrush-tufted home to coyotes and jackrabbits. Here, at the heavily
faulted and fractured edge of the Sierra range, volcanic formations
attest to the molten rock that hovers near the surface. Few people live
in the region, though it once crawled with miners.

South of Mono Lake, no road crosses the High Sierra for almost
200 miles. At all times, an unbroken jagged line of 12,000-foot to
14,000-foot peaks frown down upon you, rising as much as 2 vertical
miles above the Owens River. Nowhere else in North America can you
find such a precipitous drop from ridgecrest to valley floor. Owens
Valley is the deepest on the continent.

The steep valleys of the Eastern Sierra hide treasures of beauty
and wonder. Short miles above the dusty basins, sparkling waterfalls
dance and tumble into forested defiles, spilling across alpine meadows.
Hot springs well up, flowing into pools and channels created by grateful
bathers across the years. Barren cinder cones pepper the slopes. Atop a
high ridge to the east, trees still grow that were alive when the first
Egyptian pyramids were no more than plans scratched in the sand.

If you take U.S. 395 through the valleys east of the Sierra, you'll discover the magnificent land outside California's backdoor. Relatively few
travel this way—be one of the few if chance allows. You won't regret it. ◪

A PERFECT DAY IN THE EASTERN SIERRAS

Enjoy the overlooks and scenic drives down from Tahoe on CA 89 or from Yosemite on CA 120. Walk among the ghosts in Bodie State Historic Park, then head to Lee Vining for a picnic lunch with a view of Mono Lake. Choose an afternoon activity—perhaps a walk in the South Tufa Reserve on Mono Lake's southern shore, a visit to Devil's Postpile, a hike or horseback ride in a high valley of the Eastern Sierra, or a tour of volcanic sites. Climb out of Big Pine on CA 168 for a sunset view at 11,000 feet and camping near the ancient bristlecone groves.

SIGHTSEEING HIGHLIGHTS

★★★ **Ancient Bristlecone Pine Forest**—Making sure you have half a day available and a full tank of gas, take CA 168 east from the town of **Big Pine** to reach the forest. The road winds from the valley floor to the crest of the **White Mountains**, 11,000 feet above sea level. Two main groves of the stubby, gnarled bristlecones, some over 4,000 years old, can each be explored in one to three hours. The views westward of the **Owens Valley** and **Sierra Crest** are fabulous. **Grandview** is the highest and the best of five campgrounds along the highway. Details: Located north of CA 168 on Westgard Pass Road; (619) 873-2500; open daily from June through October. (half day)

★★★ **Bodie State Historic Park**—Seven miles south of Bridgeport on U.S. 395, desolate CA 270 heads off eastward through an empty landscape, 13 miles to the site of historic Bodie. After it was discovered in 1859, over $100 million worth of gold came from the area surrounding this rough-and-ready boom town. Some 10,000 people lived here at one time, working one of the 700 mining claims or serving those who did. Scores of bars and brothels satisfied the baser instincts of the residents—Bodie was known as much for sin and violence as it was for precious metal.

Though the buildings that still stand are only a small percentage of the original, they have never been vandalized or restored, and have been preserved by isolation and dry climate. Almost as important, no modern commercial enterprises or structures of any kind are to be found nearby. No other ghost town in the west will give you a better feel for the past.

For a bit of adventure, return to U.S. 395 via Cottonwood Canyon Road—a 20-mile back route over a low pass and down a winding arroyo to Mono Lake. It's a good gravel road that cuts up to the right just

OWENS VALLEY AND MONO LAKE

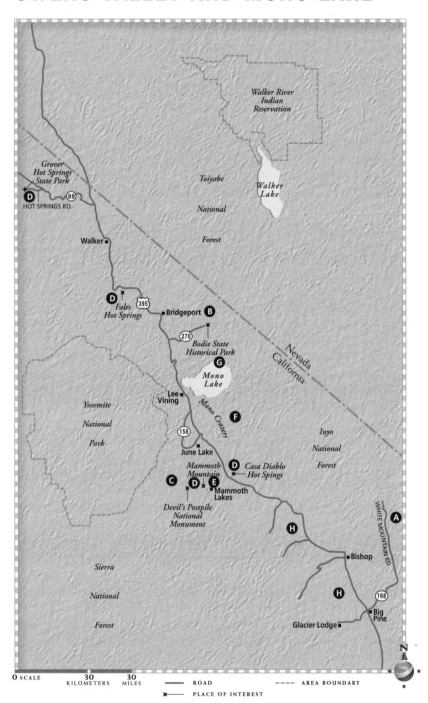

Grover
Hot Springs
State Park
D
HOT SPRINGS RD (89)

Walker River
Indian
Reservation

Toiyabe

Walker
Lake

National

Forest

Walker■

D Fales
Hot Springs (395) ■Bridgeport **B**

(270)
Bodie State
Historical Park
G

Nevada
California

Mono
Lake

Lee ■
Vining

Yosemite

Mono Craters

F

National (158)

Park

June Lake

Inyo

National

Mammoth
Mountain **D** Casa Diablo
Hot Spings

Forest

C **D** **E**
■Mammoth
Lakes

Devil's Postpile
National
Monument

A

H

Sierra

WHITE MOUNTAIN RD

National

■Bishop

H (168)

Forest

Glacier Lodge■ ■Big
Pine

N

0 SCALE | 30 KILOMETERS | 30 MILES | ——— ROAD | – – – AREA BOUNDARY
✕——— PLACE OF INTEREST

Sightseeing Highlights

Ⓐ Ancient Bristlecone Pine Forest

Ⓑ Bodie State Historic Park

Ⓒ Devil's Postpile National Monument

Ⓓ Hot Springs

Ⓔ Mammoth

Ⓕ Mono Craters

Ⓖ Mono Lake

Ⓗ Sierra Valleys

before you reach the Bodie entrance kiosk. There are no services of any kind off U.S. 395, so make sure you have at least 70 miles worth of gas in the tank when you leave Lee Vining or Bridgeport. The Bureau of Land Management (BLM) land surrounding Bodie State Historical Park is open to free, dispersed camping, though you need a permit for a campfire. Details: Located 13 miles east of U.S. 395 on CA 270; (619) 647-6445; open daily from 9 a.m. to 7 p.m. Day use fee is $5. (3 hours)

☆☆☆ **Mono Lake**—This lonely, unique lake, the remnant of an ancient inland sea, appears to be the oldest continuously filled body of water on the continent. It has been saved from extinction by rulings that limit the level of diversion from its feeder streams. Having no drainage, the lake is naturally alkaline and mineral rich. Its islands provide breeding sites for most of the world's California Gulls, which feast on the brine shrimp that thrive in the lake.

Weird crystalline formations called *tufa* rim the lake. Formed underwater, the tufa has been exposed by the gradual shrinkage of the lake's volume. A special reserve has been established to protect the moderately delicate formations. It is possible to walk among the best formations from access points in the **South Tufa Reserve** on the southern shore of the lake. Details: Take CA 120 east from U.S. 395, south of Lee Vining; (619) 647-6595. Admission is free. (1½ hours)

The town of Lee Vining, near the junction of U.S. 395 and CA 120, is the only town of consequence in the basin. Stop at the fine visitor center just north of town for information on lake access and a panoramic view.

✫ **Devil's Postpile National Monument**—The 80-foot, multi-sided basalt columns of Devil's Postpile are joined together into a scarp that is one quarter of a mile long. The formation, set in pleasant **Red's Meadow** in the **San Juaquin River Valley**, was created after the slowly cooled innards of a lava flow were exposed by time. The column tops show the shine and striations of a good polish by a glacier. A 1½-mile trail leads to lovely, 100-foot **Rainbow Falls** near the monument's south end. There are hot springs to enjoy in Red's Meadow, as well as a pack station. Five National Forest campgrounds line the river and Minaret Road.

From the end of CA 203 at **Minaret Summit** above **Mammoth Lakes**, a narrow road descends to the monument and San Juaquin River. The road is closed in the winter. During much of the summer, it is closed from 7:30 a.m. to 5:30 p.m. to private vehicles without campground reservations. Shuttles leave twice an hour from the Mammoth

Robert Holmes

Mountain Inn, stopping at several spots on the way, including the parking area for the Minaret Summit viewpoint where you can enjoy a magnificent view as you wait. Details: Open from June to October. Roundtrip shuttle is $7. (half day)

☆ **Mammoth**—Perhaps more properly called **Mammoth Lakes**, the region refers to the area around **Mammoth Mountain**, an old volcanic peak. There are indeed several lakes, the town of Mammoth Lakes, and access to the Ansel Adams Wilderness and Devil's Postpile National Monument. The famed **Mammoth Mountain Ski Area** has 27 lifts plus two gondolas. The mountain and lifts are open in the summer to mountain bikers, some of whom ride in the "Kamikaze Downhill" at the end of June—a race for the somewhat less than sane. In both winter and summer, Mammoth attracts people who like to play hard, day and night.

The lakes and wild country draw plenty of hikers, bikers, fishers, and vacationers throughout the summer. Take Lake Mary Road from CA 203 near the top of the village to enjoy the lakes. Drive 203 to its end at Minaret Summit for a fantastic view of the San Juaquin Valley and jagged Minarets. The **Mammoth Scenic Loop Road** links CA 203, a mile above town, with U.S. 395. Either take the road down from CA 203 or watch carefully for the sign a few miles above the U.S. 395 and CA 203 junction. This scenic road goes through an interesting volcanic region. Stop at the **Earthquake Fault** for a walk into a fascinating crevasse created by the forces that give Mammoth its precarious reputation.

☆ **Mono Craters**—South of Mono Lake, a distinct volcanic ridge of cinder cones parallels U.S. 395 to the east. A trailhead along CA 120 near the north cone and a couple of National Forest roads allow close inspection of these black and rust-colored rock piles. Good views are available from the roadside along U.S. 395.

☆ **Sierra Valleys**—South of the Mammoth Lakes junction, several spur roads climb quickly up to high valleys and lake basins below the Sierra crest. Drives up into any one of these valleys, or those further south, are short and rewarding. Just up from the arid valley floor are lakes, waterfalls, rushing streams, and alpine scenery. Most of the valleys have pack stations for trail rides and hiking access to high passes and remote basins.

CA 7, the **Convict Lake Road** leads in 3 short miles to a beautiful lake named for murderous escapees who hid there for a time. **Rock**

Creek Road passes upward through a beautiful valley to lovely **Rock Creek Lake**. Twelve National Forest campgrounds can be found on or near the road, which climbs to 10,000 feet above sea level. Farther south, **Pine Creek Road** would be similarly beautiful if not for the mammoth tungsten mine at the head of the valley. Still, the contrast of mineral extraction and pristine splendor is quite impressive. CA 168, out of Bishop, climbs to lakes with views of the 14,000-foot **Palisade** peaks. A café overlooking **Lake Sabrina** is a great place for lunch or a snack. **Glacier Lodge Road** leads to charming **Glacier Lodge**, (916) 938-2837, campgrounds and views of **Palisade Glacier**.

Hot Springs—The Mammoth area is one of the most seismically active in California. Volcanic features are common throughout the Eastern Sierra, and dire predictions of pending eruptions are frequent. Certainly, the abundance of hot springs in the region is pleasant proof that plenty of hot rock lies not far below the surface.

Grover Hot Springs State Park gathers warm waters into a family-style fenced pool. Details: located 3 miles west of Markleeville, off CA 89 on Hot Springs Road; (916) 694-2248; open from 9 a.m. to 9 p.m., Memorial Day through Labor Day; call for winter hours. Admission is $5 per car, plus $4 for adults and $2 for kids.

Primitive and pleasant **Buckeye Hot Springs** are about 10 miles southwest on Buckeye Road, which meets U.S. 395 4 miles north of Bridgeport. Continue up Buckeye Road to reach four National Forest campgrounds and Twin Lakes Road, which returns you to Bridgeport or to Twin Lakes. Try **Hot Creek Geological Site**, a state park a short way north of the main Mammoth Lakes junction. Caution: the water is really hot, and sudden temperature changes can be dangerous. In **Red's Meadow** next to Devil's Postpile, mineral baths are available at a nominal charge.

FITNESS AND RECREATION

Excellent hikes into the Sierras leave from the end of every road that heads up into a valley. In the bristlecones, the **Methuselah Trail** starts at Schulman Grove, looping 4¼ miles through the oldest of the old.

For a guided canoe tour of Mono Lake, join the non-profit **Mono Lake Committee** on their summer weekend trips, departing at 8 a.m., 9:30 a.m., and 11 a.m., Saturday and Sunday. Trips are $15. Call (619) 647-6595 for information.

Caldera Kayaks offers rentals and guided tours on Mono Lake. Located at the Crowley Lake Marina south of Mammoth on U.S. 395, (619) 935-4942.

Most of the Eastern Sierra Valleys have pack stations offering trail rides. Near Grand Lake on the June Lake Loop, **Frontier Pack Station** has rides ranging from one hour to all day for $20 to $65, (619) 648-7701. **Rock Creek Pack Station** is at the Rock Creek Resort up Rock Creek Road west of U.S. 395, south of Mammoth, (619) 935-4170. Take CA 168 above Bishop to reach South Lake and the **Rainbow Pack Station**. One-hour to one-day rides range from $20 to $75, (619) 873-8877.

FOOD

Two miles south of Coleville, you'll find the **Meadowcliff Restaurant**, offering American and Mexican food for breakfast, lunch, and dinner.

Bridgeport has **Bridgeport Inn** for fine dining. It's been in business since 1877, so you know they're doing something right, (619) 932-7380.

Look for the **Virginia Creek Settlement** south of Bridgeport. The restaurant has pizzas from $8, Italian dinners and steaks from $9 to $15.

In Lee Vining, basic nourishment, steady coffee, and good service can be had at **Nicely's**, (619) 647-6477. For pizza and beer, drop in at **Bodie Mike's Pizza**, (619) 647-6432.

The **Tiger Bar** in Mammoth Lakes is a favorite après-ski place for a bite and a beer, (619) 648-7551. **Paul Schat's Dutch Bakery** is a good stop for breakfast, across from the Motel 6 on CA 203. Down the street, **Slocum's Italian American Grill** has good dinners.

In Bishop, Paul's kinsman has a place called **Erick Schat's Bakkery** that people crowd into with zeal. You can come out with a strange mix of goodies, like a cup of soup, decaffeinated espresso, and a birthday cake, 763 North Main Street, (619) 873-7156. **Whiskey Creek** has a good patio for enjoying the fading evening over dinner, 524 North Main Street, (619) 873-7174.

LODGING

A mile south of Coleville is the lonely **Meadowcliff**. It's a pleasant bargain with a pool. Rooms are about $40, (916) 495-2180.

There are clean rooms and teepees at the **Toiyabe Motel** in Walker. Rooms are $35 to $45, (916) 495-2281.

OWENS VALLEY AND MONO LAKE

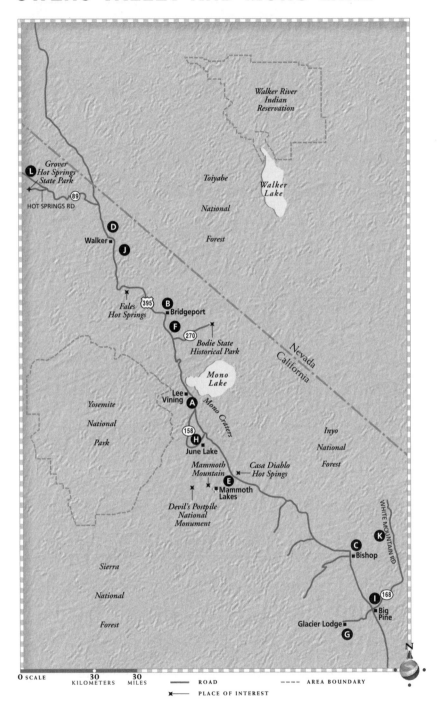

Grover Hot Springs State Park

Walker River Indian Reservation

Toiyabe

Walker Lake

National

HOT SPRINGS RD

Forest

Walker

Fales Hot Springs

Bridgeport

Bodie State Historical Park

Nevada
California

Mono Lake

Lee Vining

Mono Craters

Yosemite

National

Park

June Lake

Inyo

National

Forest

Mammoth Mountain

Casa Diablo Hot Spings

Mammoth Lakes

Devil's Postpile National Monument

WHITE MOUNTAIN RD

Bishop

Sierra

National

Forest

Big Pine

Glacier Lodge

N

O SCALE

30 KILOMETERS   30 MILES   ROAD   AREA BOUNDARY

PLACE OF INTEREST

Food

- **Ⓐ** Bodie Mike's
- **Ⓑ** Bridgeport Inn
- **Ⓒ** Erick Schat's Bakkery
- **Ⓓ** Meadowcliff Restaurant
- **Ⓐ** Nicely's
- **Ⓔ** Paul Schat's Dutch Bakery
- **Ⓔ** Slocum's Italian American Grill
- **Ⓔ** Tiger Bar
- **Ⓕ** Virginia Creek Settlement
- **Ⓒ** Whiskey Creek

Lodging

- **Ⓑ** The Cain House
- **Ⓗ** The Four Seasons
- **Ⓐ** Gateway Motel
- **Ⓖ** Glacier Lodge
- **Ⓗ** June Lake Villager Motel
- **Ⓓ** Meadowcliff
- **Ⓔ** North Village Inn
- **Ⓑ** Silver Maple Inn
- **Ⓘ** Starlight
- **Ⓙ** Toiyabe Motel

Camping

- **Ⓒ** Brown's Town
- **Ⓚ** Grandview Campground
- **Ⓛ** Grover Hot Springs State Park
- **Ⓔ** Mammoth Mountain RV Park
- **Ⓕ** Willow Springs Motel and RV Park

Note: Items with the same letter are located in the same town or area.

In the charming little town of Bridgeport, try the **Silver Maple Inn**. Rooms range from $55 to $80 (closed in winter), (619) 932-7383. For a more pampered setting, indulge yourself next door at **The Cain House**, a lovely B&B. Rooms run from $80 to $135, (619) 932-7040 or (800) 433-2246.

The town of Lee Vining has surprisingly expensive basic motels. The **Gateway Motel** offers winter rooms for $35, summer rooms for $95 (the same rooms). There is a view of Mono Lake, (619) 647-6467 or (800) 282-3929.

Along the June Lake Loop, **The Four Seasons** features A-frame cabins with splendid views of the High Sierras. Rates range from $80 to $140, depending on the season. Look for the signs south of Silver Lake, (619) 648-7476. The **June Lake Villager Motel** has rooms a nice notch up from basic at $35 to $80 and up, in the town of June Lake, (619) 648-7712 or (800) 655-6545.

In Mammoth, the **North Village Inn** is a great alternative to the big hotels on the strip. It's located just up Lake Mary Road from CA 203. Rooms are $50 to $125 in the summer, $30 more in the winter, 103 Lake Mary Road, (619) 934-2525 or (800) 257-3781.

Big Pine has several motels, including the **Starlight**, a clean, nicely kept place with HBO, 511 South Main, (619) 938-2011.

West of Big Pine up Glacier Lodge Road is **Glacier Lodge**, nestled in a gorgeous valley at 8,000 feet with views of Palisade Glacier. Rustic rooms are $65 to $75, (619) 938-2837.

CAMPING

National Forest campgrounds are renowned for their quality, and there are many along the eastern Sierras. Every road that climbs west from U.S. 395 has at least one. They don't offer hookups and only occasionally do they have pull-throughs, but the sites are almost always spacious and set away from neighbors. Areas where several campgrounds are concentrated together include CA 89 north of Markleeville, CA 120 above Mono Lake, the June Lake Loop Road, Mammoth Lakes, Rock Creek Road, and CA 168 above Bishop. Sites are usually from $8 to $11.

Grover Hot Springs State Park offers a nice campground and easy access to the hot springs pool, (916) 694-2248 for information, (800) 444-7275 for reservations.

If you need a camping night near Bodie, the friendly keepers of **Willow Springs Motel and RV Park** will take care of you. There's a campfire every evening and diversions for the kids. It's 5 miles south of Bridgeport on U.S. 395. Rooms are $45 to $65, and campsites are $18, (619) 932-7725.

Mammoth Mountain RV Park has some good tent sites too. There are a pool, jacuzzi, and recreation hall. Van tours and shuttles are available. Tent sites are $16, and RV sites are from $22 to $26, (619) 934-3822.

For an entertaining camp, stay at **Brown's Town**, 1 mile south of Bishop on U.S. 395. Most sites are shady, and there's a mock up of an old western town to explore. Rates are $10, or $13 with hookups, (619) 872-6911.

Inyo National Forest's **Grandview Campground**, at the edge of the Ancient Bristlecone Pine Forest, is a great place to spend a night if you're not bothered by high altitude (over 10,000 feet). The views are astronomical.

Free camping opportunities abound in the national forests and BLM lands that make up most of the region.

Scenic Route: June Lake Loop

As you cruise through the sagebrush basins and dry pine forests along U.S. 395, it's hard to imagine the alpine wonders to be found above. All along the eastern Sierra, streams and rivers drain into forested valleys and beautiful lake basins. The June Lake Loop (CA 158) offers easy access to such an area.

The northern end of CA 158 meets U.S. 395 6 miles south of Lee Vining. Very quickly, the land changes character as the road enters the foothills. Large Grand Lake seems to spill out of the high hills into a sage-dotted basin. The road enters a beautiful gorge, circling through a resort and recreation area to Silver Lake. From here, you drive through a pine forest with occasional views of the high peaks of the Ansel Adams Wilderness.

At the high point on the road, June Mountain Ski Basin rises above the town of June Lake, the site of some lodging and dining options. Go for a swim at the June Lake Swimming Beach, and enjoy the gorgeous mountain backdrop. From here the road slips back down to the highway.

JUNE LAKE LOOP

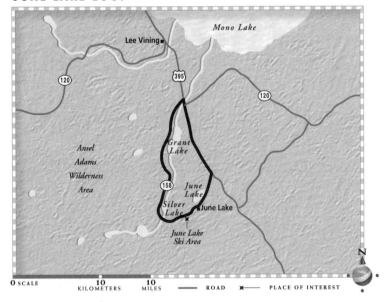

15
YOSEMITE

During the long high season, many thousands of people visit Yosemite every day. While most settle for snapshot viewpoints, the wisest escape the crowds and hit the trails. Be among the wise and find yourself a quiet spot. You will know without a doubt that you are in one of the most beautiful places on earth.

In May, Yosemite Falls, the tallest falls in North America, bursts from the valley rim to fall almost a half mile to the rocks below. In October, delicate Bridalveil spills a light stream over the edge, much of it blowing to mist before it can reach the valley floor. Incomparable walls of granite soar 3,000 feet above the gentle meadows along the Merced River. Only the perspective provided by the dots of red-jacketed climbers gives a sense of scale to the scene.

Despite the glory, there is a sadness to the valley. It is truly and utterly exhausted by overuse, overexposure, and the endless accolades it receives. You *must* visit Yosemite Valley, but it helps to imagine as it once was—silent except for the sounds of wind and water, and empty but for a small Indian group or two living along the river.

Fortunately, the glories of the park are not in the valley alone. The remarkable hard granite of the valley cliffs is found throughout the high country. Marvelous domes have surfaces that bootsoles stick to like velcro. Alpine meadows filled with wildflowers sprawl near the Tioga Pass Road. Lonely passes and lake basins are reached by over 800 miles of hiking trails. Besides, the valley is just as beautiful, if not more so, from the viewpoints and overlooks you earn with a couple of hours of hiking. ◼

YOSEMITE

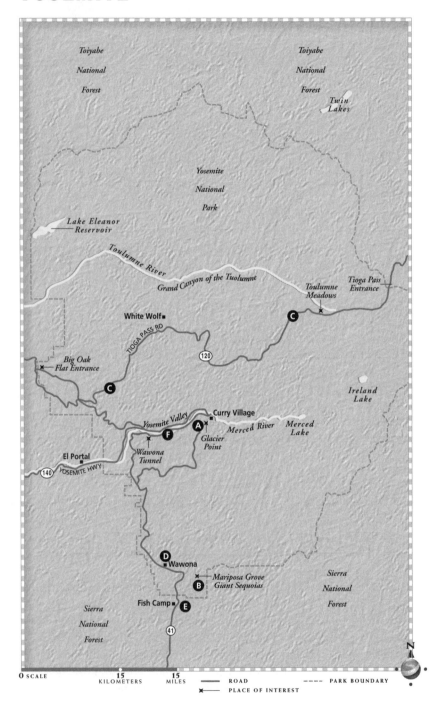

Toiyabe National Forest

Toiyabe National Forest

Twin Lakes

Yosemite National Park

Lake Eleanor Reservoir

Toulumne River

Grand Canyon of the Tuolumne

Toulumne Meadows

Tioga Pass Entrance

White Wolf■

TIOGA PASS RD

120

Big Oak Flat Entrance

C

C

Ireland Lake

Yosemite Valley

Curry Village

F

A

Merced River

Merced Lake

Glacier Point

El Portal

140

YOSEMITE HWY

Wawona Tunnel

D ■Wawona

Mariposa Grove Giant Sequoias

B

Fish Camp■ **E**

41

Sierra National Forest

Sierra National Forest

N

0 SCALE

15 KILOMETERS

15 MILES

—— ROAD

- - - PARK BOUNDARY

✕—— PLACE OF INTEREST

Sightseeing Highlights

Ⓐ Glacier Point

Ⓑ Mariposa Grove

Ⓒ Tioga Pass Road

Ⓓ Wawona

Ⓔ Yosemite Mountain Sugar Pine Railroad

Ⓕ Yosemite Valley

A PERFECT DAY IN YOSEMITE

Pick a challenge that matches your ability and walk. Hike from the Tioga Pass Road into Mono Pass for stunning views from the crest of the divide. Loop from Lambert Dome to Ragged Lakes, then back to Tuolumne Meadows. Hike to Harden Lake from White Wolf to reach views of Hetch Hetchy. Bus to Glacier Point and take a three-waterfall loop down the Panorama and John Muir Trails to Happy Isles. Hike from the valley to Yosemite Falls, Mirror Lake, or Old Inspiration Point. Stroll easily along the Merced. Stop, sit, think, breathe, and smile.

SIGHTSEEING HIGHLIGHTS

✩✩✩ **Yosemite Valley**—The three western highway approaches to the park all lead into Yosemite Valley. A one-way loop road takes visitors through the heart of the valley along the **Merced River**. As you drive in, the mighty mass of **El Capitan** anchors the north wall, rising 3,000 feet above the valley floor. To the south, **Bridalveil Fall** gushes during the spring snowmelt but is reduced to a windblown wisp of its former self at the end of the dry season. After passing the spires of the **Cathedral Rocks**, views of **Yosemite Falls** will begin to open out. At 2,450 feet, the **Upper and Lower Falls** together are the tallest in North America. In the springtime, the flow over the canyon rim is truly spectacular.

The services and accommodations in Yosemite Valley are clustered below Yosemite Falls. The **Valley Visitor Center** is located in **Yosemite Village**, above the outbound one-way road. Next door is the **Yosemite Museum Gallery** and **Indian Cultural Exhibit.** Details: Open daily from 9 a.m. to noon and from 1 p.m. to 4:45 p.m. Admission is free. (1½ hours)

Fairly short but steep hikes lead out of the valley to **Vernal Fall** and **Nevada Fall** on the Merced, **Illilouette Fall** on Illilouette Creek, Mirror Lake, and the base of **Lower Yosemite Falls**. Details: Trails are marked on the park map issued to all visitors.

East of Yosemite Falls, the valley splits, climbing up through beautiful, glacier-carved valleys and into granite basins. Inviting trails lead off in several directions. Dominating the area is mighty **Half Dome**, it's rounded summit looking 5,000 feet down to the valley floor. Half Dome's vertical north face, a daunting wall above the **Tenaya River**, looks as though it were sliced with a heavenly cleaver. With a 93 percent grade, it is the sheerest cliff on the continent. The numbers matter little; it is a stunning rock and the centerpiece of the park. Several views are particularly memorable, including the one from **Sentinel Bridge** just south of the village

Robert Holmes

and from **Mirror Lake** at the base of the north face in **Tenaya Canyon**.

Open tram tours, ranger-led walks, evening programs, and other park-sponsored activities are available. Current schedules, locations, and reservation information are printed in the park literature that all visitors receive. The Valley Visitor Center is your best source for personal assistance.

✯✯✯ **Glacier Point**—As you exit the Yosemite Valley, loop back to the south side road after you pass Valley View to reach the Wawona Road, and follow it as it climbs away from the Merced and up to a low pass at Chinquapin Junction. From here, take Glacier Point Road 16 miles up to Glacier Point for a sheer view 2,600 feet down into Curry Village. The valleys spread out before you: **Tenaya**, **Merced**, and **Illilouette**. Half Dome seems only a stone's throw away. You'll hear the echoes of roaring waters. So, too, will you hear the honking of horns, the straining of diesels, and even, on a calm day, the calls of exuberant visitors.

For an even better view, take the **Pohono Trail** to the **Sentinel Dome Trail** and climb to **Sentinel Dome**. At 900 feet above the level of Glacier Point, you'll notice that you're a notch closer to the divine. The roundtrip hike is about 2 miles from where the Pohono Trail crosses the road, about a quarter mile before the parking lot.

✯✯✯ **Tioga Pass Road**—CA 120 passes through the heart of the Yosemite high country, crosses the Sierra crest at **Tioga Pass**, and drops steeply down into the Mono Lake Basin. At its western end, CA 120 enters the park at Big Oak Flat and passes near the sequoias of **Merced Grove** and **Tuolumne Grove**. Both are a short walk from well-marked turnouts. The road winds up the divide between the Merced and Tuolumne basins through evergreen forest. There is good hiking access to the north rim of the valley from **Tamrack Flat** and **Yosemite Creek Campgrounds**.

Olmstead Point affords a magnificent view down the sculpted Tenaya Canyon to the head of the valley, with Half Dome presiding over all. Walk the short path out to the small granite knob opposite the parking area for a better look and feel. There are many points along the road where you can walk on the rocks. The granite of Yosemite is exceptionally "clean" rock, with little grit or sand to make you slip. You can walk right up steep grades without fear of slipping—though falling is still entirely possible if you're out of your league. Enjoy **Tenaya Lake** as you regret that the road couldn't have passed a bit farther from its shores.

The **John Muir Trail** comes up from the valley to meet the **Pacific Crest Trail** in **Tuolumne Meadows**. The meadows cluster around the confluence of several streams as they merge into the Tuolumne River. The meadows are still lovely, but boot traffic over the years has taken "pristine" out of the description. The visitor center can provide information on the several trails that fan out from here into the high country. If you're walking to Canada, start here.

Just over Tioga Pass, the scene changes radically. The road hugs a well-engineered grade as the land drops from sculpted highlands through a plunging valley to the basins of the eastern Sierras.

☆☆ **Mariposa Grove**—The Mariposa Grove is the largest of the three sequoia groves in Yosemite. You can drive or take a free shuttle from Wawona to the grove parking lot. From here, you can see the grove via open air tram or on foot. A free museum in the grove has exhibits on the sequoia. Details: Daily tram tours leave from the parking areas on the hour, from 9 a.m. to 6 p.m., May through October. The tram follows a 2-mile loop and includes a stop at the museum. Cost is $7.

If you're looking for solitude among these amazing trees, visit in winter or in midweek during the spring and fall—or visit groves outside of the park. (2 hours)

☆ **Wawona**—Twenty miles south of the valley mouth on CA 41, the Wawona Road, you'll come across a 120-year-old hotel set amid meadows, open forest, and a golf course. Wawona is Yosemite's southern gateway and the first site developed in the park. The **Pioneer Yosemite History Center**, a living history museum, is the chief attraction for non-golfers. Buildings from the area dating back to the 1850s are on display. Crafts and other demonstrations are scheduled throughout the summer, along with stagecoach rides. Details: At Wawona on CA 41; open Thursday through Sunday, 9:30 a.m. to 4:30 p.m. Admission is $3.

Yosemite Mountain Sugar Pine Railroad—On CA 41 in Fish Camp, you can take a short excursion on a narrow gauge rail line. There are also dinner packages and moonlight rides available. Details: Fish Camp; (209) 683-7273; the schedule has several variations, so call ahead. Regular rides leave every half hour from 9 a.m. to 4 p.m. in the summer. Cost is $6.50. The *Logger*, a steam locomotive, departs less frequently. Cost is $9.50. (1 hour)

FOOD

In Yosemite Valley, you can dine at the rustically elegant **Ahwahnee Hotel Dining Room**. Men need a jacket and tie for dinner. Reservations are usually necessary, (209) 372-1489. The **Mountain Broiler Room** in Yosemite Lodge is casual in atmosphere, but upscale in price and menu. Curry Village has the nice **Terrace Lounge** and the budget **Dining Pavilion**. Yosemite Village goes Italian at the **Pasta Place**.

The **Wawona Hotel** is the place for breakfast and dinner in Wawona. Reservations are needed for dinner, (209) 375-6556.

On the Tioga Road, you can eat at **White Wolf** or **Tuolumne Meadows**. Both are easy and casual. Groceries and snacks are available at Yosemite Village and Tuolumne Meadows. Call (209) 252-4848 for all general lodging and food information.

LODGING

Yosemite Valley has choices from luxurious to rustic. The **Ahwahnee Hotel** is at the top end with rooms for $210. It's a big step down to the **Yosemite Lodge**. Rooms here are $82; $61 with shared bath. **Curry Village** looks almost like a military camp with its cabins lined up in nice rows. The wooden ones are $53, while tent cabins go for $40. **Housekeeping Camp** has more tent cabins at $42.

In Wawona, the historic **Wawona Hotel** is an elegant choice for lodging. Rooms start at $90; $70 for shared-bath.

On the Tioga Road, **White Wolf Lodge** is a very pleasant alternative to the busy valley. Cabins with a bath are $62; tent cabins $42. The **Tuolumne Meadows Lodge** has tent cabins for $42.

Reservations for all of the above sites are made via **Yosemite Reservations**, (209) 252-4848.

Several options are found along CA 41 near the Wawona entrance. **The Narrow Gauge Inn** is close to the station of its name-sake, the Yosemite Mountain Sugar Pine Railroad. This rustic inn has great rooms, a pool, a whirlpool, and a pleasant woodsy setting. Rooms range from $85 to $130, 48751 CA 41, (209) 683-7720. On CA 41, just outside the park, the luxurious **Tenaya Lodge** has the works. The lofty lobby with its grand fireplace sends an immediate message. Rooms range from $70 (winter) to $260 (summer, suite), (209) 683-6555 or (800) 635-5807.

YOSEMITE

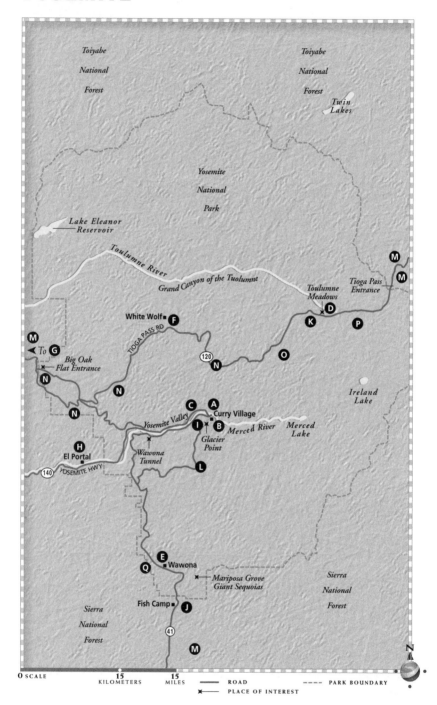

Food

Ⓐ Ahwahnee Hotel Dining Room

Ⓑ Dining Pavilion

Ⓒ Mountain Broiler Room

Ⓐ Pasta Place

Ⓑ Terrace Lounge

Ⓓ Tuolumne Meadows

Ⓔ Wawona Hotel

Ⓕ White Wolf

Lodging

Ⓐ Ahwahnee Hotel

Ⓖ Buck Meadows Lodge

Ⓑ Curry Village

Ⓗ Dell Hart Lodge

Ⓖ Groveland Motel

Ⓘ Housekeeping Camp

Ⓙ The Narrow Gauge Inn

Ⓙ Tenaya Lodge

Ⓚ Tuolumne Meadows Lodge

Ⓔ Wawona Hotel

Ⓕ White Wolf Lodge

Ⓒ Yosemite Lodge

Camping

Ⓛ Bridalveil Creek Campground

Ⓑ Lower Pines Campground

Ⓑ Lower River

Ⓜ National Forest Campgrounds

Ⓝ National Park Campgrounds

Ⓑ North Pines Campground

Ⓞ Tenaya Lake

Ⓟ Tuolumne Meadows Campgrounds

Ⓑ Upper Pines Campground

Ⓑ Upper River

Ⓠ Wawona Campground

Note: Items with the same letter are located in the same town or area.

Outside the park entrance on CA 140 is the motel village of El Portal. The **Dell Hart Lodge** has rooms from $45 to $100, (209) 379-2308. Mariposa has several chain motels.

Sonora also offers several chain motels to those entering the park via CA 120. In Groveland, the **Groveland Motel** has rooms for $55, (209) 902-7865. Closer to the park, the **Buck Meadows Lodge** has rooms from $60 to $70, (209) 962-5281.

Outside the park's east entrance, rooms are available in the town of Lee Vining.

CAMPING

Yosemite Valley has quite a few campgrounds. All of the sites in the valley must be reserved through **Destinet** by calling (800) 436-7275. There's no reservation fee beyond the cost of the campsite. If you want to stay in the valley anytime from spring through fall, you should reserve a spot. The three **Pines Campgrounds, Upper, Lower,** and **North,** are farthest from the village traffic and closer to valley trail-heads. **Lower River** and **Upper River** are on either side of the main loop and seem more crowded. None of them are particularly nice compared to National Forest or State Park campgrounds.

Bridalveil Creek Campground on the Glacier Point Road is nice for its relative isolation and easy access to south rim sunsets.

There are seven campgrounds between the Big Oak Flat entrance and Tioga Pass along CA 120. High country campgrounds don't open until they are largely clear of snow, sometimes as late as July. First-come, first-served sites may be available at one or more of these campgrounds, but it still pays to use the free reservation service. **Tenaya Lake** (walk-ins, $3) and **Tuolumne Meadows Campgrounds** are both good choices for their accessibility to the lovely granite dome country. **Wawona Campground** is an option at the south end of the park.

Many good National Forest campgrounds are located outside of the park. From Cedar Valley on CA 41, take Sky Lakes Road to reach four such campgrounds. On CA 140, the two Sierra National Forest campgrounds near Incline and Briceburg are administered by the Park Service. Call (800) 436-7275 for reservations. Five campgrounds are strung along CA 120 between Groveland and the Big Oak Flat entrance. Beyond the east entrance, six campgrounds are located in the beautiful basins above Mono Lake. Several of these campgrounds take reservations. Call (800) 280-2267 ($7.85 per reservation).

16

SEQUOIA AND KINGS CANYON NATIONAL PARKS

Together, the vast park land of Sequoia and Kings Canyon National Parks preserves the tallest mountain in the lower 48, a canyon that dips deeper than any other on the continent, and the largest living thing on the earth. All this, yet it receives relatively few visitors. For one thing, the park is well off the beaten track, too far from urban areas for most weekenders, and not on the way to or from anywhere else. For another, it is primarily wilderness. The main access road barely reaches into the park, while two others are slow, winding roads that few follow.

The most rugged stretch of the High Sierra Mountains is found in the park. No American peak outside of Alaska is taller than Mount Whitney, at 14,495 feet above sea level. Several other peaks over 14,000 feet are found along the Sierra crest, along with many exceeding 13,000 feet. The Pacific Crest National Scenic Trail passes through the parks, hugging the heights. With sheer-faced granite peaks, glacier-gouged cirques and canyons, and miles of maintained trails, it's a backpacker's paradise.

What most visitors come to see is the mighty *Sequoia giganteum*, the shorter and thicker cousins of the *Sequoia sempervirens*, the coastal redwood tree. Sequoias grow only in about 130 groves on the slopes of the western Sierras between Lake Tahoe and Bakersfield. Groves range from 1 to 4,000 acres in size. Though other species may grow taller, older, or bigger at the base, nothing contains more living mass. ◪

SEQUOIA AND KINGS CANYON NATIONAL PARKS

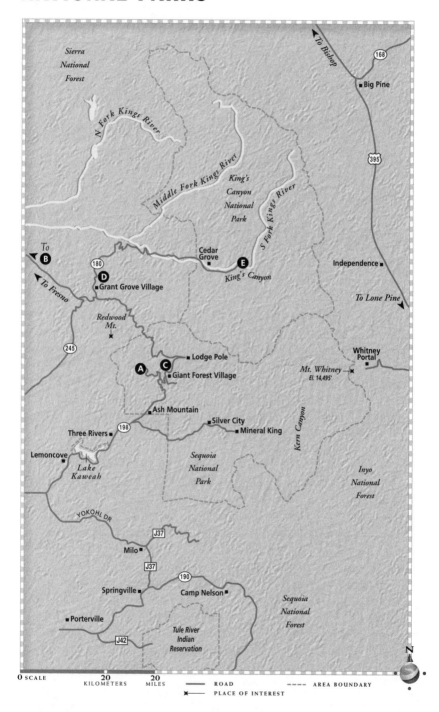

Sierra National Forest

N Fork Kings River

To Bishop

168

Big Pine

395

Middle Fork Kings River

King's Canyon National Park

S Fork Kings River

Cedar Grove

E

To **B**

180

D

Grant Grove Village

King's Canyon

Independence

To Fresno

To Lone Pine

Redwood Mt.

245

A   **C**

Lodge Pole

Giant Forest Village

Whitney Portal

Mt. Whitney
El. 14,495'

Ash Mountain

198

Silver City

Mineral King

Kern Canyon

Three Rivers

Lemoncove

Lake Kaweah

Sequoia National Park

Inyo National Forest

YOKOHL DR

J37

Milo

J37

190

Springville

Camp Nelson

Sequoia National Forest

Porterville

J42

Tule River Indian Reservation

N

0 SCALE   20 KILOMETERS   **20** MILES   ROAD   AREA BOUNDARY
PLACE OF INTEREST

Sightseeing Highlights

Ⓐ Crystal Cave

Ⓑ Forestiere Underground Gardens

Ⓒ Giant Forest

Ⓓ Grant Grove

Ⓔ Kings Canyon

A PERFECT DAY IN THE HIGH SIERRAS

From your campsite or lodge room in Kings Canyon, drive to Roads End and hike along the South Fork of the Kings River to Mist Falls or even up into Paradise Valley. Enjoy a picnic lunch along the Kings River, then drive the winding, 60-mile road to Giant Forest Village. Register at the lodge (reserved weeks ago if you're traveling in high season), then enjoy an afternoon walk along the easy Congress Trail to the General Sherman Tree, granddaddy of 'em all, returning along one of the many quieter loops through the large grove. After dinner, drive or hike the mile and a half to Moro Rock. Struggle up the steep steps to the top for an unbeatable sunset panorama.

SIGHTSEEING HIGHLIGHTS

★★★ **Forestiere Underground Gardens**—Most visitors to Sequoia and Kings Canyon arrive via Fresno and the hot highways of the Central Valley. Few want to seek out the charms of valley towns and cities, but there's one strange and compelling attraction that qualifies as a must-see on my list.

In the early 1900s, Baldasare Forestiere, an immigrant from Sicily, built himself a small room below ground level to escape from the heat. By the time he died in 1946, he had completed scores of rooms, niches, passageways, gardens, skylights, patios, a chapel, and an 800-foot auto tunnel—all below the surface, and all without plans or heavy equipment. Touring the site, you imagine a man with rare vision and passion. This is the story of an American artist and immigrant at its finest.

The site of the gardens resembles an overgrown vacant lot with a chain link fence around it. Once a rural road, Shaw Avenue has long since attracted fast food joints and ugly storefronts. Somehow, this just adds to the magic of what you find beneath it all. Details: 5021 West Shaw Avenue. Take the Shaw Avenue exit from CA 99, about 8 miles northwest of central Fresno. Go two blocks east and look for the sign on your right; (209) 271-0734. Tours are hourly from 10 a.m. to 4 p.m., Wednesday through Sunday, Memorial Day through Labor Day (noon to 3 p.m., Saturday and Sunday during the off season). Cheap at any price. Admission is $6. (1 hour)

★★★ **Giant Forest**—Here, in the largest sequoia grove of all, you'll find the **General Sherman Tree**, the largest living thing in the world at approximately 2,770,000 pounds. Trails thread through the forest, taking you well away from the road if you wish—though the traffic in Giant Forest is nothing compared to Yosemite's. The **Congress Trail** is an easy link between the General Sherman and **Giant Forest Village**. Numerous other trails wind through the trees. In the spring, the white blooms of tiny dogwood trees contrast marvelously with the huge, rust-colored trunks of trees that are as much as 3,000 years old.

South of the village, a short spur road leads through a portion of the grove to **Moro Rock**. From the parking area, a steep, narrow path of carved steps climbs a quarter mile to the summit. From the top of this bald, granite dome, the views up and down the **Kaweah River Valley** are magnificent. To the southwest, the deep valley gentles, finally opening out through the foothills into the **Central Valley**, some 20 miles distant. To the east, the valley climbs swiftly to the high cirques and basins below the **Great Western Divide**. Hidden beyond this range of 12,000-foot peaks, the amazing **Kern Canyon** drains a wilderness watershed watched over by Mount Whitney, the highest peak in the contiguous U.S.

Note that the Giant Forest Village is being phased out as a site of services. Village buildings are a threat to the health of several sequoias, and a falling sequoia could well be a threat to the health of the village buildings and those they contain. Details: Located 16 miles southeast of the park entrance on the General's Highway; (209) 565-3134. Open year-round. Admission is $5 per vehicle. (half day)

★★★ **Kings Canyon**—Driving north from Grant Grove on CA 180, you leave the park for a time and enter **Sequoia National Forest**. The

road soon begins a long, winding descent down into the canyon of the
South Fork of the Kings River. The drop to the river from **Spanish
Mountain,** the ridgeline summit you can see across the river, is over
8,200 feet, making this segment of the valley the deepest canyon in the
country.

The valley floor broadens as you enter the park and arrive in the
Cedar Grove area. Though the Kings River can rage with snowmelt
after a wet winter, its flow is often gentle. The hike through open forest lands along its banks is quite relaxing. At **Roads End,** the valley
splits around a great spur. Trails lead up **Bubbs Creek** toward the
Kings-Kern Divide and up beautiful Kings Canyon into **Paradise
Valley** and beyond.

✭✭ **Grant Grove**—Near the junction of the Kings Canyon and Giant
Forest roads, Grant Grove offers campgrounds, a ranger station, and
the chance for wonderful walks through the sequoias. Here, open park
land areas are found in parts of the grove, enhancing the majesty of the
giants. The Grant Grove visitor center is a good place to get general
information. Details: Located 3 miles from the park entrance on CA
180; (209) 565-3134; visitor center open daily from 8 a.m. to 5 p.m.
Admission is $5 per vehicle.

✭ **Crystal Cave**—A narrow road climbs to the cave; allow 20 minutes
for the drive from Giant Forest. Stalagmites, stalactites, curtains, "cave
bacon," and other formations can be seen. Details: Take Spur Road 2
miles south of Giant Forest Village; (209) 565-3134. Tours start on the
hour, 8 a.m. to 4 p.m., May through September. You must obtain your
reservation and $4 ticket for a tour of this interesting cave at either the
Lodgepole or Ash Mountain visitor center. (2 hours)

FITNESS AND RECREATION

A beautiful day hike through the large, roadless **Redwood Mountain
Grove** is the best way to get a real feel for the primeval sequoia tree. A
trail runs down Redwood Creek from the General's Highway, about 6
miles south of Grant Grove Village. Two side trails circle across the
slopes to the east and west of the valley path, allowing for loop choices
of between 5 and 12 miles or so.

Another good hiking option is from **Kings Canyon** into **Paradise
Valley** and beyond. The 2½-mile hike to the **Mist Falls** is an easy

SEQUOIA AND KINGS CANYON NATIONAL PARKS

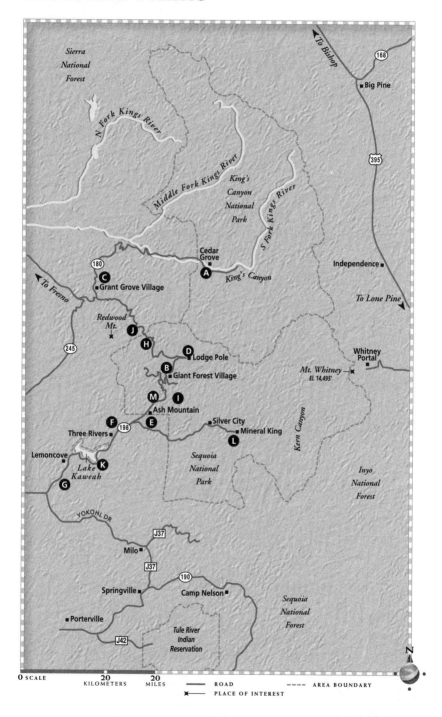

Sierra National Forest

N Fork Kings River

Middle Fork Kings River

King's Canyon National Park

S Fork Kings River

To Bishop

168

Big Pine

395

Cedar Grove

Independence

180

To Fresno

C Grant Grove Village

King's Canyon

A

To Lone Pine

Redwood Mt.

J

H

245

D Lodge Pole

B Giant Forest Village

Whitney Portal

Mt. Whitney
El. 14,495'

M

I

Ash Mountain

E

F

198

Three Rivers

Silver City

Mineral King

L

Kern Canyon

Lemoncove

Lake Kaweah

K

G

Sequoia National Park

Inyo National Forest

YOKOHL DR

J37

Milo

J37

190

Springville

Camp Nelson

Sequoia National Forest

Porterville

J42

Tule River Indian Reservation

N

0 SCALE   **20** KILOMETERS   **20** MILES   ROAD   AREA BOUNDARY

✕ PLACE OF INTEREST

Food

- Ⓐ Cedar Grove Snack Bar & Market
- Ⓑ Giant Forest Village Cafeteria & Market
- Ⓒ Grant Grove Restaurant & Market
- Ⓓ Lodgepole Deli & Market

Lodging

- Ⓔ Buckeye Tree Lodge
- Ⓐ Cedar Grove
- Ⓑ Giant Forest
- Ⓒ Grant Grove
- Ⓕ Lazy J Ranch & Motel
- Ⓖ Lemon Cove Bed & Breakfast
- Ⓗ Stony Creek

Camping

- Ⓘ Buckeye Flat Campground
- Ⓐ Cedar Grove Campground
- Ⓙ Dorst Campground
- Ⓒ Grant Grove Campground
- Ⓚ Lake Kaweah Campground
- Ⓖ Lemon Cove Sequoia Campground
- Ⓓ Lodgepole Campground
- Ⓛ Mineral King Campground
- Ⓜ Potwisha Campground
- Ⓗ Stony Creek Campground

Note: Items with the same letter are located in the same town or area.

option. The additional 2 miles to Paradise Valley involves a 1,000-foot elevation gain.

FOOD

The **Giant Forest Village Cafeteria** is open for breakfast, lunch, and dinner, offering basic American fare. Picnic supplies can be purchased at the **Giant Forest Market**. Both are open daily in the summer from 8 a.m. to 7 p.m.

The Lodgepole area has the **Lodgepole Market**, open daily from 10 a.m. to 6 p.m., and the **Lodgepole Deli,** serving sandwiches and pizza from 11 a.m. to 7 p.m.

In Grant Grove, the **Grant Grove Restaurant** is somewhat nicer than the rest, serving three meals a day and offering cocktail service in the evening, open 7 a.m. to 9 p.m. The **Grant Grove Market** has food and other supplies, open 8 a.m. to 9 p.m.

Cedar Grove, in Kings Canyon, has a snack bar and a market at the Cedar Grove Lodge, open daily from 7 a.m. to 9 p.m.

Hours for all facilities are shorter before Memorial Day.

LODGING

Sequoia and Kings Canyon National Parks offer four lodging locations with several options. **Giant Forest** has motel rooms ranging from $70 to $90 and cabins from $60 to $115. Giant Forest is only open mid-May through mid-October. In **Grant Grove**, cabins are $32 to $71 in the high season, $28 to $58 in the low season. Lodge rooms in **Cedar Grove** are $84 (summer only). In **Stony Creek**, rooms are $90. Reservations for all rooms and cabins are made through Sequoia Guest Services, (209) 561-3314.

When approaching the park from CA 198 from Visalia, there are several good lodging options. The **Lemon Cove Bed & Breakfast** has nice rooms and a lovely yard. Prices are very reasonable at $55 to $90, 33038 Sierra Highway (CA 198), Lemon Cove, (209) 597-2555 or (800) 240-1466. In Three Rivers, the **Lazy J Ranch & Motel** has a wonderful, sprawling lawn with a pool, shade trees, and nice rooms starting at $45, 39625 Sierra Drive (CA 198), (209) 561-4449 or (800) 341-8000. A minute from the park entrance, the **Buckeye Tree Lodge** is right on the Kaweah River, with a pool and rooms from $46 to $71, 46000 Sierra Drive (CA 198), (209) 561-5900.

For approaches via CA 180 and the General's Highway, Fresno has many chain motels. They include **Best Western, Marriott, Days Inn, Hilton, Holiday Inn, Ramada, Sheraton, Super 8**, and **Motel 6**. Most are concentrated at exits from CA 99.

CAMPING

The park has campgrounds at **Lodgepole, Grant Grove, Mineral King**, and **Cedar Grove**, as well as two campgrounds along the General's Highway—**Stony Creek** and **Dorst**—and two in the Kaweah Valley—**Buckeye Flat** and **Potwisha**. Grant Grove is the busiest area and is very close to the actual Grant Grove sequoia grove. Dorst has a trailhead for the 2-mile walk to Muir Grove. All four Cedar Grove campgrounds are along the Kings River. Lodgepole is the closest to Giant Forest.

Outside of the park, there are several good campgrounds. Four National Forest campgrounds are near Grant Grove, two to the north in the Kings Valley, and two to the east along the road to Big Meadows and Horse Corral Meadow (from the General's Highway). On CA 198 below Three Rivers, **Lake Kaweah** has a campground operated by the U.S. Army Corps of Engineers. Also on CA 198, the **Lemon Cove Sequoia Campground** is quiet and shady, with sites from $14 to $18, a store, and a pool, 32075 Sierra Drive, (209) 597-2346.

APPENDIX

METRIC CONVERSION CHART

1 U.S. gallon = approximately 4 liters
1 liter = about 1 quart
1 Canadian gallon = approximately 4.5 liters

1 pound = approximately ½ kilogram
1 kilogram = about 2 pounds

1 foot = approximately ½ meter
1 meter = about 1 yard
1 yard = a little less than a meter
1 mile = approximately 1.6 kilometers
1 kilometer = about ⅔ mile

90°F = about 30°C
20°C = approximately 70°F

Planning Map: Northern California

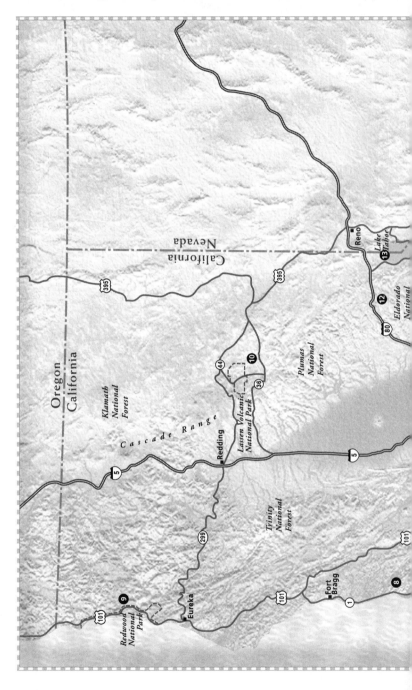

You have permission to photocopy this map.

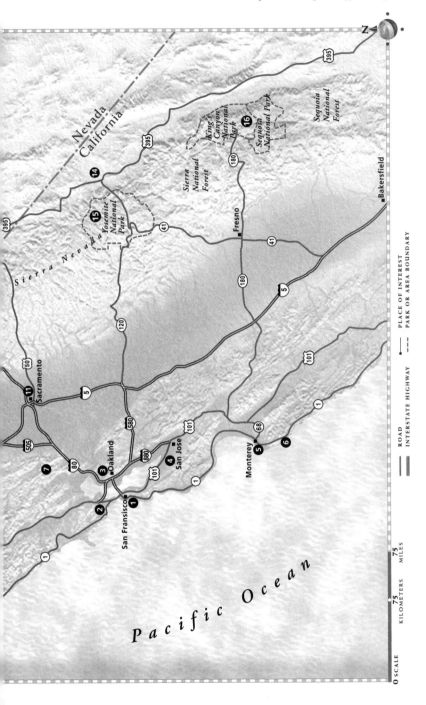

Maps Index

Other Books from John Muir Publications

Rick Steves' Books

Asia Through the Back Door, 400 pp., $17.95
Europe 101: History and Art for the Traveler, 352 pp., $17.95
Mona Winks: Self-Guided Tours of Europe's Top Museums, 432 pp., $18.95
Rick Steves' Baltics & Russia, 160 pp., $9.95
Rick Steves' Europe, 560 pp., $18.95
Rick Steves' France, Belgium & the Netherlands, 304 pp., $15.95
Rick Steves' Germany, Austria & Switzerland, 272 pp., $14.95
Rick Steves' Great Britain & Ireland, 320 pp., $15.95
Rick Steves' Italy, 240 pp., $13.95
Rick Steves' Scandinavia, 208 pp., $13.95
Rick Steves' Spain & Portugal, 240 pp., $13.95
Rick Steves' Europe Through the Back Door, 520 pp., $19.95
Rick Steves' French Phrase Book, 192 pp., $5.95
Rick Steves' German Phrase Book, 192 pp., $5.95
Rick Steves' Italian Phrase Book, 192 pp., $5.95
Rick Steves' Spanish & Portugese Phrase Book, 336 pp., $7.95
Rick Steves' French/German/Italian Phrase Book, 320 pp., $7.95

A Natural Destination Series

Belize: A Natural Destination, 344 pp., $16.95
Costa Rica: A Natural Destination, 416 pp., $18.95
Guatemala: A Natural Destination, 360 pp., $16.95

City·Smart™ Guidebook Series

City·Smart Guidebook: Cleveland, 208 pp., $14.95
City·Smart Guidebook: Denver, 256 pp., $14.95
City·Smart Guidebook: Minneapolis/St. Paul, 232 pp., $14.95
City·Smart Guidebook: Nashville, 256 pp., $14.95
City·Smart Guidebook: Portland, 232 pp., $14.95
City·Smart Guidebook: Tampa/St. Petersburg, 256 pp., $14.95

Travel+Smart™ Trip Planners

American Southwest Travel+Smart Trip Planner, 256 pp., $14.95
Colorado Travel+Smart Trip Planner, 248 pp., $14.95
Eastern Canada Travel+Smart Trip Planner, 272 pp., $15.95
Florida Gulf Coast Travel+Smart Trip Planner, 240 pp., $14.95
Hawaii Travel+Smart Trip Planner, 256 pp., $14.95
Kentucky/Tennessee Travel+Smart Trip Planner, 248 pp., $14.95
Minnesota/Wisconsin Travel+Smart Trip Planner, 240 pp., $14.95
New England Travel+Smart Trip Planner, 256 pp., $14.95
Northern California Travel+Smart Trip Planner, 272 pp., $15.95
Pacific Northwest Travel+Smart Trip Planner, 240 pp., $14.95

Other Terrific Travel Titles

The 100 Best Small Art Towns in America, 256 pp., $15.95
The Big Book of Adventure Travel, 384 pp., $17.95

Indian America: A Traveler's Companion, 480 pp., $18.95
The People's Guide to Mexico, 608 pp., $19.95
Ranch Vacations: The Complete Guide to Guest and Resort, Fly-Fishing, and Cross-Country Skiing Ranches, 632 pp., $22.95
Understanding Europeans, 272 pp., $14.95
Undiscovered Islands of the Caribbean, 336 pp., $16.95
Watch It Made in the U.S.A.: A Visitor's Guide to the Companies that Make Your Favorite Products, 328 pp., $16.95
The World Awaits, 280 pp., $16.95
The Birder's Guide to Bed and Breakfasts: U.S. and Canada, 416 pp., $17.95

Automotive Titles

The Greaseless Guide to Car Care, 272 pp., $19.95
How to Keep Your Subaru Alive, 480 pp., $21.95
How to Keep Your Toyota Pickup Alive, 392 pp., $21.95
How to Keep Your VW Alive, 464 pp., $25

Ordering Information

Please check your local bookstore for our books, or call **1-800-888-7504** to order direct and to receive a complete catalog. A shipping charge will be added to your order total.

Send all inquiries to:
John Muir Publications
P.O. Box 613
Santa Fe, NM 87504